THE MANAGEMENT OF THE WORLD ECONOMY

By the same author

THE ECONOMIC DEVELOPMENT OF COMMUNIST CHINA
(*co-author*)

BRITAIN AND CHINA

NATIONALITY AND WEALTH

CONFLICT AND PEACE IN THE MODERN INTERNATIONAL
SYSTEM

THE CONTROL OF THE SEABED

INTERNATIONAL AGENCIES: The Emerging Framework of
Interdependence

TYPES OF INTERNATIONAL SOCIETY

THE UNITED NATIONS: How it Works and What it Does

SOCIALISM WITHOUT THE STATE

THE INTERNATIONAL PROTECTION OF HUMAN RIGHTS
(*editor*)

THE EVOLUTION OF INTERNATIONAL ORGANISATIONS
(*editor*)

A HISTORY OF THE UNITED NATIONS, vol. 1: The Years of
Western Domination, 1945–1955

ECONOMIC RELATIONSHIPS AMONG STATES

THE MANAGEMENT OF THE WORLD ECONOMY

Evan Luard

So distribution should undo excess,
And each man have enough

(*King Lear*, IV. i. 73–7)

St. Martin's Press   New York

© Evan Luard 1983

All rights reserved. For information, write:
St. Martin's Press, Inc., 175 Fifth Avenue, New York, NY 10010
Printed in Hong Kong
First published in the United States of America in 1983

ISBN 0–312–50950–2

Library of Congress Cataloging in Publication Data

Luard, Evan, 1926–
   The management of the world economy.

   Includes index.
   1. International economic relations. I. Title.
HF1411.L8   1983   337   82–23109
ISBN 0–312–50950–2

Contents

List of Tables

List of Figures

Preface

This book has two basic aims: to provide a simple and non-technical introduction to the problems of the modern international economy; and to consider how some of these problems might be overcome, or at least lessened, by more effective management of that economy than exists today. It is not an economic textbook. It is designed as much for the educated layman as for the student; and it is concerned as much with international politics as it is with international economies.

Political and economic issues are anyway not easy to disentangle. It is sometimes said that in domestic societies today most of the problems of politics are economic in origin. This is as true in the international as in the domestic field: many of the most fundamental political issues between states today are the economic conflicts that divide them.

The book is thus concerned with the politics of international economics: what is nowadays sometimes, somewhat inaccurately, termed political economy (that term was originally applied to what is simply now called economics). It therefore examines the problems that arise among states concerning trade, concerning the international monetary system, concerning development aid, energy and energy prices, resources, food and employment questions. It considers the principal causes of dispute among states about such matters. It describes the international institutions which already exist for examining these problems and how far they have proved adequate in confronting them. Finally, the book considers the changes in institutions and policies which would be required to create a more stable economic system as well as a more just world economic order than the one we have today.

E. L.

Acknowledgements

The author wishes to express his grateful thanks to his friends Professor Amartya Sen and Professor David Henderson for their valuable comments on parts or all of the text.

List of Abbreviations

AIOC	Anglo-Iranian Oil Company
BIS	Bank of International Settlement
BP	British Petroleum
Ecosoc	(UN) Economic and Social Council
EEC	European Economic Community
EFTA	European Free Trade Area
FAO	Food and Agriculture Organisation (s.a.)
GATT	General Agreement on Tariffs and Trade
GNP	Gross national product
GSP	Generalised System of Preferences
IBRD	International Bank for Reconstruction of Development (World Bank) (s.a.)
IDA	International Development Association (affiliate of the World Bank)
IEA	International Energy Agency
IFAD	International Fund for Agricultural Development (s.a.)
ILO	International Labour Organisation (s.a.)
IMF	International Monetary Fund (s.a.)
IPC	Iraq Petroleum Company
NIC	Newly industrialising country
OAPEC	Organisation of Arab Petroleum Exporting States
ODA	Official development assistance
OECD	Organisation for Economic Co-operation and Development
OPEC	Organisation of Petroleum Exporting Countries
RIIA	Royal Institute of International Affairs
SDR	Special drawing right
Socal	Standard Oil of California
Socony	Standard Oil Company of New York
Texaco	Texas Oil Company
Uncitral	UN Commission on International Trade Law
UNCTAD	UN Conference on Trade and Development

UNDP	UN Development Programme
VAT	Value-added tax
WHO	World Health Organisation (s.a.)

s.a. = specialised agency. Specialised agencies are part of the UN system, or UN 'family', but do not fall under the jurisdiction of the United Nations proper, being autonomous agencies. Other UN bodies mentioned are part of the United Nations itself, though some, being voluntary programmes, have a different membership from the United Nations and have their own governing bodies. UNCTAD, though not a specialised agency or a voluntary programme, is virtually autonomous, being controlled by its own board. The Administrative Committee on Co-ordination brings together the heads of the United Nations and the specialised agencies. Other bodies listed are not part of the UN system.

Introduction

THE COLLAPSE OF THE POST-WAR SYSTEM

At the end of the Second World War, a new world economic system was established. It was intended to be very different from any which had existed earlier. It was to be above all an advance on the system that had prevailed between the wars, constricted and contorted as that had been by governmental import controls, exchange regulations, export subsidies, managed exchange rates and nationalist interventions of many kinds.

There were four guiding principles underlying the new arrangements.

First, and most crucial, was the principle of *liberalisation*. Tariffs, quota restrictions, exchange controls, multiple exchange rates, and all the other interferences with a free market so widely practised before were now to be progressively eliminated. After a somewhat hesitant beginning, some progress was made towards achieving that aim. Successive negotiations reduced tariffs among the developed countries to a fraction of their pre-war level: to 5 per cent or so on average against over 20 per cent in the late forties. By the seventies attempts were being made to restrain other types of trade restriction that increasingly replaced tariffs for excluding imports. A similar process took place in the monetary sphere: by the end of the fifties convertibility of non-resident currencies was introduced in most industrialised countries, and a decade or so later currencies were allowed to float freely in the market.

Yet this process of liberalisation was always highly selective. Whole areas of trade were omitted from the beginning. Trade in agriculture was scarcely touched. Other types of trade were little affected: for example, trade in processed products and in simple manufactures. Each of the areas omitted was vital to some countries, mainly in the developing world. In other words, the industrialised states, while willing to seek the benefits of increased specialisation and comparative costs in trade with each other, were not generally prepared to extend the same principles to their trade with poor countries. Those countries themselves, with heavy import requirements and large balance of payments deficits, mostly showed equally little ardour for liberalisation, even for trade with each other. So liberalisation from the beginning, though widely extolled in principle, was not always so enthusiastically implemented in practice.

Secondly, the new system was to be based on the principle of *non-discrimination*. In place of the special favours which under the previous system were often accorded to traditional partners or political associates – in the form of preferences, bilateral trading agreements, barter arrangements or special tariff regimes – economic relations would now be based on the strict application of the most-favoured-nation principle (under which privileges accorded to one nation were to be extended impartially to others applying the same principle). The principle of non-discrimination was widely accepted in theory; and was explicitly endorsed in the rules laid down for the new trading and monetary system. But, again, it was less universally adopted in practice. Colonial preferences were long maintained by Britain, France and other countries; and were continued in a new form in the special treatment given to 'associates' by the EEC. The United States kept preferential arrangements with the Philippines, Hawaii and Puerto Rico. Political discrimination was widespread: communist countries were excluded from the benefits of most-favoured-nation treatment by the United States for political reasons, while special trading arrangements were equally made between the Soviet Union and her allies. So here too practice did not always match principles. But, in theory at least, non-discrimination now became, in the West at least, the norm to which lip-service was paid.

The third principle of the new system was *multilateralism*. The new arrangements were not to be private pacts among small groups, such as had been made between the wars. They would be set up on a basis agreed among the principal nations of the world and would be subsequently supervised and regulated, where necessary, by international institutions set up for the purpose. In other words, some degree of economic sovereignty was to be lost by each participant. Multilateral systems for supervising and regulating trade and monetary affairs were indeed successfully established: in GATT and the IMF respectively. In each case member states were obliged to make undertakings removing a part of their former independence: for example, in raising tariffs and in changing exchange rates. Here too the practice did not always exactly match the principle. When crisis arose, individual countries would halt particular imports, would devalue their currencies, with barely a pretence of consultation. Even so, far more than at any earlier time in human history, a system for the international management of the economic system did seem now to have been created.

Finally, the system was designed to promote *full employment* among the populations of those countries that took part; and therefore required a rapid rate of economic growth. Full employment was an explicit aim (laid down for example in the UN Charter). And it was a condition for participation in the system by some countries: Britain, for example, from the beginning reserved the right to opt out of the new arrangements, in both the commercial and the monetary spheres, if full employment appeared threatened. Here, above all, success seemed to have been secured. For more than two decades, rapid and sustained economic growth was successfully achieved in industrialised countries. It brought with it very low rates of unemployment, which appeared to justify and sustain the new system. During the fifties and sixties, the economies of the rich countries of the world grew faster than at any earlier time in their history: by 4–5 per cent a year. This in turn helped to stimulate rapid development among poor countries too; which on average, indeed, grew faster still. World employment expanded rapidly. A new era seemed to have dawned, more prosperous than any before.

These were the four guiding principles of the new system. From about 1970 onwards, however, each of them became more difficult to fulfil. The most important single change was that high growth was replaced by low growth. Especially from the time of the oil-price rise in 1973, the steady expansion of the world economy ceased. Inflationary pressures, partly stimulated by the oil-price rise, caused governments deliberately to introduce deflation to counter them. This brought, in place of low unemployment, the highest experienced at any time since the 1930s (occasionally still higher). This in turn caused serious problems for poor countries which found that their chief markets declined, the prices of their exports fell, while the price of their imports, from rich countries as well as from oil-producers, rose faster than ever. The failure to fulfil this objective, the maintenance of high employment, in turn threatened each of the others.

The whole process of liberalisation was checked. During the seventies, with declining growth in income and trade, increasing unemployment and increasing competition from elsewhere, there were everywhere calls to save jobs by reducing imports (in other words, by destroying jobs elsewhere). While the old forms of protection – such as tariffs and strict exchange controls – were not usually restored, new types of restriction – non-tariff barriers, anti-dumping regulations, 'voluntary restrictions', 'trigger prices', 'safeguards', and similar methods – were now invented to take their place. So the whole goal of liberalisation, on which the post-war system had above all been based, was increasingly under threat.

The principle of non-discrimination too began to be eroded. Regional grants, industrial subventions, export subsidies and other discriminatory measures to assist home industries were introduced, in the universal effort to save jobs. Discrimination began to take place between whole groups of nations. Regional arrangements were made, discriminating in favour of those within the region: as within the EEC in Europe and within other groups elsewhere. There was discrimination between rich countries and poor. Occasionally this was discrimination in _favour_ of the poor: as in the Generalised System of Preferences for some exports of poor countries. More often it was against: as in the arrangements made for restricting textile imports to rich countries, which were applied only to poor countries, even though imports of textiles from other rich countries grew faster.

Finally, the principle of multilateralism was now increasingly challenged. From the beginning the new multilateral institutions had been established on a somewhat one-sided basis. Communist states, by their own choice, played little or no part in them from the start. Most poor countries were not independent at the time when the new bodies came into being and so had no share in shaping them. In practice, therefore, the new 'multilateral' institutions were from the beginning dominated by a restricted group of Western developed states, applying principles which they themselves had chosen. Even after poor states had become the great majority of their members, the structure and voting mechanisms established ensured that they were still dominated by rich ones. In the early years the United States alone enjoyed over 30 per cent of the votes in the IMF and the World Bank; the developed countries as a whole had nearly 80 per cent (as well as most of the seats in the governing council of each body). Even thirty years later, when each had a large majority of poor members, that domination was only marginally reduced (p. 107 below). But it now began to be contested. A 'new international economic order' was increasingly demanded. Developing countries now claimed the right to a share in power in world institutions proportionate to their numbers. Rich countries in reaction made new arrangements for meeting together to reach decisions on their own. Though the _principle_ of multilateralism was still widely endorsed, it was a new kind of multilateralism that increasingly emerged.

The entire post-war economic system was therefore under threat. Conditions had become quite different from those at the end of the Second World War, when the post-war system had been established. US power, economic and political, was now dramatically less. The dollar, on which the world's monetary system had been primarily based, was unstable, no longer linked to gold and for long declined in value. The trade of industrialised countries was now threatened, for the first time since 1945, by the rapidly increasing exports of newly industrialising countries (NICs), which, with much lower labour costs and often higher efficiency, could produce similar products for a fraction of the price. Energy, which had been abundant at prices which did not properly reflect its scarcity, under the control of Western companies, now suddenly became exorbitantly expensive, and under the control of producer governments. In many industries – steel, shipbuilding, electronics, textiles and petrochemicals – huge overcapacity emerged. Unemployment rose inexorably, in rich countries and poor alike. And inflation, formerly relatively modest, was now rampant everywhere.

The comfortable assumptions which more than two decades of prosperity had fostered were thus no longer tenable. The two objectives which the post-war system had been mainly designed to secure – liberalisation and full employment – now seemed increasingly difficult to reconcile. In the new conditions the question arose: should the main emphasis of policy be placed on reducing unemployment, even if this involved the abandonment of liberalisation and the persistence of inflation; or should the control of inflation have the greatest priority in economic policy, even if this meant slowing the rate of economic growth and leaving larger and larger sections of the population without work? This question was bitterly disputed, between nations as within them.

It was evident that the economic system of the immediate post-war years was now coming to an end. The question was: what kind of system would replace it?

THE NEED FOR MANAGEMENT

One possible answer to these problems in the world economy was to try to bring it under a more effective international management.

It seemed an obvious conclusion that, since so many of the problems from which individual national economies now suffered had international rather than national causes – world inflation, world energy prices, world recession, world monetary problems – international answers were required. The same type of economic regulation as had been practised for decades, with considerable success, within states should now be used to overcome the instabilities of the international economic system. All the main needs which had brought about regulation by national governments now brought a similar need for management at the international level.

The world trading system, for example, clearly required better international regulation. National governments had for many years intervened to influence trade, internal and external; to protect the interests of producers and consumers alike; to restrain monopolies and other barriers to free trade; and to provide the basis for fair competition. But these aims were now more urgent internationally than nationally. Not only had international trade become a far higher proportion of all trade for every nation; it was internationally that the main barriers to trade, the main distortions and the main inequalities now existed. It was no longer internal tolls, market sharing, monopoly practices and pricing policies within states which required controlling. It was the tariffs and quotas imposed by governments against each other; combinations among national producers of particular commodities; monopolies and special pricing arrangements among private corporations that operated internationally; instabilities in world, not national prices: it was now these that required regulating action.

In the monetary field, again, better international arrangements were required. Here too national governments had over many years controlled the level of credit in domestic markets: by influencing the supply of money, by restraints on lending and by influencing prevailing interest rates. This was required to check inflationary tendencies within each economy, to stimulate demand at times of depression, and to regulate the level of activity generally. But here too it was now at the international level that such action was mainly needed. No state was any longer an island: in establishing its interest rates, budget deficit or money supply, national authorities created immediate effects on other economies too. The rate of interest in the United States, or the level of credit restriction there, affected the world economy as a whole. Inflation had become an international as much as a local phenomenon, exported from one state to another. Recession too was international: still more obviously it was transmitted from state to state and could only be overcome by international action. At the very least, multilateral guidance was needed to co-ordinate national responses: for example, to influence interest-rate policy or trade policy, or to encourage reflation or deflation (so that all were not engaged in deflating or reflating at the same time, with calamitous results). Many felt that more was required than this: that the credit policies of international bodies, such as the

IMF, needed to be adjusted in the common interest, to raise demand in time of recession and to dampen it in boom. Increasingly, to reduce the instabilities of the modern world economy, international counter-cyclical strategies were seen to be necessary.

International action was also required to maintain and conserve threatened world resources. For years national governments had been concerned about the husbanding and development of their national resources, the conservation of their land, and the assurance of energy supplies for their people. But this task too had now become an international responsibility. The rapid depletion of the earth's remaining resources was a disaster that would be felt by all nations: and the conservation of those that remained was therefore a task for the entire international community. Conversely, there was an international interest in ensuring that those resources that existed were accessible and became available at prices that conformed with the economic realities of the day and not with the restrictive practices of a few producers. Again, therefore, the management of the world's remaining resources had become a task which could only be undertaken on an international basis.

The internationalisation of the economy had transformed another task previously performed by individual states. National governments had intervened to promote regional policies: to ensure that the economic development of particular regions did not fall too far behind that of the more prosperous localities within the same state. But to the regional problems of the modern world national action was irrelevant. For inequalities now lay between nations rather than within them. With the growing speed of travel and of knowledge, these inequalities became increasingly conspicuous, and so increasingly unacceptable. Policies designed to spread wealth and investment, therefore, now needed to be undertaken at the international rather than the national level: the transfer of resources to those countries most needing, yet least able, to attract them, in a common effort to promote the development of a common world.

Finally, it was not only geographical inequalities that needed tackling at a wider level. The same was true of inequalities between individuals. Traditionally, national governments had intervened not only to reduce inequalities between regions but also to secure economic justice among their peoples generally; they had done this through progressive taxation and through the creation of social services, paid for primarily by the rich yet benefiting primarily the poor. But in the modern world it was only through international measures that such inequalities could be remedied. Embryonic international social services already existed; in the work of the UN agencies operating in the areas of health, education, labour affairs, children's welfare, food, communications and other fields. But the budgets of these organisations were so small, and their activities consequently so restricted, that they exercised virtually no visible impact on the inequalities that existed in each area. Only the establishment of programmes on a scale far exceeding those set up so far could have any significant effect. And, whatever the scale, the responsibility for organising and administering these services could only be an international one. Here again, therefore, functions that were previously those of national governments could now only be effectively undertaken, given the nature of the inequalities of the modern world, on an international basis.

So in many fields better international arrangements were required. But, even if it were accepted that some more effective management of the world economy was needed, there was a wider question to be considered. What were the purposes which such management should seek to procure? And in whose interests should it be undertaken?

WHAT TYPE OF ECONOMIC MANAGEMENT?

The type of economic policy chosen by those responsible for managing the international economy will depend on the analysis they make of the way that the economy operates at present and the causes of its underlying problems.

There are two main views today about the character of the international economy and the kind of international measures necessary. They differ (like corresponding theories concerning domestic economies) in their assessment of the major problem to be dealt with, and therefore in their choice of the policies to be adopted.

The first might be defined as a broadly monetarist approach (although the precise importance attached to money supply as such would vary considerably). This is the view that has prevailed on international problems among most governments in recent times; certainly, among most rich countries and within international institutions. Under this view the main problem to be tackled, internationally as domestically, is inflation. The main cause of inflation is excess demand, both within individual economies, and, as a result, within the world economy. The principal cause of excess demand is the excessive volume of money and credit generally within the system: again, both in the domestic system (the money supply created or allowed by governments, through government borrowing and lax credit policies) and in the international system (money created by large Euro-currency lending and easy IMF credit policies). The proper remedy for the inflationary pressures in the domestic economy is tighter credit, higher interest rates, balanced budgets and cuts in government borrowing (and therefore cuts in government spending generally). Even national measures of this kind, if applied generally, should reduce inflation elsewhere. Internationally, corresponding measures are needed for the same purpose; tight credit policies (for example, by restricting the volume of funds borrowers can acquire from the IMF), strict repayment terms, and severe conditions for loans (whether from bilateral donors or the IMF), including demands for deflationary policies as the price of credit, restraint in the issue of special drawing rights (SDRs), and restrictions on lending in the Euro-currency market. Development assistance would be limited and conditional, and used for non-inflationary purposes only (for example, for developing new sources of raw materials, and for project rather than programme lending). Trade should be liberalised to maximise the benefits of a market economy and to reduce domestic costs.

The second approach can be styled as broadly Keynesian. Under this approach (reflected, for example, recently in the recommendations of the Brandt Report) the central problem to be confronted is unemployment: in other words, not excessive but inadequate demand. Domestically, this creates a need for more ample credit, for lower interest rates, for higher public spending, for budget deficits: designed to raise demand to meet productive capacity and so create jobs. Internationally, similar remedies are required. More ample credit should be provided: the IMF should thus be willing to provide larger loans, for longer periods, on less rigorous terms; and it should issue SDRs specifically to poor countries to help them import more for development purposes. Bilateral donors and international institutions should be willing to provide greater transfers, in loans and grants, to raise purchasing power among poor countries. And greater assistance should be given in rescheduling or cancelling debts. Rich countries should allow increased access to their markets for the exports of developing countries, without necessarily demanding corresponding concessions in return. The increase in demand so created within the poor countries would enable them to increase their purchases in rich countries; and so help to boost the economies of the latter too. So, world economic activity would be revived; and unemployment, the main problem, gradually reduced.

Each of these analyses corresponds to a widely held view about the modern international economy. The former is more commonly held in rich countries, the latter in poor; the former by conservative economists, the latter by progressive ones. Each, however, is open to question in the analysis it makes of the modern world economy.

The criticism to be made about the international monetarist approach is similar to that which can be raised against such an analysis of domestic economies. Even if the initial assumption were accepted – that inflation rather than unemployment is the primary problem to be tackled (or, at least, that its solution is the precondition for solving the unemployment problem) – it is open to question whether, in the international as in the domestic economy, rigid control of the money supply and of credit generally will necessarily succeed in overcoming it. In the domestic economy *general* deflation (of which restriction the money supply is only a small part) may in time bring a reduction in the rate of wage increases; and so a temporary reduction in the rate of inflation. But it will achieve this, even in the short term, only at the cost of a severe loss of production and a decline in the living standards which could otherwise have been secured. Even while the policy lasts, the reduction in wage costs, if achieved, will be offset by increases of costs in other areas: through higher interest rates, reduced turnover, reduced productivity and (for the government) reduced tax revenues and increased costs (for example, of unemployment benefits). Recession indeed may bring *higher* not lower demands for credit from enterprises in difficulty, public and private.[1] More important, any reduction in the rate of inflation is likely to be temporary only. For the holding back of living standards over a period, which is an intrinsic element of the policy, may only *increase* the pressure for larger increases in income as soon as growth resumes, as unions determine in an expanding economy to win back the loss in earning power their members have suffered earlier. Inflation over the long term, therefore, may not be affected. Yet meanwhile a severe loss of standards of living has been suffered which cannot later be made good.

At the international level similar difficulties arise. Here too it is open to question whether rigid control of the volume of lending, high interest rates and a restriction in the supply of money will bring any long-term reduction in world rates of inflation. Internationally as domestically, these measures (if implemented by the IMF and other institutions) mainly have the effect of slowing world growth and reducing world employment. Whether they bring any significant relief in inflationary pressures can be doubted. Poor countries which lose their markets in recession become still more dependent on loans from elsewhere; and the volume of credit is increased. Periods of severe deflation, very high interest rates and restrictive IMF policy in 1973–5 and 1979–82 left average rates of inflation, at around 10 per cent in developed countries, no lower than before they began and far higher than at any earlier period. Conversely, periods of strong growth and easy money from 1950 to 1970 produced the lowest inflation rates of the post-war period: 1–4 per cent within developed countries. This suggests that other causes of inflation may be of at least equal importance: for example, combination among producers – whether these are *countries* restricting supply (such as the members of OPEC), *companies* influencing price (such as those producing uranium, pharmaceuticals, computers and others), or *unions* influencing wage costs – declining world resources (for example, of energy, minerals, food and land), and new types of consumer credit. Many of these factors are little affected by restrictions in the money supply and other deflationary policies. At the international as at the domestic level, therefore, the monetarist remedies, while they have a significant effect in reducing growth and living standards, may do little to contain deep-seated inflationary pressures. Their chief effect is that all over the world the numbers of those without jobs dramatically increases, while the standard of living of all is deliberately depressed.

The neo-Keynesian analysis, however, though less wrong-headed than the monetarist one, also appears inadequate. Whether applied nationally or internationally, it suffers from the same defects. It correctly recognises in both cases that unemployment is a far worse disaster than inflation (and will not always do much to cure it). But the remedy it seeks – the reflation of demand – is itself inadequate, for it proposes an expansion of demand that is indiscriminate. Domestically, it advocates measures of general reflation – lower interest rates, reductions of taxation, increases in government spending, and budget deficits – which are undifferentiated in their effect. All types of economic activity and all types of income will be promoted, directly or indirectly. The effect of such measures is not only socially inequitable, in that it most increases the purchasing power of those who are already best off – the wealthy (who benefit most from tax reductions), private companies (which benefit most from lower interest rates and increased demand), and those belonging to powerful unions (who will benefit most from the increased bargaining power which reflation provides); it also will have less effect in its primary purpose, the restimulation of the economy. For purchasing power is on average increased most among the wealthiest sections of the population, who may use much of it for saving, or for the purchase of property, pictures, and holidays abroad, with little impact on economic activity, employment and income elsewhere in the economy; while least benefit will go to the poorest sections, who would be most likely to use their purchasing power within the home economy in ways which will create jobs. Finally, because much of the increased wealth will quickly find its way into the banking system, credit will be expanded, and inflation will be quickly restimulated. Thus, not only will levels of unemployment (and levels of inequality) be reduced far less than if a more *selective* type of reflation had been adopted: inflation will be increased far more.

This applies even more clearly to the effect of the neo-Keynesian policy in the international economy. The measures it demands – a relaxation of credit by the IMF and other financial institutions, more generous lending policies by the World Bank and other aid-givers, the provision of greater access to the markets of developed countries for the products of poor states – all of these will primarily benefit a small number of relatively prosperous poor countries, rather than developing countries as a whole. And the poorest countries of all will benefit least of all. Equally important, *within* those countries it will only be relatively small and privileged groups in each population who will be assisted: those who work in the industrial sector or in producing export crops; those who work in the government, to which much of the external aid is provided; or those who belong to the dominant elite within each country, who may be able to ensure that external assistance mainly benefits their group. Finally, assistance that benefits these groups, feeding demands for increased consumption among a privileged wealthy group – demands that can be met only by increased imports or higher prices (usually both) – will most stimulate inflation. Here too, more selective reflation, designed explicitly to transfer purchasing power to the least developed countries, where the potential for development is greatest, and to the poorest groups *within* each country, would not only be more socially just: it would both do more to restimulate the world economy and create less inflationary pressure in doing so.

Each of these views, therefore, though widely held, has weaknesses. However, there is a third view possible of the problems of the current international economy and of the remedies which are therefore required.

Under this view the most basic problem which the economy confronts is neither inflation nor unemployment (though both are serious). It is the *maldistribution* of resources, both among countries and among individuals, within the world economy as a whole (for this reason it might be called the *distributionist* approach). The existing distribution has the effect that large numbers of individuals and groups, scattered about many countries of the world, are virtually propertyless and thus play no effective part in the international economy as a whole. Both the main problems of the world economy we have examined to some extent derive from this fact. If there is widespread inflation in the modern world, it is partly because a substantial section of its population, amounting to at least a fifth, are without work or without significant work, and therefore, while they add marginally to overall international demand, contribute nothing or virtually nothing on the supply side. If they survive at all it is through marginal transfer payments, whether made nationally (through embryonic social services or charity) or internationally (through food aid and other programmes). If there is unemployment in the international economy, that too is the result of maldistribution of purchasing power: for the effect of the concentration of wealth is excessive saving, or spending on land, or on expensive consumer products often obtained from abroad, which create little employment; while a more equal distribution would increase demand for the basic supplies which can be locally produced – food, housing and clothing – and so at least go some way to creating more employment.

This third view, therefore, is concerned not only with the overall *level* of demand in the world economy, but also with the *type* of demand; and above all with its overall distribution. So far as the type of demand is concerned, it holds that demand-management policies should be of a kind that will relate new demands to available resources. They should not, therefore, be such as to increase pressure on resources already in very short supply, such as energy and minerals. This implies that new demand should not be created for types of industrialisation which make the greatest demands on such resources. It should rather be concentrated on developing traditional and service sectors which use least resources and create the greatest employment; and above all on increasing food supplies, of which future needs are greatest. For while food is in short supply, like hydrocarbons and minerals, it is not, as they are, non-renewable, and in this case therefore opposite considerations apply: an increase in demand, and so in price, can be expected over the long term to increase the available supply.

So far as the *distribution* of demand is concerned, this view holds that the primary aim must be to increase demand where *needs* are greatest and there are most unused resources, including unused labour. Among countries this will mainly be in the poorest countries of all, where there are large numbers of unemployed living in great poverty. But this view also holds that it is not the distribution among countries which is of primary importance. A simple transfer from rich countries to poor countries, though it may create a somewhat less unjust world, will not reduce many of the most extreme inequalities in the modern world – which are within states – and will not stimulate the kind of demand that is necessary for reviving the world economy. For it may only create demand among privileged groups within those countries whose needs are smallest and whose purchases, as we have seen, create least work.

An essential feature of the distributionist approach is that it is transnational: unconcerned by national boundaries. Most current approaches to 'north–south' relations remain bemused by the old-fashioned nation-state fallacy: that is, they still conceive of the world economy in terms of economic relations between *countries*. In this way they ignore the relations which are ultimately of most importance: between individuals, groups and enterprises, within the world economy as a whole. Under the distributionist view, the need is to consider economic relations without regard to national frontiers. And in increasing demand the aim must be above all to increase it most among those in all countries where at present demand is lowest and needs are highest: the landless, workless, foodless, propertyless, all over the world. This is necessary not only on grounds of justice, but also because it is here that a sustained expansion of demand will have the greatest long-term impact. This must be so since it is here that unsatisfied demand is greatest. And, since the higher the income the greater the proportion of any increment in it that will be saved, it follows that the higher the income among those who benefit from demand creation, the less will be the effect on the world economy generally.

But a distributionist strategy may not only be best at solving problems of distribution. Paradoxically, it may also be more successful in confronting each of the two problems with which the other theories are mainly concerned. It is more likely to reduce unemployment. An increase in demand among the most deprived sections of the population all over the world will raise demand mainly for food, for housing and clothing. Production of all of these is highly labour-intensive. Policies specifically directed to raising demand among such people will therefore do more to increase the opportunities for employment than any more general boost in demand. For, given the existing structure of the world economy, undiscriminating expansion will mainly raise production of those goods purchased by the wealthy, many of them highly sophisticated products produced by capital-intensive methods creating few jobs; and raise the demand of companies, including further capital investment, the effect of which may be to destroy rather than to create jobs.

Similarly, the distributionist strategy may also be less likely to create inflationary pressures. For the most part demand will be created for simple products – clothing, housing and simple manufactures – the supply of which can usually be raised without increasing pressures on scarce resources. Demand would, it is true, also be created for food, where there is the appearance of deficiency. Yet, since there is room for significant increases in yield (and so food supply) in most developing countries, higher demand, by raising prices, might provide precisely the incentive, now lacking, needed to produce increasing quantities.

We shall consider the implications of the distributionist strategy for managing the world economy in greater detail in the final chapter of this book. What is certain is that any such attempt to discriminate in the distribution of benefits from increased growth would require better instruments for managing the international economy than exist today. Many indeed would hold that better management of this kind is anyway required: to avoid the instabilities and uncertainties that have bedevilled the international economy in recent years and to overcome the combination of high inflation, high employment, high interest rates and low growth which have characterised it. It is to the ways in which better management of this kind might be achieved that the following chapters are devoted.

1 Growth

1.1 GROWTH AMONG INDUSTRIALISED COUNTRIES

It is only very recently that, even within states, governments have been expected to take a responsibility for stimulating economic growth. During the nineteenth century neither statesmen, industrialists nor economists thought much in terms of 'growth' at all. They were concerned with 'flourishing markets', 'plentiful money', 'prosperity' – sometimes with '*rising* prosperity'. But they did not have the statistical basis needed for measuring precisely the increase in production from year to year; still less for making comparisons between the rates of growth achieved in different states. There was far greater concern about the *immediate* factors influencing prosperity in each country – harvest failures, banking collapses, new discoveries of gold or other minerals, the development of new technology, above all the vagaries of the trade cycle – than with exact comparisons between the fortunes of different economies or the policies that produced them.

There was a general impression that until the middle of the century Britain was the most advanced and prosperous nation in the world; and that before the century's end the United States overtook her in that position. Even this impression was hazy. Today, though our knowledge is greater, it is still not possible to give an accurate picture of relative levels of economic growth at that time. Reasonably precise figures can be given for rates of growth in individual countries at least from 1880, and sometimes from the early nineteenth century.[1] But, because of differing price structures and variations in statistical practice, there is no sure basis for comparison between them. In the middle of the century, income a head was probably highest in Britain, followed by the United States, France, Belgium and Germany, in approximately that order. But the pre-eminent position which Britain had acquired, as a result of the industrial revolution and her trade dominance, began to decline soon afterwards. By 1870 the standard of living in the United States had probably at least equalled that of Britain, while those of Canada,

Australia and New Zealand were almost as high. By the end of the century the United States had clearly moved ahead; Germany was catching up fast; and France was now declining even compared with Britain (see Table 1.1).

But there was little sense that rates of growth depended on government policies. They seemed to depend on 'market conditions', themselves largely beyond control. Economic growth in all the industrialised states at this time was influenced, for example, by the prolonged depression which affected the whole Western world for over two decades after 1873. The depression was a depression of prices rather than of industrial activity (which flourished for much of the period, especially in the United States and Germany). It started with a normal downturn of the business cycle, especially pronounced because it coincided for all the four main industrial countries, bringing a reduction in the prices of manufactures. At about the same time, the development of improved and cheaper shipping brought a big increase in imports of food from overseas. This, together with the drop in economic activity generally, caused a severe depression of agricultural prices. By the end of the seventies this had intensified the industrial recession and brought a fall in other prices. There was a reversion to protectionism, which, while it eventually revived European agriculture (except in Britain, which in the interest of cheap food declined to protect her farmers), intensified the contraction of trade and production.

TABLE 1.1   *Average earnings and GNP a head, 1895*
(£ a year)

	Average earnings (Mulhall)	GNP a head (Kuznets)
Australia	49	39
United States	39	47
Britain	31	42
Canada	27	37
France	23	28
Belgium	14	31
Denmark	44	27
Germany	36	26
Switzerland	28	36
Sweden	25	34
Italy	22	12

SOURCES   M. G. Mulhall, *Dictionary of Statistics* (London, 1895); S. Kuznets, *Economic Growth of Nations* (Cambridge, 1961) p. 26.

From 1895, when a better balance between agricultural supplies and demand had been restored, the price level of both agricultural and manufactured goods began to rise once more. Money wages rose roughly at the same speed during the period of falling prices and in the subsequent revival. So, while in the early part of the period there was a shift of real income in favour of the industrial workers (whose wages could buy more with declining prices), in the second as the price of food rose and farmers were able to increase wages, it was the standard of living of agricultural workers which improved. The next two decades were a period of unparalleled prosperity. In the short period between 1900 and 1913, world trade in manufactures doubled.

National rates of growth, however, were affected not so much by this *long-term* movement of prices as by the age-old cycle of boom and depression. Such cycles usually had a periodicity of six to ten years between crests. At this time, though the cycle in one country would influence economies elsewhere, they did not normally coincide. The United States suffered severe depressions in the early seventies, the early nineties and in 1906, but experienced very rapid growth during most of the rest of the period. Germany underwent a severe recession in the mid-seventies but otherwise enjoyed almost uninterrupted growth. France suffered serious depressions in the early seventies, the mid-eighties and the early 1900s, but enjoyed boom conditions in the early eighties and late nineties, and immediately before the First World War. Britain experienced recession early in each decade but attained modest levels of growth at other times.

The rapid economic growth which took place at this time was based on a new pattern of world production. The initial impetus of the industrial revolution, based on coal, iron, railways, steamships, textiles and clothing, was now, after an interlude of slower technical innovation during the seventies and eighties, succeeded by the development of steel, electricity, chemicals, telecommunications, automobiles, and new consumer goods such as cameras, bicycles and typewriters. At the same time, cheaper shipping made possible far bigger imports of grains, meat, wool, rubber and oil to Europe. This created new economic growth points in the countries of the periphery where those commodities were produced. These became flourishing markets for the manufactured goods produced in Europe and North America, and especially from Britain and the United States.

The result was that there were considerable variations in the growth rates of individual countries. Britain continued to dominate in textiles (even in 1913 she still accounted for two-thirds of the world's trade in textiles), iron, coal and other traditional industries, for which she found new markets overseas to replace traditional European markets. But these were not growth industries and productivity growth was slow. Relying too much on her traditional industries, and on her income from foreign investment, she did not exploit the opportunities for growth in new industries such as steel, chemicals, telecommunications, electrical engineering and automobiles. France enjoyed periods of great prosperity, but remained predominantly an agricultural country. The countries that did best were those that were able to increase their exports fastest: the United States and Germany among industrial states, Australia, Canada and Argentina among agricultural producers. Among the industrial countries, Germany and the United States grew fastest because they were most successful in applying the benefits of scientific advance and research to industry, and so developing new technology. Productivity grew most quickly in Germany; to a rather lesser extent in the United States.

The average rates of growth of the major economies during this period have been estimated as shown in Table 1.2. The average rate of growth throughout Western Europe and North America was 2.7 per cent: faster than was to be achieved for the next 30 years but considerably less than was to be normal for the first 30 years after 1945. In terms of income a head, by 1913 the United States, Canada and Australia were undoubtedly in the lead. Britain, benefiting from a considerable income from overseas investment (amounting to 10 per cent of her whole national income immediately before the First World War), probably still came next. Germany and Denmark were not far behind. In total national income Germany, with a considerably larger population, now easily outstripped Britain, while the United States,

TABLE 1.2   *Growth rates, 1870–1913*

	Industrial production (Lewis)	Total output (Maddison)
United States	4.9	4.3
Germany	3.9	2.9
Britain	2.2	2.2
France	1.8	1.6

SOURCES W. A. Lewis, *Growth and Fluctuations, 1870–1914* (London, 1979) p. 17; A. Maddison, *Economic Growth in the West* (London, 1964) p. 28.

with three times the population of either, was still further ahead: by this time the United States was producing about a third of the manufacturing output of the entire world, including 43 per cent of the world's steel (against 26 per cent in 1870). The United States, Britain, Germany and France together accounted for 72 per cent of all world industrial production.

Outside the main industrialised countries, growth was fastest in the states of European settlement on the periphery. Cheaper shipping now made it possible for these to export large quantities of grain, wool, meat, rubber, oil and other products in return for imports of manufactures. This brought rapid growth in Canada, Australia, New Zealand and Argentina (exporting mainly wheat, wool, lamb and beef, respectively). Within Europe (apart from Belgium, which was almost an extension of the French economy), Sweden secured a fairly rapid rate of growth, exploiting her natural endowment by exporting timber, and later pulp and paper, all over Europe. Switzerland, Denmark and the Netherlands embarked on the process of industrialisation, mainly pulled by the momentum of the larger industrial countries around them. Russia, though starting late, had by 1914, through rapid investment, largely with French capital, become a significant industrial power by virtue of her sheer size. Finally, Japan, with few natural resources except coal, and no tradition of industry or science, was already beginning, through the intense application of the methods tried successfully in Western countries, to develop both her agricultural and her industrial potential. For the most part it was those countries that had a developing foreign trade, a reasonably productive agriculture to provide the markets for industrial goods, a fair level of education and technology, an effective financial system and a substantial middle class that grew fastest. For this reason the countries of Central and Eastern Europe, which lacked most of these assets, and still more the majority of countries in Latin America, Asia and Africa, did not achieve any significant industrialisation (though among them it was those, such as Egypt, Burma, Indo-China and Thailand, which had significant agricultural exports, or those, such as Chile and Malaya, which had significant mineral exports, that grew the fastest).

The First World War brought to an end this rapid spurt of growth. During the war the gold standard was abandoned, international investment almost came to an end, production was concentrated on war needs, and exports declined. When the war was over, there was a brief period of very high inflation, brought about by the coincidence of worldwide shortages with rapidly renewed demand. This was followed, in 1920, by a period of serious depression, which for some countries eased only gradually during the course of the twenties. Large-scale debts between states, the creation of totally new states with little economic viability, and financial chaos in some of them, inhibited growth in parts of Europe. European output thus only regained the 1913 level in 1925. But from that point it grew fast for a few years: by 4 or 5 per cent a year.

There was at least one way in which government policies at this time began to affect growth. Performance in Europe during the twenties was partly determined by exchange rates. Britain, concerned with stability rather than growth, in 1925 pegged her currency to gold at the pre-war level, and then found it impossible to export on a scale that would mop up her high unemployment, especially as many of her exports went to countries outside Europe whose economies were depressed by low agricultural prices. France, on the other hand, which fixed the franc at an undervalued level, restored her markets abroad and recovered fast. Germany, at first held back by very heavy reparations payments and a bout of hyper-inflation, underwent a rapid economic recovery in the second half of the twenties, aided by large-scale investment and loans from the United States. The United States herself, the only economy that had been little affected by the war, grew rapidly during much of the twenties and so further increased her share of world production and world trade. By 1929, therefore, the United States was overwhelmingly the most prosperous country of the world, followed by Britain, France and Germany among European countries; while Canada, Australia, New Zealand and South Africa, weakened by depressed agricultural prices, now stood at a generally similar level.

The stock-exchange crash of 1929 in the United States, and the financial crises which followed both in Europe and in North America, ushered in a period of very low growth – even economic decline for a time. From 1929 to 1933 output in the United States fell by a third, in Eastern Europe by 20 per cent, in Germany by 16 per cent, and in Europe as a whole by about 10 per cent. Commodity prices now sank even more disastrously than in the two decades after 1873. This not only reduced income in the producing countries, but also reduced demand for the manufactures produced in Western Europe. Investment fell both at home and abroad. Levels of economic activity throughout the Western world were thus intensely depressed, and unemployment in most countries rose to heights not previously experienced (or at least not previously recorded). Only in the latter half of the thirties did a slow recovery take place. In Western Europe this was sustained by rearmament, but in the United States it was followed by a further decline at the end of the decade.

The long depression severely restricted growth in the inter-war period as a whole. Annual growth rates averaged well under 2 per cent a year, compared with over 3 per cent for the main industrial countries before the First World War. Britain's growth rate was barely more than 1 per cent a year, and that of France was below 1 per cent. Germany's, on the other hand, was above the average, while a few smaller states – the Netherlands, Sweden, Norway and Finland – achieved higher rates still, of up to 3 per cent.[2]

The Second World War again distorted the normal pattern of growth. The US economy was once more little disrupted by the war, and now grew more rapidly than ever, with production increasing by 50 per cent during the course of that conflict. By 1950, therefore, the United States had attained an average rate of growth of 2.9 per cent a year since 1913. In other countries the rate was only 1.9 per cent (0.7 per cent for France, 1.2 per cent for Germany, 1.7 per cent for Britain and 2–2.3 per cent for the Scandinavian countries and the Netherlands). The balance of prosperity had thus altered yet again. The United States, Switzerland and the Scandinavian countries, all economies little affected by the war, had improved their position; that of Britain, France and especially Germany had declined. By that time income a head among the principal developed countries is estimated to have been as shown in Table 1.3.

The next 23 years, between 1950 and 1973, saw the most rapid period of economic growth of recent times. After the disruption of the war and

TABLE 1.3 *GDP a head, 1950 (1973 US $ '000)*

United States	3.6
Canada	2.7
Sweden	2.3
Australia	2.1
Switzerland	1.9
Britain	1.8
Denmark	1.7
France	1.6
West Germany	1.1
Italy	0.84
Japan	0.45
Soviet Union	0.36

SOURCE C. P. Kindleberger and B. Herrick, *Economic Development* (New York, 1977) p. 16.

the difficult period of economic recovery thereafter, the main industrialised countries of the Western world achieved, over nearly 25 years, a growth rate never attained before or since. When the period began there was a marked imbalance between the strength of the US and West European economies: the US economy was stronger than ever before, but the war had brought severe disruption and physical destruction in most of the West European countries. For the first ten years after 1945, recovery in Europe was inhibited by a shortage of capital goods and the hard currency required to purchase these. But the massive injection of US aid to Europe through the Marshall programme, the devaluation of European currencies against the dollar in 1949 and the gradual liberalisation of trade and payments brought a rapid recovery to Europe. The growth of European economic power meant that even before the end of the fifties the dollar shortage, the basic problem of the early post-war years, had been transformed into a chronic US deficit, leading to a continual drain of dollars to Europe (p. 98 below).

There were a number of reasons for the rapid rate of growth achieved at this time. The first was that by now it was assumed that governments did have a role in creating growth. Most were committed to full employment and so to high levels of demand, and adopted monetary and tax policies to secure that end. Other reasons were rapidly expanding world trade, assisted by progressive liberalisation (especially within the EEC, where, after 1957, barriers were removed altogether) and efficient management by governments which were able to ensure a steady level of demand without excessive inflation; the resulting high confidence among businessmen, leading to steady investment; the economies of scale which larger companies secured; a high level of research and innovation; better forecasting and business planning; the development in Europe of new technical and business methods and of consumption patterns often first developed in the United States.[3] Investment was sustained by government incentives and tax concessions. Even when there was some recession in the private sector, high levels of public spending and welfare payments maintained incomes, so reducing the scale of downturns. Fiscal and monetary policy reflected the explicit commitment of most governments to full employment policies, which meant they were not willing to sacrifice growth for the sake of containing inflation (which by later standards was not high anyway). There was a high level of consumer demand, stimulated by heavy advertising and much market research. And there were rapid improvements in productivity, especially in agriculture. Growth was particularly strong in those countries, such as West Germany, Italy,

Austria and Japan, which had suffered the most disruption during the war and were therefore able to develop a totally new industrial structure. It was also fast where the available labour force could be increased from elsewhere: as in West Germany (from East Germany and Southern Europe), in France (from Algeria and Portugal), and in northern Italy (from the south).

As a result the average rate of growth in the West during the fifties was over 4 per cent a year (4.4 per cent in Western Europe). In the decade that followed, growth was faster still, about 5 per cent in the West as a whole (8 per cent in Japan, over 5 per cent in Western Europe and just over 3 per cent in the United States). In both decades there were only mild fluctuations in activity, sometimes beginning in the United States (with small and brief recessions in 1948–9, 1953–4, 1958–9, 1962–3, 1968 and 1970–1). In Eastern Europe too there was fairly rapid growth, resulting from very high rates of saving and investment, the movement of labour from the land to the towns, and low rates of pay in industry and agriculture, though efficiency was reduced by excessive centralisation of decision-making, lack of incentive, poor management and lack of genuine consumer choice.[4]

From the early seventies, however, this period of development came to an end. The rapid rate of growth slowed considerably; the average for Western developed countries generally fell to about 2.8 per cent in the first half of the decade and was even slower in the second half.

There were two main reasons for the lower rates of growth. First, the large rise in the cost of oil, and subsequently of other fuels, in 1973 brought sharp deficits in the balance of payments of developed countries, causing them to slow growth and so reduce imports. Secondly, high levels of inflation, partly as a result of this rise in energy costs, also induced governments to resort to severe deflation, slowing growth still further. There was considerable instability in exchange rates, now allowed to float freely, resulting mainly from big variations in rates of inflation and in interest rates. Confidence, and therefore investment, declined. Government spending was cut. Unemployment rose to levels higher than had been known since the slump of the early thirties.

Though these problems were common to all the industrialised countries, rates of growth continued to vary widely. Both in the period of rapid growth before 1973 and in the slow growth period thereafter, performances differed considerably. The highest rates of growth were achieved by Japan, West Germany, Switzerland, Sweden and the Netherlands; and the slowest by the United States and Britain.

TABLE 1.4   *Annual average growth rates, 1960–80*

	1960–73	1974–80
Britain	3.1	0.7
Canada	5.6	2.7
France	5.6	2.8
Italy	5.2	2.7
Japan	10.4	4.3
United States	4.2	2.4
West Germany	4.5	2.4
Developed market economies	5.6	2.6

SOURCE   United Nations, *World Economic Survey, 1980–81*, p. 18.

Table 1.4 gives the rates of growth achieved by the main industrialised countries from 1960 to 1980. As these figures show, there were very substantial variations in rates of growth among these countries. By 1980 the more successful had secured a standard of living more than double that of the slow-growing countries. However, the rates of growth of all alike were far lower than before. Increasingly they were slowed by instabilities deriving from the international economy as a whole.

The commitment of governments at the national level to seek growth for their economies was thus no longer enough. Since inflation, recession and high interest rates – the main obstacles to growth – were international rather than national in origin, international measures were now needed if the rates of growth of earlier times were to be restored.

1.2   GROWTH AMONG POOR COUNTRIES

Variations in the standard of living attained by rich countries were, anyway, trivial compared with the huge gap that existed between income a head in this group as a whole and that of the inhabitants of poor countries. It is to the rates of growth secured among this latter group that we must now turn.

Most third-world countries had achieved little industrialisation before the Second World War. Even where some industry had been established – as in India, Argentina, China and Egypt – it represented only a small proportion of the whole economy. Rates of growth therefore depended mainly on the success of their agriculture. This varied with climatic conditions, availability of water and land, systems of inheritance and land tenure, and similar factors. It depended partly on the development of communications, making possible the establishment of flourishing national markets. But it depended even more on how far such countries had access to wider markets beyond the seas, making possible the development of export crops and export industries. Even if they were so integrated within the world economic system, however, it was mainly as suppliers of food and raw materials. For this reason, there was often little significant development, even in those cases, outside the enclaves where these were produced.

Whether growth was achieved was, anyway, largely outside the control of the peoples of these countries. Most had for two or three centuries been colonies, and, outside Latin America, remained so until after the Second World War. Only within the last 20 or 30 years have such states ceased to be controlled by governments whose main interest was in the success of their own economies far across the seas.

Statistics for most of these territories are so inadequate, and the proportion of subsistence activity was so high, that it is impossible to obtain reliable figures for rates of growth or standards of living before the Second World War. In 1950 the average income a head in all developing countries was about 150 current dollars a head (something like a tenth of the average among rich countries at that time). But this average covered very wide variations: between countries which had substantial resources of their own, especially oil or other minerals, and those that did not; between those where general levels of education were high and those where they were low; between those that had ample fertile land and adequate food supplies and those that did not; between those that already enjoyed some degree of industrial development, usually financed by external investment (as in Argentina, India, and the Philippines), and those that had little. For all these reasons, income a head, even at the beginning of this period, varied widely: from around 50 to well over 500 current dollars a head. Table 1.5 shows the variation among some typical poor countries at that time.

All developing countries encountered severe problems in seeking to improve their rates of growth. The whole structure of their societies often inhibited the development of an industrial economy. Traditional ways of life – conditions of land tenure, the system of inheritance, customary obligations to the family, the traditional role of women, patterns of consumption, the use of savings to finance weddings and other festivals – often reduced social mobility and the readiness to undertake new types of economic activity. Usually there were low rates

TABLE 1.5   *GDP a head, 1950 (1973 US $)*

Argentina	864
Cyprus	560
Chile	431
Mexico	402
Jamaica	313
Colombia	295
Brazil	284
Morocco	301
Philippines	293
Syria	246
Sri Lanka	192
South Korea	157
Egypt	146
Thailand	129
China	112
India	105
Indonesia	98

SOURCE Kindleberger   and   Herrick,   *Economic Development*, p. 16.

of savings and small opportunities for investment. Society was often divided between a wealthy landowning class, which had little inclination or incentive to engage in risky industrial ventures, and the vast majority of cultivators and small traders, without the resources, the opportunity or the ambition to do so. Activities in commerce or industry had low social status, while the high regard attached to landownership meant that most savings were invested in land, raising its price without raising the price of its products or stimulating improved methods of production. In many cases inadequate administration, archaic political structures, regressive tax policies (often reflecting the interests of a narrow ruling class), strong tribal and family loyalties, and sometimes widespread corruption created an environment unfavourable to economic growth. Levels of education were low and illiteracy widespread. Frequently the traditions of discipline, punctuality, foresight, ambition and co-operation required for economic progress were weak; while instability, economic and political, undermined confidence. And often, as a result, capital and brain-power were drawn abroad by the gravity force of more prosperous economies elsewhere.

These general problems were compounded by special difficulties in achieving economic development. A necessary precondition for this was to create an efficient agriculture, both to feed the urban population which industrialisation created and to produce the export surpluses required to finance imports of capital goods, of many consumer goods and of some food and raw materials, as well as to repay foreign debts. But agricultural productivity could not usually quickly be raised. Communications were often inadequate to create effective markets, either at home or abroad, and so to stimulate production. Prices for agricultural produce were usually low and unstable. There was difficulty in replacing traditional methods and crops with those needed to create an exportable surplus: it was usually easier to increase the production of existing crops, which only depressed prices further. There were many physical constraints. Sometimes there was little unused land and an expanding population seeking to work on it. Soil was often poor. Usually there was either too little water or too much, while the dams, drainage, and irrigation works needed to control it were very expensive. Supplies of fertiliser were inadequate but especially necessary for land that was often already eroded by primitive agricultural techniques.

Even if they could improve agricultural productivity, such countries faced other problems impeding industrialisation. Roads and railways were poor; power was inadequate and unreliable; banking and insurance facilities were lacking; telephone services were inefficient; specialised supplies and services were unavailable. Usually there was no significant middle or moneyed class which might, as in Europe and North America, become the agents of enterprise and innovation. The low level of education meant that productivity stayed generally low. Above all, local income usually was too small to create an adequate home market to stimulate production of manufactured goods.

Finally, even if all these domestic difficulties could be overcome, there were other problems deriving from the international environment. Access to markets abroad, which might have encouraged investment and made trade the engine of growth, was often restricted by the protectionism of developed states, which especially affected the type of product such countries were best equipped to manufacture (see p. 75 below). Foreign investment, while it flowed in large quantities to a handful of more advanced developing countries, was in general not attracted to economies suffering the types of problem just described. Even when it was available, investment often favoured a type of production that was inappropriate for poor countries: capital-intensive and geared usually to production of consumer goods unsuited to such a country. The level of technology and basic science was inadequate to promote industrial advance, or sometimes even to apply industrial techniques effectively. On the contrary, both savings and profits and skilled manpower tended to be drained away in the opposite direction, to rich countries elsewhere. There were serious shortages of the foreign exchange needed to import capital goods and other necessities. Balance of payments deficits were large. Debts rapidly accumulated. And in consequence dependence on creditors, whether foreign governments, international banks or international financial institutions, steadily increased.

The remarkable thing is that, despite all these problems, many poor countries secured high rates of growth: even higher than those achieved at the same time by the rich countries, themselves extremely high; and much higher than those which rich countries had secured at the same stage of development. Developing countries benefited at this time from the fact that the economies of rich countries, their main markets, were themselves growing fast; from the fact that they started from a very backward position and benefited from technological advances already made by rich countries; and from the fact that they received considerable injections of foreign capital and economic aid. During the fifties the poor countries grew on average by 4.5 per cent a year (against 4.2 per cent a year among rich countries). During the sixties their growth was 5.6 per cent a year (against 5 per cent a year among rich countries). And during the seventies, despite all the special problems that then arose, especially the high price of energy, which affected poor countries even more acutely than the rich, their growth remained high at 5.3 per cent (against 3.1 per cent for the rich countries).

But this average rate of growth was misleading, for it concealed huge variations between particular countries and groups of countries. The total includes very wealthy 'capital-surplus' oil-producing states: if they are omitted, the rate of growth of developing countries in the seventies immediately declines. The total also includes the so-called newly indus-trialising countries (NICs), such as Brazil, Mexico, South Korea, Singapore and Taiwan, countries which had secured large-scale foreign investment, had developed substantial manufacturing capacity and large export trades, and so had secured rates of growth well above the average, sometimes of 10 per cent or more. Other middle-income countries, even without such large exports of manufactures, secured rates of growth of 6–7 per cent a year, relying mainly on exports of minerals and agricultural production.

This left a substantial number of other third-world countries where growth was very low indeed. Among the 30 or so 'least developed' states, a large proportion of them landlocked, often mountainous or desert countries, rates of growth were often below 2 per cent. That rate was declining towards the end of the period. And some were not growing at all, even in aggregate terms.

In any case, these rates of overall growth gave no indication of standards of living. Not only did such countries start from a position of acute poverty, which for the least developed meant a bare subsistence income for most of the population; more important, the *effect* of growth depended on rates of population increase. The important figure is income a head – the measure of standard of living. This rose far more slowly than the absolute growth in national income. Among developing countries generally, the growth in income a head was only 2.3 per cent during the fifties (against 3.1 per cent in rich countries); thus the gap in living standards, already enormous, was then steadily widening. During the next two decades, as population growth in poor countries began to slow while their national incomes grew faster, the situation began to change. During the sixties income a head grew by 3.1 per cent among poor countries against 3.9 per cent in industrialised countries. But in the following decade, during which the severe recessions of 1974–5 and 1979–80 affected rich countries far more, the position was reversed. Even income a head grew faster in the poor countries (about 2.9 per cent against 2.4 per cent among the rich).[5] For the first time the gap began to narrow.

But these figures too, cover huge variations among poor countries. As

TABLE 1.6   *Growth of GNP a head, 1960–80*

	1960–70		1970–80	
All developing countries	3.1		2.9	
Low-income countries	1.8		1.7	
Sub-Saharan Africa		1.7		0.2
Asia		1.8		2.0
Middle-income countries	3.5		3.1	
East Asia and Pacific		4.9		5.7
Latin America and Caribbean		2.9		3.2
Middle East and North Africa		1.1		3.8
Sub-Saharan Africa		2.3		1.6
Oil-exporting developing countries	2.8		3.5	
Industrialised countries	3.9		2.4	
Centrally planned economies	n.a.		3.8	

SOURCE   World Bank, *World Development Report, 1980*, p. 99.

Table 1.6 shows, the increase in income a head among the different regions of the world varied widely. Income a head in Africa and Southern Asia barely increased at all. Among the very poorest countries in each region (those with incomes a head under $350 in the late seventies)[6] absolute growth was only 1.5 per cent on average in the seventies; and the growth in income a head was less than 1 per cent, sometimes nil, and occasionally even negative. Thus it was in the poorest countries of all, where standards of living were already lowest, that the rates of growth were also lowest.

This reflected the fact that to some extent the differences in growth rate corresponded with the extent of industrialisation. Industry was nearly always the fastest growing sector; and where it was largest (as in the NICs) overall growth was also fastest. Industrial production grew by 8 per cent in the middle-income countries, but by only 5.5 per cent in the low-income countries. Agricultural production, on the other hand, grew slowly in both groups, sometimes not keeping up with the rise in population. Thus by the end of the seventies food production a head was 10 per cent less in Africa than it had been in the sixties. Nearly all poor countries became increasingly dependent on imports of food, mainly from rich countries. This situation was likely to get worse: according to the FAO, by 1990 the total food deficit of developing countries could be 120—50 million tons (Chapter 7 below, p. 172).

At first sight some of these figures might seem to provide grounds for optimism about the situation of poor countries. By historical standards their rate of growth in recent years has been very high. It has been almost twice as high as that of rich countries; and over the last few years even the growth in income a head has been higher. These facts, however, are misleading. First, the absolute gap in wealth between the two groups is so large that, even if all poor countries are taken as a group, any marginal improvement in the relative situation of the latter is so slow as to be almost invisible. A growth of 3 per cent in income a head for a rich country, having an income a head of say $5000, would be an increase of $150 a year for each person. In poor countries with an income a head of say, $400, even growth in income a head that is faster, say 4 per cent a year, gives a growth in income of only $16 a year. In that sense the gap is continuing to widen, even if now at a slower pace. Thus, even if poor countries on average continued to grow faster than rich (which is by no means certain), it would still take well over 250 years, it has been estimated, for the gap to disappear.

But in addition, as we have seen, the figures for poor countries as a whole conceal great variations. Among the poorest countries of all, both

TABLE 1.7   *Rates of growth per head, 1960–80 (per cent)*

	1960–70	1970–80
Industrialised countries	4.1	2.5
Middle-income countries	3.5	2.7
Low-income countries	1.8	1.8

SOURCE   World Bank, *World Development Report, 1981*, p. 3.

total rates of growth and increases in income a head are far lower (see Table 1.7). In their case the gap is not just continuing to widen temporarily but is getting worse all the time (with income a head

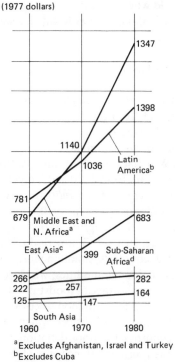

SOURCE   World Bank, *World Development Report, 1980*, p. 8.

FIGURE 1.1   *Growth in GNP a head by region, 1960–80*

growing by little more than 1 per cent, compared with double that rate among rich states).

Finally, and most important of all, comparison between entire states is itself misleading. More significant is the comparison between groups *within* states. Even in faster-growing poor states there exist, as the World Bank has often pointed out, large pools of absolute poverty, especially in the rural areas where there is virtually no growth visible at all, and sometimes with growing populations, a decline in absolute living standards; where already income is barely adequate to sustain life; and where levels of nutrition, health and housing are all totally insufficient for a reasonable existence. To define areas of poverty in terms of types of *country* is therefore wholly inaccurate. The real source of concern should be the groups and individuals living in poverty, in rich countries and poor, throughout the world whose welfare is almost totally unaffected by the overall rate of growth of the country in which they live (Fig. 1.1).

1.3   CONSTRAINTS ON GROWTH

Thus rich countries and poor alike, though still *pursuing* the highest possible rates of growth, had from the early seventies onwards faced increasing difficulties in achieving these.

What were the reasons for the dramatic slowing of growth which occurred in this decade? Why had the era of unprecedented expansion which lasted for nearly 25 years from 1950 suddenly come to an end?

The reason was partly the increasing *instability* of the world economy. The collapse of the Bretton Woods system in 1970–1 (p. 101 below) was followed shortly afterwards by the adoption of floating exchange rates that were inherently unstable. In 1972–3, a period of intensive boom, occurring in all developed countries simultaneously, led to a huge increase in the prices of all major commodities, which roughly doubled in the course of a year. A severe shortage of foodstuffs at about the same time brought an equally sharp increase in food prices all over the world. Above all, the fivefold increase in oil prices which occurred during 1973–4 caused the rich countries to adopt deflationary policies while they sought to overcome their serious balance of payments deficits. This in turn led to a sharp reduction in the earnings of poor countries too. From that point there was only a slow recovery in the world economy, before a further sharp rise in oil prices in 1979–80 heralded another bout of severe recession in rich states.

The increase in the price of oil and of some other commodities, however, was only one manifestation of a far wider problem affecting all countries, rich and poor alike, during this period. This was the increasingly high rate of domestic inflation which prevailed in all economies throughout this decade. The average rate of inflation in developed countries rose steadily, from an average of 3 per cent in 1950–65, to 5 per cent in the second half of the sixties, to about 10 per cent at the end of the seventies. It was the effort to contain this inflation, as much as to restore their large balance of payments deficits, which caused Western governments in the second half of the decade to impose severely deflationary policies, and so led to a dramatic slowing of growth.

Why did inflation become so high in this period? First, there were many features of developed economies at this period which created high levels of demand there. Most governments attempted, in accordance with the Keynesian doctrines which prevailed almost everywhere, to bring about, by appropriate budgetary and monetary policies, the necessary volume of demand to maintain purchasing power and employment – for the first part of the period, indeed, to maintain 'full employment'. During the fifties and sixties employment was probably at higher levels than had ever previously been known; (though the fact that inflation was considerably higher after 1970, when rates of unemployment rose, suggests that the level of employment was not, as was sometimes believed, the fundamental cause of inflation). There was everywhere a very high level of public spending, including expenditure in many areas, such as defence, social services and administration generally, which created little corresponding outlet for consumer demand. There were strong political pressures on governments, from both domestic and external sources, to maintain high levels of growth and the types of policy, including large investment incentives and regional policies (again increasing demand), likely to produce it. Large budget deficits increasingly became the norm; and were not significantly lower in times of boom or balance of payments surplus than in times of recession or deficit. There was a huge extension of credit of all kinds; including large-scale borrowing on the market by industry, public and private, bank lending, hire purchase, bank cards, and other forms of consumer credit. High interest rates, intended to contain inflation, had little effect (as had long ago been forecast[7]) in deterring borrowing, but increased costs, both for governments and for all other borrowers. The index-linking of many benefits, pensions and, in some countries, wages, intended as a response to inflation, inevitably further stimulated it. The share of the service sector in each economy became very much larger, and costs in this sector rose twice as fast as the cost of manufactures. As prices rose in response to all these factors, *expectations* of inflation rose still further, again feeding further inflation, since they increased the concern to spend rather than to save (or induced to save in a way which involved spending, as on housing or land or pictures).

Secondly, other causes of inflation stemmed from the supply side. It was widely believed that a major cause was the increased bargaining power of labour, resulting from the unions' monopoly power, legal protection of their position, social security benefits cushioning them and their families from the effect of strikes, and overfull employment policies. Though this is a simple and attractive explanation, however, it is one that is scarcely supported by the evidence. Overfull employment can scarcely itself have been a factor, since, as we have seen, inflation was highest during the seventies, at a time when unemployment was growing steadily higher throughout the industrial world. Inflation was no less in countries such as the United States and France, where only a small proportion of the workforce was unionised. Increases in income were scarcely less among those, such as women, parts of the agricultural population and the managerial classes, who did not belong to unions, than among those who did. Above all, the real power of unions was no greater at this time than in earlier ages when inflation was minimal. The only objective measure of union power is the willingness of their members to strike. But strikes had been far more numerous, and had lasted longer, immediately before and after the First World War, without causing rapid inflation at either of these times. The real difference in the post-war world was on the side not of the unions but of the employers. If inflation was higher it was not because of the greater power of the former but the greater weakness of the latter. Employers had less reason to resist demands. The big increase in the public sector, which could easily add wage costs to prices; a wide degree of monopoly and of oligopoly within the private sector; a greater degree of product differentiation, reducing the effect of competition; greater reliance on advertising, packaging and servicing rather than price competition to sell products; a greater interdependence of industry, leading to pressure from suppliers and customers for quick settlements; greater reliance on external finance, also leading to the need for quickly resumed production; and a greater concern generally to maintain production, turnover and cash flow even at the price of higher wage costs – these were far more important in causing inflationary settlements than was greater militancy among unions, which overall showed no more willingness to strike at this period than in earlier times and often (as in the United States) were suffering a decline in membership as well as in finances.

These two domestic causes of inflation, therefore – very high levels of internal demand and an increasing unwillingness of employers to risk prolonged stoppages – were important enough. But there was a third reason, deriving from the international environment, which was still more fundamental. This was the increasing pressure of population and industrial growth on limited resources: resources that were either finite or could not easily or rapidly be increased. The most obvious case was land: the pressure of increasing population and increasing demand for food brought in most countries an increase in land prices which far outstripped the general rate of inflation but which itself contributed to higher prices of almost all other products, especially food. The increase in the demand for housing, which rising income stimulated, was almost equally intense, especially since housing could more easily be acquired than land as a hedge against inflation: and here too prices rose far faster than other prices (the average price of a three-bedroomed house in Britain, for example, quadrupled between 1945 and 1965, from about £1000 to £4000) and multiplied by six or seven times more in the fifteen years after that (to £25,000–30,000); a total increase of 20–30 times. The pressure of demand for food in relation to supply rose almost equally rapidly, especially in developing countries, where the rise in population was heaviest and the increase in food supply lowest, leading (where governments permitted it) to substantial increases in prices there too. Demand for particular minerals in limited supply – uranium, cobalt, chrome, copper and tin, for example, as well as silver and gold, which are special cases – could cause huge price rises over the years: at times of boom, such as 1972–3, prices sometimes more than doubled in the course of a year. The most dramatic case of pressure on supply arose in the case of energy (see Chapter 6 below), a factor adding to the prices of almost all other products. The pressure of rising world demand on these various resources counted for a substantial proportion of the inflation which affected developed economies during the seventies. And there was every indication that, if existing rates of growth were maintained, such pressure would be continued.

Developing countries suffered even more than rich ones from very high rates of inflation. The average, even when extreme cases are excluded, was over 20 per cent.[8] This resulted partly from poor economic management, partly from the rapid increases in the price of the capital goods and other manufactures they bought from the West and in energy prices. But it also derived from the development situation in which they found themselves. This created rapid increases in demand and income, derived from large government programmes and high investment. These could not easily be matched by increases in food, housing and other consumer goods to satisfy the new purchasing power so created, so that price levels rapidly rose.

Whatever the cause of inflation, the consequences for world growth were decisive. During the fifties and sixties, Western governments were willing to tolerate inflation at levels of up to 5 per cent, while still maintaining expansionary policies. During the seventies they were unwilling to tolerate inflation levels of 10–15 per cent or even higher, as now became common. Though most people, both within governments and outside, accepted that the best means of containing the problem, without sacrifice of growth, was the adoption of policies regulating the growth of income, there was also widespread scepticism about how these policies could be made to succeed.[9] In consequence governments all over the developed world resorted to severe deflation (an ancient remedy now sometimes dignified by the title 'monetarism'). Credit was restricted, interest rates were raised, public spending was cut, and in consequence unemployment was increased and demand held back. This was, as we have seen, the prime reason for the drastic reduction in growth rates which occurred after 1973. The reduction in growth was thus the result of a deliberate choice by governments: by the governments of rich countries, which concluded that they would prefer to forgo growth if in so doing they could contain inflation.

But, though the new policy (or rather the old policy, since it was not unlike that adopted in many countries during the twenties and early thirties, or indeed the impact of the gold standard during the nineteenth century) was adopted by rich countries to meet the problems which they themselves faced, its effect was felt equally in poor countries. The latter continued to grow faster than rich countries, but their rate of growth was none the less held back. The reduction of economic activity in the rich states drastically reduced the demand for the products of poor countries, whether raw materials, food or simple manufactures. That reduction in demand brought a corresponding reduction in the prices of their products. Finally, the deliberately induced recession in the north brought with it a reversion to protectionism there which still further restricted market access and earnings for poor countries. This reduction in their earnings in turn reduced their own demand for the exports of rich countries, so even further accentuating the decline in world production. A descending spiral set in which threatened to bring back world depression on the scale of the thirties.

Not only, however, was there a reduction in the capacity of states to maintain high growth rates at this time: there was also a reduction in the desire to do so. This was not only because of the concern to reduce inflation. There was increasing doubt, at least in rich countries, whether the maximising of economic growth was a sensible or appropriate policy. There was a growing awareness of the finite character of many of the resources which continuous growth progressively consumed. There were fears that some at least would be exhausted within a few decades if the pressure for further growth continued unabated. There were doubts about the costs and feasibility of recycling and waste disposal. According to the most alarmist view,[10] food supplies could be inadequate to support the likely population of the future (expected then to rise to 7 billion* by the year 2000). If existing rates of growth were maintained, according to this view, at some point between 2000 and 2100 a crisis of huge proportions would occur when energy, resources and food would be exhausted, industrial and agricultural production would rapidly decline, and deaths from starvation and pollution would occur on a vast scale. Even if new sources of energy were found, population controlled, pollution reduced and agricultural productivity increased, the crisis could only be delayed by two or three decades. Only a stable-state economy could, under this assessment, prevent the cataclysm. This would require an immediate halt to population growth, a drastic reduction in the consumption of resources (to a quarter of the previous level for each unit of industrial production), a similar reduction in pollution (by three-quarters for each unit of production), an increase in capital expenditure devoted to agriculture, an improvement in the fertility of the soil and a transfer of consumption to services. Though this judgement was in the view of most a somewhat wild one, there were none the less widespread doubts about the heavy costs of growth in human terms: through the increase of large-scale organisation, bureaucracy, urbanisation, congestion, pollution, inequality, work impoverishment and the acquisitive life-style which must result.

Others doubted the validity of these fears. Some suggested that the degree of pressure on resources had been greatly exaggerated by the opponents of growth. Many new sources of minerals already used, it was held, would be found through more intensive exploration both on land and beneath the seas. Alternative materials would be developed through research in chemical synthetics and other methods and these would prove virtually inexhaustible. New forms of energy would be discovered: either through harnessing sun, wind and wave power, biomass and other methods, as environmentalists wished; or through developing nuclear

---

* 'Billion' is used throughout to denote a thousand millions.

power, especially the fast-breeder and fusion power, as others felt inevitable. Some argued that it was not the fact of growth which gave rise to problems but its distribution. It was growth in rich countries which created the worst environmental problems and the greatest pressure on resources. Faster growth in poor countries, with low or nil growth among the rich, would not only create a fairer distribution of wealth and welfare in the world but would, because poor countries still accounted for a small proportion of world industrial production, bring far less depletion of resources. In any case, the standard of living in poor countries was so low that growth, even if for rich countries it was only a luxury, was there an absolute necessity. New types of technology, industry and life-style would be developed that were not environmentally damaging. Certainly, so long as the growth of population continued – and any reduction would take a considerable time to bring about – reasonable rates of growth were essential to provide even a minimum standard of living for the peoples of tomorrow.

While the former of these arguments was persuasive among some sections of the population in wealthier countries, it was the latter view which prevailed among *governments*, in rich countries and poor alike. The aim at least of the administrations in all countries continued to be to secure the fastest possible growth for their economies. If in the following decade or so that aim was not to be achieved, it would not be because of a far-sighted renunciation of the goal of growth by governments. It would be, on the contrary, because the refusal to renounce growth would even further intensify the pressure of demand on inadequate resources all over the world and so fuel still sharper inflation than before, leading in turn to still more severe deflation to contain it. At the same time, growing protectionism might hold back levels of world trade and of production. On these grounds it was not unrealistic to suppose that the 2 per cent growth of the late seventies might decline to 1 per cent or even nil growth in the following decade.

It thus seemed altogether possible that the aim demanded by the environmentalists would indeed be accomplished, but despite, not because of, the will of governments: because they were not able to overcome the problems of the international economy – above all that of rampant inflation – in a way which would, as in earlier years, allow the world as a whole to combine sustained economic growth with reasonable stability of prices.

1.4 INTERNATIONAL DEMAND MANAGEMENT

Whether or not these fears are justified, and the world is now moving towards an era of nil growth – or at least very low growth among rich countries – it is too soon to say. What is certain is that by the early 1980s the era of spectacular growth which the world experienced from 1950 onwards appeared to have come to an end. That growth had been fairly widely distributed between states. Though it had been mainly powered by the engine-room provided by the rich countries, the demand these created helped to stimulate rapid growth in most poor countries as well.

The rapid expansion of the previous decades had been stimulated above all by four conditions: rapid liberalisation of trade, relatively stable supplies of raw materials, reasonable price stability in most countries (and so reasonable exchange-rate stability) and steadily expanding consumer demand sustained by reasonably expansionist government policy. From the early seventies all four of these conditions ceased to be fulfilled. Liberalisation was replaced by increasing protectionism, not only against the exports of poor countries but also by rich countries against rich. The supply of raw materials, especially of oil, became increasingly erratic, leading to sharp increases in price and a large transfer of funds to oil-producing states which were not well equipped to spend them. Relative price stability was replaced by rampant inflation in most countries, leading to increased instability in exchange rates. This in turn led to a significant curtailment of consumer demand within some developed economies, brought about by the increasingly deflationary policies pursued by governments.

There was no longer, therefore, a stable and self-sustaining world economy. Stability and growth were now likely to be attained only through a far more effective and deliberate management of the international economy than had ever previously been attempted. What was chiefly required was a form of demand management applied at the world level. The techniques for reducing excessive fluctuations in activity, which had been applied at the national level for nearly fifty years, were now urgently needed at the world level too.

Economic 'interdependence' between states had been recognised theoretically for years. The need for joint consultation about economic relations among states was continually reiterated. This recognition had even been reflected in a growing number of international institutions designed to confront the world's economic problems through collective action: from formal institutions within the UN framework, to less formal arrangements for mutual consultation, mainly among rich countries. Most of the formal institutions were relatively specialised: world bodies to consider specific problems, money, trade, labour, agriculture, education and others (some of which we shall consider in later chapters). They met for the most part in isolation from each other and confined themselves to the problems arising in their own spheres (though there was endless discussion of 'co-ordination' of these various autonomous bodies, for the most part this did not succeed even in bringing about effective co-operation between them[11]).

A few more general economic institutions emerged. The United Nations had an Economic and Social Council, which was supposed to supervise the institutions of the UN system as a whole. But in practice it devoted itself mainly to the activities of purely UN bodies (that is, programmes undertaken within the UN proper rather than in its agencies). Its discussions were too diffuse, and representation far too low-grade, for its discussions and resolutions to exercise any effective influence on governments. Periodic 'dialogues' took place between the rich countries and the poor countries as a group: for example, in the regular conferences of the UN Conference on Trade and Development (UNCTAD), which took place every three or four years; in occasional special assemblies of the United Nations on north–south questions (in 1974, 1975 and 1980); in the once-and-for-all negotiations in 1975–6, known as the Conference on International Economic Co-operation, which agreed little; in the UN committee entitled the Committee of the Whole, which was established to undertake such negotiations after the end of that conference; and innumerable other lesser negotiating bodies. More significant, probably, were the periodic get-togethers of the rich states which conferred among each other on the problems confronting them: both in the Organisation for Economic Co-operation and Development (OECD), the economic body which linked them, and in the periodic summits at heads of government level. But, despite all these multifarious organisations and activities, there existed no permanent body, representing both rich and poor countries, to keep under review the state of the world's economy and to agree on common action.

Yet some such body was clearly badly needed. No effective solutions were likely to be reached without a joint approach. The economic future of the rich countries was crucially dependent on decisions reached within the poor states. More than 30 per cent of their exports of manufactured goods went to poor countries (the proportion for the United States was 34 per cent and for Japan 45 per cent[12]) so that maintaining the purchasing power and foreign-exchange reserves of poor states was vital to rich countries too. Many of their essential raw materials and foods came from these countries. Some of their major companies operated there. And decisions – for example, concerning the price of oil or other commodities, or concerning investment or trade policy – reached within those countries were vital to the future of the rich states' economies.

The poor countries were even more dependent on the rich. They depended on them for markets for their manufactures, for investment funds, for aid and for technical and management assistance. Growth in the rich world was essential to them, to improve the prices of their commodities, to provide better markets for their manufactures, which were sold almost entirely in the rich countries, and to reduce pressures for protection against those imports in the rich states.

It was self-evident that, if the economic interests of either party were to be effectively protected, there must be joint discussion of the management of the world economy as a whole. Decisions on international monetary questions, trade policy, development aid and international investment had to be reached on a joint basis. Even decisions concerning interest rates, public spending, rates of growth, capital flows or restrictions on imports in any *one* country, at first sight purely domestic matters, could now have an immediate impact elsewhere. Yet for the most part decisions on all of these continued to be made unilaterally, and with little regard for the interests of other countries.

If a more stable international economy is to the achieved, far closer co-ordination of the decisions of states – even about questions that appear purely matters of national policy – will clearly be required than takes place today. Such joint decision-making would need to involve senior ministers, and not the lowly officials often involved in international consultations at present. It would have to bring together not only representatives of rich countries, as do the economic 'summits' today, but those of poor countries too, whose interests are vitally affected and whose co-operation may be essential to effective action. And it would have to take place on a regular and frequent basis, unlike the occasional and spasmodic get-togethers that are usual today.

In other words, a new type of body, whether or not within the UN system, is required: a kind of international economic council. This would consist perhaps of the ministers of finance of 20 or at most 25 states. It would be balanced between rich countries and poor, and so far as possible between regions (but would always include the six or seven most powerful economic states). It would meet at least quarterly, to discuss the state of the world economy. There are already two UN bodies that bring together a representative group of ministers of finance at regular intervals: the Interim Committee of the IMF; and the Development Committee, which comes under the aegis of the World Bank and the IMF together. These could well be merged into a single body. They could then, with new terms of reference, be adapted to perform the function required. Though the creation of new institutions will not in itself solve problems, it may be the first step without which those problems will not be adequately confronted.

Perhaps the first task of such a body would be to seek to promote *balanced* world growth. It is, for example, essential that, so far as possible, the impact of the trade cycle should be desynchronised, so that it falls on different countries at different times, rather than, as so often today, with a mutually reinforcing effect which intensifies the problems for all countries. During the early post-war period it was generally believed that the US economy was so dominant that it must automatically exert a decisive effect on all other countries: when the United States sneezed, it was said, the rest of the world caught pneumonia. The reality of that period happily belied those fears. The US recessions of 1949 and 1954 had little impact elsewhere, coinciding with periods of growth in Western Europe; and that of 1958, while it was reflected in most other countries, was not a serious downturn. During the sixties the cycles coincided still less. The United States suffered a short decline in 1961 which affected no other country except Britain. After this the United States maintained a steady growth (partly sustained by the Vietnam War), while other countries suffered successive downturns: Britain in 1962-3, France in 1964, Japan in 1964-5, West Germany in 1967. The United States then suffered a slight recession in 1969-70 which coincided with a period of boom elsewhere.[13] As a result, throughout that period the pressure of high demand in one area was to a large extent balanced by low demand elsewhere. The forces of expansion in Europe were generally so powerful that they could withstand the weakening effect of recession in the United States, while the US economy was autonomous and little affected by developments elsewhere.

During the seventies this situation dramatically changed. All the Western economies boomed together in 1971-2, setting off an explosion of high demand and a doubling of commodity prices. Subsequently, shattered by the increase in oil prices, all entered depression together in 1974-5; and then slowly recovered, led by the United States, during 1976-8. In 1979-80, in response to a further increase in the price of oil and rising inflation at home, all together reintroduced tight money, high interest rates and cuts in public spending, so that rates of growth universally fell once more. Thus, instead of counteracting each other, booms and depressions were now mutually reinforcing.

One of the main aims, therefore, of any body seeking to bring about more effective management of the world economy would be to reverse this situation. It would seek to ensure that, if some countries were obliged to deflate their economies because of high inflation or serious balance of payments deficits, those that were in surplus, or suffering a lower rate of inflation, would correspondingly expand. The main difficulty in achieving this in the past has been the reluctance of governments in surplus to reflate, often on the grounds that such action would stimulate inflationary pressures (this was the difficulty that occurred during 1977–8, when West Germany and Japan, enjoying at the time substantial balance of payments surpluses, were vainly begged to allow their economies to grow, to relieve pressure on those countries, such as the United States and Britain, with balance of payments deficits). One of the problems has been (as then) that the pressure for expansion has come from countries with an obvious self-interest in bringing that about.

If attempts at management are to be more effective in the future, four things are probably necessary. First, more impartial figures than at present should be available to press the case with the governments from which action is required. The representatives of governments with no obvious interest, perhaps smaller European countries or poor countries, which have been scarcely represented in most such discussions before, would, if represented on the world economic council, be in a position to fill this role. The same might be done by international officials, perhaps noted economists working in a non-national capacity (a kind of international council of economic advisers). Either of these might be better able to bring influential pressure to bear than could the representatives of governments with an obvious axe to grind. Secondly, there is need for better machinery through which such influence could be exerted: such as the council of economic management suggested, meeting regularly. Thirdly, there might be need of objective indicators of the circumstances requiring expansion by a country, whether defined by balance of payments surplus or by some other measure. Finally, there would be need for some inducements that could be offered by the governments that did not expand, to lead others to do so: perhaps firm undertakings of the reciprocal measures they would take to reduce inflation or balance of payments deficits (and to expand in time in due course).

Another subject which such discussions would need to cover would be levels of interest rates in individual countries. The need to co-ordinate policies on this question has been recognised over many years. Interest rates today all over the industrialised world are several times as high, even in real terms, as they were in the period immediately after the Second World War. This creates heavy burdens for all borrowers, excessive profits for banks and other lenders of funds, and huge costs to governments in repaying their own debt. The cost to poor countries, compelled to borrow on a large scale in international markets, is especially heavy. Rates of interest are high not only because of the efforts of governments to restrain credit to contain inflation, but also because the support of their currencies compels them to compete with each other in attracting funds from abroad (or at least in avoiding the loss of funds to other centres). Fifteen years ago the British government initiated discussions designed to bring about some degree of 'interest-rate disarmament'; understandings between governments which might help to reduce the effect of mutual competition in keeping rates high. Those discussions came to nothing. But the need for such undertakings is as great as ever today. At present US interest rates determine the level of activity of the entire world economy: so no reflation becomes possible without US reflation.[14] One of the tasks of any new mechanism for managing the international economy must thus be to seek such understandings once more. These would need to cover both the *relative* level of interest rates between states, according to their different economic circumstances; and *average* levels, having regard to the needs of the international economy and the need to reduce the burden which high rates at present create.

Another factor affecting growth rates which would require international discussion is the volume of credit within the international economy. The policies of international bodies such as the IMF and the World Bank, still more those of bilateral donors and of the international banking system, are at present almost entirely unco-ordinated. Yet they can have a vital influence on the levels of demand which poor countries can maintain. If sustained and balanced growth in the world economy is to be possible, the policies of these various bodies will need to be brought into alignment. And their decisions need to take account not only of their normal policy considerations but also of the needs of demand management in the world economy as a whole. Thus the IMF, for example, might be asked to regulate the issue of SDRs – on which decisions are at present reached for three or four years at a time, in an almost arbitrary manner – on a far more short-term basis, according to the needs of cyclical policy. More SDRs would be issued at times of severe recession and fewer at times of boom or high inflation. When depression was sufficiently severe, additional SDRs might need to be distributed, and distribution might be in accordance with need rather than, as at present, according to existing quotas. Conversely, at times of especially severe inflation the IMF might be called on to restrict its credit creation accordingly. If some effective influence over the level of credit in the world economy is to be obtained, however, international bodies will need to be able to regulate the levels of lending from private as well as from public sources. Such a policy would therefore require international bodies to secure some influence over the private international banking system, at present almost entirely uncontrolled, though it accounts for the greater part of the volume of international credit today (p. 119 below).

International demand management would also require measures affecting international trade. At present the trade policies of most countries tend to reinforce, rather than to counteract, the instabilities of the business cycle. At times of recession (and so of contraction of world trade), the threat to jobs at home causes governments to introduce measures of protection, which in turn further reduce international trade and activity. Effective management of the world economy would require the opposite of this: a mutual opening of markets to counteract recession. The international bodies concerned with trade, such as GATT and UNCTAD, may be required to define the rules for bringing this about. Nations might need to commit themselves to reduce restrictions as trade declined (or at the very least to undertake not to raise them in such circumstances). If such measures were to be effective, some system of multilateral surveillance would be needed so as to subject governments to constant cross-examination of their policies in this field. This is the technique which was adopted within the Organisation for European Economic Co-operation at the time when liberalisation of trade restrictions was being brought about after the Second World War. A similar procedure, applied worldwide, would be valuable today in order to *maintain* liberalisation, and to adjust it to the needs of the world economy today.

Multilateral surveillance is equally needed in the field of aid and investment if equilibrium within the world economy is to be maintained. Again, the unilateral policies of governments often intensify imbalances rather than counteract them. For example, on demand-management grounds aid from rich countries should clearly be raised at periods of declining activity (as, for example, at the end of the seventies): to increase the purchasing power of developing countries and so help sustain the world economy as a whole. In practice at such periods, rich countries, determined on retrenchment, have more commonly contracted their aid programmes and so exacerbated world recession. Again, outside influences are required. An international body responsible for managing the international economy might be able to make governments better aware of their responsibilities – and above all of their self-interest – in this respect: that is, it could bring pressure for an adjustment in aid levels to meet the needs of the international economy as a whole. And a multilateral approach could reduce distortions in both the type and direction of aid supplied at present (pp. 56–7). In the same way governments might be expected to liberalise their regulations concerning capital exports at times of recession so that foreign private investment might at such periods help to restore activity in the world as a whole.

As we have seen, one of the reasons why deflationary policies have been so widely pursued in recent years has been the concern to counter inflation, from which every country, rich and poor, has suffered. It is thus, perhaps, above all in containing inflation that joint action is necessary. An international body concerned with managing the world economy might, more effectively than governments acting bilaterally, discourage irresponsible fiscal and monetary policies which serve to intensify world inflation (and, unlike the IMF, should be in a position to make representations on such matters to all states, whether or not any request for drawing rights had been made). The concern felt by many European states at the inflationary policies of the United States during the late sixties and seventies, for example, might have had more impact in influencing US policy if expressed through the pressures of an international body of this kind. Such a body could exert joint influence on the producers of commodities, such as oil, to reduce the inflationary effect that sharp increases in their prices have for the entire world economy. They could seek similarly to deter excessive price increases for the manufactured goods sold by rich countries (which between 1974 and 1979 increased in price considerably more than the price of oil), which can equally serve to restrict growth. They could examine the shortages of minerals, food and energy that lead to rapid price increases and recommend the policies to relieve them. And they could encourage appropriate incomes policies as a less destructive counter-inflationary strategy than prolonged deflation.

But perhaps the most fundamental responsibility of any body established to survey the growth of the world economy would be to consider the regional policies needed to sustain a healthy world economy. The huge inequalities in standards of living between different regions of the world today have become as unacceptable, given their visibility in the shrinking world within which we live, as have been for several decades very large inequalities between regions within states. In both cases glaring disparities offend the sense of propriety as much as the sense of injustice: none can feel comfortable in the face of such gross inequalities in ways of living. One of the prime tasks of international economic management, therefore, will be to seek the policies, in the field of investment, trade, money and other areas, which best reduce these manifest inequalities and injustices (see Chapters 2–4 below).

We have here been able only briefly to sketch some of the types of international economic strategy that might be needed to bring about more sustained and better balanced growth in the world economy. Precisely what type of policy is required for this purpose will be considered in more detail in subsequent chapters. What can scarcely be doubted is that balanced world growth could be better achieved through an attempt to secure common policies and common action, rather than allowing economic events to remain dependent on the vagaries of individual governments, each pursuing their own narrow objectives, and governed by economic forces they are unable, acting alone, to bring under control.

2 Investment

2.1 THE GROWTH OF INTERNATIONAL INVESTMENT

One of the factors influencing rates of growth in different parts of the world has been the flow of resources between states and regions.

There was little international investment before the middle of the nineteenth century. At that time foreign investment mainly took the form of the purchase of fixed-interest bonds issued by governments and other authorities in need of funds on foreign stock markets. European governments, Latin American governments, US cities and states all raised funds in this way: mainly in London, sometimes in other European capital markets. The issues were floated by banks which specialised in such business, such as Rothschild's and Baring's. The money was used for building railways in the United States, France and Belgium, sinking mines in Latin America, buying property and land in the United States, Canada and Australia, and for government spending everywhere.

The total remained extremely small at first. Until 1845, British foreign investment, though far the largest at the time, was only about £5 million a year. By 1850 the total stock was little more than £200 million.[1] By 1870 the annual rate had risen to £30 million a year, and by 1873 the accumulated total had reached about £1 billion.[2] By that time French foreign investment, the next largest, was about £500 million, Germany's was about £250 million. French and German investment was primarily in Europe; Britain's went mainly to other parts of the world, especially the United States, Canada, India and Latin America.

From that point British investment began to increase rapidly. The yield to be obtained from foreign investment at this time was higher than could be secured at home (on average $1-1\frac{1}{2}$ per cent more).[3] And particular investments, for example foreign holdings of land and mortgages, though risky, could yield 16 per cent (against an average of 4 per cent for Consols in 1870–80). There was substantial investment in railways, mines, ports, electric power and gas and in rubber and cotton plantations. Foreign governments, especially the financially insolvent and dependent governments of semi-colonies, such as Turkey, Egypt, Persia and China, but also the more impoverished governments of South-Eastern Europe and Latin America, came to the London market to borrow funds. Thus, in the 40 years from 1873 British investment quadrupled, reaching £4 billion by 1913. By that time the income from it represented 10 per cent of total national income, a phenomenal proportion, never approached by any other nation at any period. Whether borrowed by governments or by railway and other undertakings, the investment was still mainly in the form of fixed-interest securities. There was little direct investment by companies. Most of the British investment was in primary producing countries outside Europe (about half within the British empire),[4] which mainly exported food and materials to Europe in return for British manufactured goods.

Most French investment on the other hand, mainly in government bonds, went to other parts of Europe. In 1900 70 per cent of French foreign holdings were in Europe, though there began to be increasing investment elsewhere, especially in the French empire, above all North Africa and Indo-China. French foreign investment was strongly influenced by political factors: the government only allowed access to the Paris market to foreign governments to which it was well disposed.[5] It was not allowed, for example, to the German government, nor for a decade or so to the Italians. Russia, on the other hand, immediately the alliance with that country was concluded in 1893, was given every possible facility for raising money in Paris. By 1913 lending to Russia came to represent 25 per cent of all French foreign investment. Of the rest 18 per cent went elsewhere in Eastern Europe, 18 per cent to the rest of Europe, 14 per cent to Latin America, 10 per cent to the French colonies, 7 per cent to Africa, and about 5 per cent each to North America and Asia.[6] Often the loans were tied to the purchase of French equipment or manufactures. The total investment rose to £1.8 billion in 1914. By that time the income from the investment was equal to 5–6 per cent of French national income.

German investment abroad started slowly. There were ample opportunities for investment in the rapidly expanding German industry, and interest rates at home, which were higher than in most other European states, made domestic issues more attractive to the great German banks which were the source of much of the investment. But by 1914, with growing German political interest in other parts of the world and strong encouragement from the German government, foreign investment had risen to about £1200 million. More than 50 per cent of the total was in other parts of Europe, especially Eastern Europe, 17 per cent in the United States and 17 per cent in Latin America.

US investment abroad was still relatively small. Until 1914 it was consistently exceeded by inward investment, mainly from Europe. By 1914 US foreign investment was still only about £500 million. It went mainly to North and South America: 40 per cent to Mexico alone and 30 per cent to Canada.

After the First World War this situation changed radically. European foreign investments had fallen drastically. Investors in Britain and France had been obliged by their governments to sell their holdings to win foreign exchange. Controls on new foreign investment had been imposed which were only gradually removed. After the war, yields on foreign bonds were little higher than those available at home, so making them less attractive to investors. Moreover, the areas which had been the chief recipients of foreign loans before 1914, the food-producing lands of the periphery and South-Eastern Europe, were now in considerable economic difficulties (despite special assistance by the League of Nations to the countries of Eastern Europe and privileged access to the London market for the British dominions and empire). The United States, now far the most prosperous country in the world, with a substantial capital surplus, became easily the most important foreign investor. She began to invest substantially abroad, both in Latin America and in Europe: above all in Germany, then rapidly recovering from the war and subsequent economic disasters, and in urgent need of foreign exchange. US interest rates were now lower than those in Europe, so attracting borrowers to that market. By 1930 total US foreign investment was over £3 billion and outward investment exceeded inward investment by about £1.7 billion.

With stagnation at home British foreign investment recovered fairly rapidly: by the mid-1930s it had again reached £3.7 billion, little short of the 1914 figure. An even larger proportion, nearly 60 per cent, was now in the Commonwealth (of the rest 20 per cent was in Latin America, 8 per cent in Europe and 5 per cent in the United States).[7] French foreign investment, which had been reduced to less than half by the war, especially by the loss of investments in Russia, revived slowly during the twenties, especially through new colonial issues. In 1928 it is estimated to have been about £400 million, of which about 30 per cent was newly invested since 1918.[8] This rose to about £750 million by 1935.[9] The investment, still influenced by political considerations, went particularly to Eastern Europe, especially the countries of the Little Entente. Some consisted of direct advances by the government rather than the holdings of small investors (so anticipating the bilateral loans which became common after 1945).

During the depression, foreign investment fell rapidly. It had already declined by 1930. In 1932 it almost ceased for two or three years. Confidence, already low, evaporated altogether for a time. US funds were rapidly withdrawn from Europe, while some European funds sought security in US markets. The London capital market was closed to foreign borrowers in 1931 and only gradually reopened. The repudiation of debts by a considerable number of governments, especially in Latin America, made it increasingly difficult to raise new loans. Highly unstable exchange rates created a risk of exchange loss. Balance of payments problems brought strict government controls of foreign lending. The low prices of food and raw materials deterred investment in the producing countries where much had been attracted in earlier days. Finally, the nationalistic spirit of the age brought a general concern to build up industry at home rather than risk investment in remote parts of the world. European governments now had little reason, as before 1914, to try to shore up tottering governments overseas with loans (though some French loans to Eastern European and Italian loans to Albania were essentially of the old kind). And often they prevented or limited foreign investment through exchange controls.

There was a slight change in the character of investment at this time. Much still consisted of loans raised by governments and municipalities: 40 per cent of British foreign investment remained of this kind in 1933.[10] But there was some increase in portfolio investment – the buying of foreign securities – when exchange regulations permitted it. And there was now for the first time a small amount of direct investment by companies, especially US companies, seeking to expand their activities abroad, above all in Latin America. This meant that now a rather higher proportion was genuine investment in production facilities, including manufacturing abroad, as against loans to governments, much of which had gone for day-to-day expenditure or for the repayment of loans.

During the Second World War much foreign investment was sold off (for example, by Britain and France). Much became valueless because of the destruction of assets, expropriation or other reasons. As a result three out of the four main lenders of funds in the pre-war era – Britain, France and Germany – ceased for a time to be significant net investors abroad. The United States became more than ever the dominant investor.

But there was a more important change in the *type* of investment. The three types of foreign investment which had been most common in pre-war times – borrowing by governments through the sale of bonds in foreign markets, borrowing by municipalities, railways and public utilities in the same way, and the purchase of foreign securities by individuals (portfolio investment) – now became much less significant. Four relatively new forms of investment came to be of primary importance: direct investment by companies in production facilities in other lands; direct lending by one government to another; lending by international institutions to governments; and, ultimately the most important of all, bank lending both to companies and to governments.

By far the most significant of these at first was direct investment by companies. This now took place on a scale never known before. There were a number of reasons why direct investment of this kind grew so rapidly. The world economy as a whole was flourishing, with high and consistent rates of growth in both developed and developing countries, and therefore promising new opportunities for investment. Large private companies became increasingly dominant abroad as well as at home. The rapid growth in their scale, as well as improvements in transport and communications, made worldwide operations a more practical proposition than ever before. Major companies looked for opportunities to secure further returns for the heavy investment already undertaken in research and development by manufacturing established products abroad. In that way production facilities could be established closer to the final markets. Customs duties and many other restrictions on imports could be avoided. Advantage could be taken of investment incentives, regional grants, tax holidays and other inducements widely offered by governments seeking foreign investment. Above all, wage rates and other costs were generally lower, sometimes substantially lower. As a result, after 1945 direct investment by companies multiplied many times. Investment to some extent represented trade of a different sort: instead of the export of finished products, companies exported the specialised technology for making them, often with a view to trading them in new markets.

There was, however, a still more significant change in the character of this foreign investment. Before 1914 foreign investment had helped to spread wealth around the world. It had gone from the most developed regions of the world to areas in the periphery that were less developed: especially to the economies which supplied food and raw materials to Europe – Canada, Australia, Argentina, South Africa, and other overseas areas. A substantial amount had been invested in very poor countries, especially in Latin America but also in Asia (for example, India and China). Even in colonial territories there had been significant investment by the colonial powers responsible, especially in infrastructure: for roads, railways, irrigation and ports. Now, however, private investment was primarily in manufacture, and, while it still came overwhelmingly from countries which were already developed, it went to countries that were equally or almost equally developed – in other words from rich countries to rich. Nearly 65 per cent of all foreign investment during the 1960s, for example, was in Western Europe and Canada, 10 per cent in the United States, another 6–8 per cent in Australia, New Zealand and South Africa.[11] During the seventies there was a substantial increase in the volume of investment from Western Europe in the United States: still from rich to rich. Altogether nearly four-fifths of total foreign investment went to the countries already most developed, having only a quarter of the world's population and needing the investment least; only about 20 per cent went to poor countries whose need of capital resources was greatest.

There were many reasons for this. Poor countries were believed to be politically and economically unstable: educational standards, and therefore productivity were low; communications were poor; skills were lacking; services were inadequate; above all the markets were restricted and so profitability likely to be small. On these grounds the flow of private investment to those countries at first grew only slowly: to about $2 billion a year in 1960 and under $4 billion in 1970 (see Table 2.1).[12] By 1975, only about a quarter of the world's total stock of foreign investment was in developing countries, though they had more than three-quarters of the world's population.[13] Direct investment to such countries grew more rapidly during the seventies and the flow was over $13 billion by 1979. But it remained a small proportion of all foreign investment; and was still less than the funds received by poor countries as development assistance from governments.

TABLE 2.1   *Private flows to developing countries, 1960–80 (US $billion)*

	1960	1965	1970	1975	1980
Direct investment	1.8	2.5	3.7	11.5	9.7
Bank loans	–	–	3.0	12.0	18.0[a]
Bond lending	–	–	0.3	0.4	2.0[a]
Export credits	0.5	0.8	2.1	4.4	12.2

[a] Provisional figures.
SOURCE   OECD, *Development cooperation*, 1971, p. 34; 1981, p. 172.

The sources of foreign investment were also highly concentrated. Because private investment was now primarily direct investment by companies, it inevitably came from the countries where such companies were mainly based. A high proportion came from a single country, the United States. Until 1970 about four-fifths of all international direct investment was undertaken by US or UK companies and the share of the United States alone was about 60 per cent.[14] Though other countries, including France, West Germany and Japan, gradually built up their share, it remained a relatively small proportion of the total. Even when, after 1973, substantial funds became available to oil-producing countries it did not fundamentally affect the concentration of industrial ownership: their funds were placed mainly in Western bank deposits and were invested by Western, primarily US banks. A substantial part of the modern industrial sector in poor countries was owned by Western companies.

From the early seventies, direct investment was overtaken by a new type of international lending to developing countries: investment through the international banking system. The surpluses of the oil-producing states were mainly deposited in Western banks, which were then able to lend them elsewhere, mainly in developing countries. The greater part of this was lent by the banks to governments. A small but significant part, however, went into industrial investment, though mainly in a small number of relatively advanced countries.[15] The total of bank lending to poor countries rose to nearly $20 billion a year by 1980. The total of outstanding loans to non-oil developing countries therefore grew from $33 billion in 1974 to $200 billion by the beginning of the eighties.

Finally, after 1975 there was a reversion to the type of foreign borrowing which had been common before the First World War. A modest but increasing amount of money was raised by placing bonds in the markets of rich countries. This was done however almost exclusively by the wealthier developing countries. By the end of the decade something like $5 billion a year was lent in this way and the total was rising.

If these various flows could have been increased, and if a significant proportion could have gone, directly or indirectly, to investment in industry, whether private or public, there would have been some progress in meeting the industrial needs at least of some poor countries. But nearly all these private funds went to a small group of better-off developing countries. And by 1980 increasing doubts began to affect even investment in these countries.

By this time a crippling level of debt had been incurred by the more advanced poor countries. This was hugely increased after 1973 by the borrowing they were obliged to undertake to meet their deficits on oil imports, over and above their many other needs (see Table 2.2). In the six years from the end of 1973 to the end of 1979 the external debts of oil-importing countries tripled (that is, twice as much debt was accumulated in these six years as in all the preceding years). The total level of medium and long-term debt of all such countries by the end of the decade was well over $400 billion (against $75 billion in 1970) and their annual debt-servicing payments were of the order of $45 billion a year. 40 per cent was to commercial banks (against 16 per cent in 1970), 30 per cent in export credits, the rest official loans. As a result the debt-servicing ratio – that is, the proportion of export earnings needed to service the debt – averaged 12–15 per cent and for some was well over 20 per cent (20 per cent was once regarded as the danger point beyond which it should never be allowed to go). For advanced developing countries such as Brazil and Mexico the ratio was over 50 per cent.[16] Since poor countries were likely to need to borrow still more in order to repay these loans, as well as to meet their general balance of payments deficits, the overall level of debt would multiply still further. Rates of interest were higher than ever. And, as inflation declined, the *real* rate of interest (which during the seventies had sometimes been negative) rose faster still.

The performance of developing countries in the period after the Second World War in meeting their debt obligations had been remarkably good: far better than that of similar countries in the inter-

TABLE 2.2 *Medium- and long-term debts of developing countries, 1970–80*

Country group	Billions of current dollars		Billions of 1978 dollars		Percentage real growth 1970–80[a]
	1970	1980	1970	1980	
Oil importers	48.0	301.3	102.6	250.9	9.4
Low-income	14.5	48.0	31.0	40.0	2.6
Middle-income	33.5	253.3	71.6	210.9	11.4
Oil exporters	19.7	137.4	42.1	114.4	10.5
All developing countries	67.7	438.7	144.7	365.3	9.7

[a] Compound annual rate of change.
Note: Includes private nonguaranteed debt.

SOURCE   World Bank, *World Development Report, 1981,* p. 57.

war and pre-war periods. But there was now increasing doubt whether, without substantial rescheduling or cancellation of debts, that performance could be maintained. On these grounds in 1978–9 there was some readjustment of terms of the debts of very poor countries through 'retrospective terms adjustment'. In some cases debts were cancelled altogether. In a number of other cases, rescheduling took place. But, if poor countries were able to remain solvent, it seemed likely that far more radical measures to write off or reduce debts might be required in the future.

Thus all three main types of private investment in poor countries – direct investment by companies, bank loans, and bonds issued by governments in capital markets elsewhere – were now threatened. The flow was, moreover, very unevenly distributed. Nearly 50 percent of all bank lending to poor countries went to five countries only. Over a quarter went to only two (Brazil and Mexico). Conversely, 80 per cent of developing countries received under 20 per cent of these funds between them.[17] And the 30 or 40 least developed countries of all received almost none. Direct investment too went mainly to the developing countries already most advanced: since the poorest could not normally offer the markets or the skilled labour forces which such investment demanded. Finally, bond issues benefited only a few wealthier developing countries which could command confidence in the bond markets.[18]

Private investment, therefore, though larger than at any earlier time, no longer served, as it had before 1914, to bring about a wider distribution of capital resources throughout the world, by exploiting the advantages of raw-materials availability or low wage costs. Both of these assets now counted for much less in relation to the deficiency of markets and skills in the poor countries of the periphery. The high level of international private investment which began to take place at this time, therefore, far from reducing the inequalities in production potential among states, if anything increased them. For it now ensured that production potential remained still more concentrated in the areas where it was already highest: either the rich countries themselves or a dozen or so of the more industrialised poor countries.

2.2 TRANSNATIONAL CORPORATIONS IN THE MODERN INTERNATIONAL ECONOMY

The huge increase in foreign investment had transformed the role which private companies played within the world economy.

Even in developed countries a dominant position often came to be held by companies based abroad: and for long that meant mainly US companies. That dominance often aroused concern. In France in the sixties, there was widespread hostility to the powerful position occupied within the economy by US corporations; as there was in Britain and other countries during the seventies. In smaller developed countries, such as Canada and Australia, the problem was even more acute. There was increasing discussion about the ways in which the host countries could better control economic activity by such companies.

Yet even in more developed countries the dominance of a small number of companies increased. Whole industries came to be controlled by a few large companies. So the oil industry, the computer industry, the aircraft industry, the chemical industry, the automobile industry, the nuclear-power and pharmaceutical industries, among others, came to be almost entirely dominated by a few major firms, often US firms.

In poor countries the dominance which such giant companies could acquire was inevitably greater. Because their own industry was far smaller and weaker, it was far less able to compete. Because their own governments were less experienced, they were less well equipped to control the companies effectively. In some cases even a single large firm (Firestone in Liberia, Anaconda in Chile, United Fruit Corporation in several Central American states, the United Africa Company in several West African countries) could acquire an overwhelming position. More often there were several such companies, each dominant in a particular sphere.

The governments of a few developing countries adopted a position of overt hostility to the companies, sometimes expropriating them with little or no compensation. Most, however, felt ambivalent about the role played by such corporations. Investment from foreign companies could help them in overcoming some of the most serious deficiencies from which their countries suffered: shortages of savings, of resources, of foreign exchange and of technology. It could bring about industrialisation which might not otherwise occur. It brought tax revenues for the local government. It created jobs. It brought a transfer of managerial skills, marketing techniques, administrative abilities, as well as industrial technologies, at every level. It could stimulate local production of components, servicing industries, retailing organisations, and financial services. In many cases it saved imports or created exports (on average foreign-owned companies exported more than local companies). And, since there was often a limitation on the remittance of profits abroad, it often also produced substantial reinvestment of profits in other productive operations. On all these grounds a large number of governments in poor countries did everything possible to attract foreign investment: through tax holidays, investment grants, rapid depreciation, regional policies and other means – sometimes in mutually destructive competition.

Foreign investment, however, also brought considerable costs. It was often concentrated in capital-intensive production not well suited to a poor country with a large unemployed labour force. It promoted a type of product and a pattern of consumption borrowed from developed countries and not necessarily appropriate to local traditions. It brought a long-term drain of foreign exchange in the remission of profits and dividends. It distorted the local wage structure by offering wages far higher than local companies could afford. It often caused increased imports as well as increased exports. It pre-empted resources, including skilled labour, materials and equipment, which could otherwise have been exploited by local businessmen, employing a more appropriate technology and at far less cost to the economy as a whole. It could reduce the local rate of savings and of enterprise by absorbing the few investment opportunities available. And it meant that decisions of vital importance to the domestic economy were taken, in boardrooms in foreign countries thousands of miles away, by those who were more concerned with the profit of their own company than with the interests of the host country.

Poor countries therefore faced a cruel dilemma. Either they could encourage foreign investment, for the sake of acquiring foreign exchange and other advantages, but in so doing accept increasing foreign domination of their economy as a whole; or they could halt the inflow of capital to prevent this, and in so doing slow their own development and deprive themselves of the resources, technology and other benefits which the investment might have brought. In other words, the price of progress in developing countries could be the mortgaging of a large part of their economy to foreign owners. These might then acquire increasing control over the types and levels of production, over the distribution of investment, over how much was exported and imported to and from which countries, over the proportion of local and foreign nationals employed, over staffing levels and levels of pay, over the prices charged for their products (as well as for the components shipped from the same company in the home country): all decisions which were determined in the light of their own interests, rather than of the needs of the economy in which they operated.

Rich countries too, though for different reasons, were ambivalent about the benefits of investment in poor countries. In principle most governments of such countries favoured the expansion of activities by their own companies all over the world (and often the spread of the 'private enterprise system' generally). But in practice they placed many restraints on these companies if they wished to expand their operations abroad. They limited or prohibited all investment in states that were ideologically or in other ways not favoured by them. They imposed, for most of the time,[19] a strict control of all outward investment for balance of payment reasons: even if it was not banned altogether, it was usually subject to heavy fiscal burdens or subject to assent by government officials. They were also usually highly cautious about providing any guarantees against political risks, without which companies might be unwilling to undertake such ventures.

Private investment in poor countries was thus uncertain in volume and unpredictable in effect. Such countries therefore began to look to other kinds of financial flow to aid them in their development efforts.

2.3 THE GROWTH OF DEVELOPMENT ASSISTANCE

The capital needs of poor countries might have been adequately met if private investment could have been made good by assistance from governments. After 1945 a wholly new type of international transfer of funds had emerged. As we have seen, before the First World War foreign lending had been almost entirely by *individuals*. These had lent abroad by purchasing the bonds issued by foreign governments, public utilities and occasionally by companies operating abroad. Between the wars lending was still mainly by individuals: either buying bonds as before or purchasing shares issued by foreign companies. After 1945 investment was mainly by *companies* and later by *banks* lending to governments or companies abroad. But from the 1950s there began also substantial programmes of lending, and later giving, by the *governments* of rich countries to those of poor countries.

This development was barely foreseen at the end of the Second World War. Attention was focused mainly on the reconstruction of the developed world. Most poor countries at that time were still dependent territories. In so far as their needs were considered at all, it was widely assumed that their development would depend on their own resources, or on whatever private investment they could attract from abroad. Only at the end of the forties did it begin to be recognised that substantial assistance from richer countries would be needed as well if poor countries were to be in a position to overcome the state of underdevelopment in which they lived. In 1950 President Truman announced his Point 4 programme for providing aid, especially technical assistance, to developing countries. During the course of the fifties the US aid programme, directed at first mainly to countries which that country regarded as politically important, or as reliable friends, increased rapidly. By 1960 it had reached nearly $3 billion or 0.5 per cent of US national income. Colonial powers such as Britain and France also gave increasing sums in assistance, especially for those countries that had formerly been their colonies: France was giving 1.5 per cent of her national income for such purposes at that time. A few other countries began to give small amounts of aid.

At this time much of the aid took the form of loans, at market rates of interest: transactions that would not be classified today as development assistance at all. Moreover, the total transferred to poor countries in this way was for long only a fraction of the volume of development assistance that had been provided for *developed* countries through the Marshall Plan for Western Europe (about $17 billion). From 1960, however, aid programmes to poor countries began to increase fairly steadily. The United States remained, in absolute terms, the largest 'donor' (though the word was a misnomer so long as most of the money was still lent), but from 1965 the proportion of her national income going in aid fell steadily. The programmes of most other countries grew gradually. In absolute terms, therefore, the total volume of aid grew steadily, though not as fast as national incomes. But the aid was not co-ordinated. There was little attempt at a comparative assessment of needs. And in practice aid was still concentrated among particular states which, for one reason or another were favourably regarded by the donors, whether on political or strategic grounds, many of them not the poorest developing countries.

The terms on which aid was given were gradually improved. A significant proportion came to be lent on 'soft' terms: that is, at low rates of interest, with long periods of repayment, and often with the first payments deferred. An increasing part was given as outright grants, for which no repayment had to be made at all (a few countries gave all their aid in that form). Only aid which included at least some concessionary element – such as lower than normal interest rates or deferred repayment – was now officially classified as 'development assistance'. And an increasing proportion came to be given as outright grants. There was also some attempt at local co-ordination: for many countries the World Bank established consortia of the chief donors to discuss aid policy with the recipients, usually on the basis of 'country programmes'.

These improvements could not make up for the inadequacies in quantity. Official development assistance (ODA) grew slowly to $7 billion in 1970 (including multilateral aid); and then to over $20 billion, at current prices, in 1980 (see Table 2.3). In real terms, however, it had only increased by 25 per cent since 1965. By 1980 it was only 30 per cent of financial flows to poor countries, as against 50 per cent in 1970. The share going to very poor countries was declining. And aid represented a smaller proportion of the national income of donor countries than in the early sixties (0.37 against 0.45 per cent).

TABLE 2.3   *Official development assistance 1960–80 (US $ billion)*

	1960	*1965*	*1970*	*1975*	*1980 (est.)*
United States	2.7	4.0	3.2	4.2	4.6
France	0.82	0.75	0.97	2.1	3.8
Britain	0.4	0.47	0.5	0.9	2.5
West Germany	0.2	0.46	0.6	1.7	3.6
Japan	0.1	0.24	0.46	1.1	3.0
Netherlands	0.03	0.07	0.2	0.6	1.5
Sweden	0.007	0.04	0.1	0.6	1.1
Total OECD	4.6	6.5	7.0	13.8	25.0
(constant 1978 prices)	13.1	16.7	14.9	17.9	20.2
Total OPEC				5.5	4.7(1979)

SOURCE   World Bank, *World Development Report, 1980*, pp. 140–1.

US dominance declined: as a proportion of GNP, US aid dropped consistently from 0.5 per cent in 1960 to under 0.2 per cent at the end of the seventies (see Table 2.4). France and, to a lesser extent, Britain remained significant donors, giving 0.6 and 0.5 per cent by the latter date. West Germany and Japan, two of the fastest growing industrialised states, had reached only 0.4 and 0.27 per cent of national income by the end of the seventies, but the proportion was rising. The most generous, in terms of income a head, were the Netherlands and the Scandinavian countries. These almost alone managed, by the second half of the seventies, to exceed the UN target of 0.7 per cent of national income. The Soviet Union and East European countries gave only insignificant quantities of aid and had the worst record of all (according to some estimates 0.04 per cent of their national income). OPEC

Table 2.4   *Percentage of GNP devoted to ODA, 1960–80*

	1960	1965	1970	1975	1980 (est.)
United States	0.53	0.58	0.32	0.27	0.18
France	1.3	0.76	0.66	0.62	0.59
Britain	0.56	0.47	0.41	0.39	0.52
West Germany	0.31	0.40	0.32	0.40	0.44
Japan	0.24	0.27	0.23	0.23	0.27
Netherlands	0.31	0.36	0.61	0.75	0.94
Sweden	0.05	0.19	0.38	0.82	0.95
Total OECD	0.51	0.49	0.34	0.36	0.37
Total OPEC				2.71	1.28

SOURCE   World Bank, *World Development Report, 1980*, pp. 29, 140–1.

countries gave nearly 2 per cent of national income through various funds.

By this time there was increasing dissatisfaction with bilateral aid on the part of both recipients and donors. The recipients felt that such aid often placed them in a position of dependence. Whether explicitly or implicitly, its granting was subjected to conditions (as was shown, for example, when sudden political changes took place in Cuba, Chile and elsewhere). They resented the fact that aid was so unequally distributed. They disliked the influence of political factors in determining that distribution. And they preferred the concept of assistance given by multilateral organisations which could be expected to be more impartial in their decisions.

Donors equally became disenchanted with bilateral aid. With the moderation of the cold war, they felt less political incentive to offer handouts to those who might become disaffected (and less sure that goodwill was always to be bought with generous aid in any case). They were not convinced that the aid which they gave was always spent wisely (or even honestly). They were inhibited by balance of payments as well as budgetary constraints. And they were increasingly preoccupied by purely domestic problems – inflation, unemployment and environmental questions – which they believed required their limited resources to be spent at home. Above all, there was in the rich countries less and less a sense of moral obligation to help those who were far worse off in other countries.

For these reasons, from the early sixties, and especially from 1970 onwards, an increasing proportion of aid came to be given through multilateral institutions. About 10 per cent of OECD aid was given through multilateral institutions in the sixties, and the proportion grew to 27 per cent by the end of the seventies (30 per cent if EEC assistance is included). Multilateral aid had begun, on a very small scale, at the same time as the bilateral programmes: at the end of the forties. Apart from limited League financial assistance to several East European countries – a little akin to IMF assistance in the later period – there had been no multilateral aid in previous ages. In 1948 a very small UN technical assistance programme, provided from the regular budget of the organisation, was established. It was soon followed by the Expanded Programme of Technical Assistance, which was on a larger scale but financed by voluntary contributions. This was followed in 1958 by the Special Fund, also run by the United Nations, designed to provide pre-investment aid to developing countries. In 1964 the Special Fund and the Expanded Programme were merged in the UN Development Programme (UNDP). This continued to be financed by voluntary contributions. Many of the projects it financed were executed by specialised agencies of the United Nations. However, the total amount of finance provided in this way remained limited: it was still well under $1 billion at the end of the 1970s.

Far more significant was the assistance provided through the World Bank (IBRD). This lent to governments at commercial rates of interest, using funds raised on the world's money markets. Officially concerned with 'reconstruction' as much as with development, it had at first lent more of its money to rich countries than to poor. By the mid-fifties it was still only lending about half a billion dollars a year, of which more than half went to Europe, Australasia and other rich regions. Many developing countries could not afford its high rates of interest. To meet their needs, therefore, in 1962 the Bank established a 'soft' loan affiliate, the International Development Association (IDA), to lend to poor countries at a nominal rate of interest or 'service charge' (normally $\frac{3}{4}$ per cent). During the sixties lending by both the Bank and the IDA increased significantly: to about $1 billion a year in 1965 and 2 billion between them in 1970. At about that time it decided to devote an increasing proportion of its resources to agricultural projects, education and population programmes rather than to the large-scale infrastructure projects – dams, highways, power and ports – for which earlier loans had been provided. Its lending continued to increase rapidly and by the early eighties it was 'committing' (that is, agreeing to lend, subject to the necessary detailed conditions) around $12 billion a year. There were also regional development banks (with soft loan affiliates): for Latin

America, Africa and Asia. And there were a number of OPEC institutions lending to poor countries.[20]

A number of other, more specialised development funds were established within the UN system: for family planning (UN Fund for Population Activities), spending $100 million a year; for agricultural development (the International Fund for Agricultural Development); for industrial development (the UN Capital Fund), and so on. Most of these were financed by voluntary contributions. The sums available were therefore usually limited. More significant was the spending from the regular budgets of the specialised agencies of the UN, some of which went on assistance work of one kind or another: the budgets of the agencies taken together, to which all their members had to contribute, amounted to well over $1 billion by the end of the 1970s.

The total amount of aid provided continued to grow. It increased by 50 per cent in real terms during the seventies. But there was little effort at co-ordination of all these efforts, even among the multilateral bodies, and still less between the multilateral and the private. Each of the agencies of the UN system, including the World Bank itself, was an 'autonomous' agency and not therefore under the control of the United Nations. Each had separate governing bodies and different memberships. There were a number of co-ordinating bodies: the Administrative Committee on Co-ordination, which brought together the heads of all the agencies; the Economic and Social Council (Ecosoc), an intergovernmental body which concerned itself mainly with the many programmes within the United Nations proper; and the Committee on Programme and Co-ordination, the committee of Ecosoc with special responsibility for co-ordination, also mainly concerned with the activities of the United Nations itself. None of these achieved any effective co-ordination of the mass of separate programmes, even within the United Nations, let alone among the family of specialised agencies as a whole. The World Bank itself went almost entirely its own way. There were advisory bodies on development questions: especially the Committee for Development Programmes, a body of development experts whose reports were however little regarded; and the Development Committee, attended by ministers of finance, which was intended to bridge the gap between the World Bank and the IMF, but in practice became little more than a discussion forum.

Thus, though multilateral assistance was in general far more acceptable to poor countries than bilateral aid, and though it gradually grew in scale in proportion to the latter, it remained disorganised, dispersed and, above all, deficient in amount.

In any case, the growth of multilateral aid did not dispel criticisms of all assistance programmes. Among poor countries there were some who doubted the value and desirability of any aid, whether from governments or international institutions. In either form, it was held, it created a form of dependence on those who ultimately provided the funds. Such assistance normally promoted an alien type of development, determined, or at least influenced, by outsiders who were accustomed to totally different types of economy. It instilled alien values and economic concepts. If frequently deterred indigenous types of development, indigenous production patterns and indigenous enterprises. If it benefited anybody it was only the governments or the dominant elites in the receiving countries and not their people generally. There was little sign of a 'trickle-down', from the agencies, contractors and construction workers who directly benefited, to the disadvantaged, mainly in the countryside, who most needed help. It was channelled through the governing forces who held power and usually served only to strengthen their position, without significantly benefiting the mass of the population. And it did nothing to alter the unequal structure of power within the receiving country, which was often the main barrier to development. It was thus far less relevant to the real economic needs of such countries than better trading opportunities, improved agricultural prices, and above all a change in the distribution of wealth and income, which would release new productive forces in every developing country.

Against this, others argued, again both in rich countries and poor, that almost all development assistance represented a net transfer of resources from countries that were already rich to countries that were exceedingly poor. It helped, like private investment, to redress the main deficiencies from which such countries suffered: in savings, in resources, in foreign exchange and in technology and skills. In many cases, and increasingly, it took the form of assistance to agriculture, education and family planning, which must be of direct benefit to large sections of the population. Even large-scale capital projects – dams, highways, power stations and fertiliser factories – must bring some help to poor people: by bringing water for their land, access to markets, or power for small-scale industry. External aid, by promoting the development process, far from maintaining elites in power, could stimulate the transfer of power to wider sections of the population, who were made economically more significant, while, conversely, the more backward a country remained economically, the more political power would remain in traditional hands. In any case, the need for assistance was urgent: to await until radical changes in the power structures had occurred before offering development aid would be to condemn already underprivileged peoples to an unnecessary prolongation of their misery without in any way contributing to promoting political change.

There were comparable differences of view, again in both poor countries and rich, about the practicability of alternative forms of development. Many in poor countries demanded a policy of 'self-reliance', involving the renunciation of foreign aid and foreign investment and a reduction of foreign trading links; and a 'de-linking' of their economies from the dominant capitalist world system of the day. Although the pace of development that resulted might be slower than in countries which sought flourishing interchange with developed economies (such as the NICs), it would in the long run bring about a form of development that was more balanced, more appropriate to the life-style and culture of their own region of the world and less dependent on the economies of the Western world.

Against this, it was argued that the attempt at autarkic development of this sort must bring growth so slow that it would be self-defeating. Internal tensions would threaten the entire experiment. The demonstration effect of higher standards of living elsewhere could not be obliterated and would cause a drain of resources, both material and human, to countries of higher standards of living, and a decline of faith in the viability of the experiment (a decline said to be already seen in such countries as Tanzania and Cuba which had embarked on that route). The cutting-off of trade links with the outside world, far from benefiting them, would sacrifice the superior division of labour, based on comparative costs, which an integrated world economy could afford, and prevent trade becoming, as it had for those poor countries which had developed fastest, the engine of growth. While rich countries could sacrifice growth for environmental or other reasons if they so chose, since their standard of living was already sufficiently high, it was not open to poor countries to choose this slower path except at unacceptable cost to the welfare of peoples who were already living near or below subsistence levels. Only rapid development could bring the independence that was desired; and that required close integration with the world economy outside. 'Self-reliance' would bring only backwardness.

Such disputes about desirable roads to development partly reflected the glaring division in standards of living which still prevailed and the fear of economic domination that resulted. The demand for autarky would decline only when levels of development were less far apart than they were. And that would only be achieved when the international community had evolved a more rational strategy for influencing the flow of resources across the world, so as to bring a more balanced pattern of development in the international economy as a whole.

2.4 INTERNATIONAL INVESTMENT POLICY

Classical economic theory held that a rational international distribution of investment funds would come about as a result of market forces. Such funds would automatically gravitate to the areas where the marginal productivity of capital was highest. Since raw materials and food supplies were widely distributed about the world, capital too would become equally dispersed. Because labour costs were lower in the least developed areas, capital would be especially attracted to those areas (if no artificial controls on its movement were imposed). And in this way development itself would spread from more advanced to less developed regions. The fact that in the last part of the last century a considerable volume of investment did flow from the more developed to less developed areas of the world perhaps gave some colour to these theories. It is questionable, however, if the pattern of international investment has ever been mainly determined by rational economic criteria of this sort.

In the first place, national governments have at all times intervened to influence the flow of investment funds, for political or other reasons. This was seen even before 1914 in the closure of stock markets to particular governments (for example, by France) or in the offer of special rights to raise capital to colonial territories and other favoured borrowers (for example, by Britain). More recently, it has been seen in the use of government controls, for balance of payments or other reasons, to prevent foreign investment; or to restrict it to particular areas or particular purposes. Secondly, money has been borrowed rather than lent; and who borrowed depended on the needs and capacities of particular governments, not the needs and capacities of their territories. Foreign lending has never been mainly for investment in industry: for most of this time, both before 1914 and since – above all in the last 10 years, when the flow has been greatest – it has been primarily to governments, to enable them to finance their own spending or to repay earlier loans. Even where true investment has taken place, it has been for the creation of infrastructure, such as communications or power supplies, rather than for industrial purposes. The safety of such investment, and even investment in manufacture, has depended more on confidence in the political and economic strength of a government or economy than on the relative productivity of capital. Thirdly, a number of factors, including caution, inertia and patriotism, have had the effect that the available investment funds have often been more easily and readily reinvested in the relative safety of the home economy, with larger and more predictable markets, than in unfamiliar and hazardous economies abroad. Fourthly, the attraction of low labour costs and of available raw-material supplies abroad, though not insignificant, have usually been much smaller factors in determining the location of manufacturing capacity, especially in recent times, than has the characters of governments, the availability of flourishing markets, of skilled labour forces, of adequate financial and other services, of good communications and supply organisations of many kinds: assets which are usually more widely available in rich countries than in poor.

All of these factors have inhibited international investment, at most times. Over the last 30 years there have been factors working in the opposite direction. The dynamism of some developing economies, growing much faster than those of industrialised countries, has made them more favourable locations for investment from elsewhere. The existence of large volumes of internationally mobile capital, especially within the international banking system, looking for suitable investment opportunities, has provided ample resources for such flows. Against this, the political risks of investing abroad have often seemed greater than ever. An increasing proportion of all investment has been by governments or state corporations rather than by private companies, almost exclusively within the home territory. Where investments in poor countries has taken place, it has been primarily in the procurement of energy and raw-material supplies, especially oil, needed for the benefit of the developed countries from which the investment came, rather than for that of the recipient state, and not usually for manufacture. And while there has been a large volume of lending to *governments* in poor countries, little of this too has found its way into industrial investment.

Better management of the international economy, therefore, requires not only higher growth, as we considered in the last chapter, but also a more *balanced* growth than occurs today and so more balanced investment. Much of the world's potential work-force is never reached by investment today. If it is to be reached it will at first be only by aid. Aid can take account of the *needs* of different localities in a way that private investment, concerned only with relative returns, is never likely to do. At present, however, development assistance fails to do this. Not only is it inadequate in amount to offset the differential attractions of more prosperous areas. Because of the multiplicity of aid-giving governments and institutions, and because of the political factors which still continue to influence their decisions, its distribution is not governed by any clear economic criteria: while India receives about $3 a head richer Réunion gets over $1000; while Bangladesh gets about $8 a head, Israel receives over $200. The burdens of aid *giving* are equally illogically distributed: the Netherlands gives five times as much as the United States in proportion to GNP. If international development is to take place on a more coherent basis, there is clearly need for a more rational system to govern both.

The distribution among *receiving* countries is at present manifestly unjust (see Table 2.5). At present, better-off developing countries receive more international aid a head than the lower-income countries which have greatest need of it and least chance of securing funds from elsewhere. This was sometimes justified in the past on the grounds of the greater 'absorptive capacity' of the former. But it is doubtful if, so long as the *type* of aid given is appropriate, there is any limit to a country's capacity to benefit from aid. There is no real limit, for example to the amount of assistance that even the poorest country can use in improving its education, its water supplies, its health services and its infrastructure generally. The poorer countries, unlike middle-income countries, are unable to obtain loans from the international banking system or private investors. They are therefore totally dependent on aid for foreign exchange. Over recent years this has been recognised by the main international development institutions: 90 per cent of the concessional funds provided by such bodies (mainly the IDA and regional banks) today goes to very poor states. Bilateral donors act differently: only

TABLE 2.5 *Aid per head among groups of countries (US $)*

Type of country	ODA a head
Least developed countries	23.84
Other low-income countries	9.31
of which	
India	3.36
Pakistan	15.23
Middle-income countries	30.12
OPEC	4.73
NICs	1.34

SOURCE OECD, *Development Cooperation, 1981*, p. 87.

about 35 per cent of the aid provided bilaterally (aid which is much more subject to political influence) goes to such countries (for the United States and France the proportion is little more than 20 per cent). The result is that at present better-off developing countries on average receive more international aid a head than the low-income countries,which have greater need of it and less chance of securing funds from elsewhere.[21] If a more rational distribution of funds is to be established, that situation should be reversed.

Ideally there would be a system of *graduation*. As the level of income a head in a poor country rose, so its eligibility for concessional assistance would decline. If this came to be a generally accepted principle, the political bias which at present distorts the distribution of aid (so that most of the aid given by the United States and the Soviet Union goes to politically favoured regimes, most of that given by France and Britain to their former overseas territories, and most of that given by OPEC goes to Muslim countries, regardless of relative needs) would decline. Such a change, designed to make the levels of aid received conform with rational criteria, can only come about if there is some integration between private and public aid: if, that is, bilateral programmes become subject to a greater degree of international discussion and international surveillance than is the case today. This would demand the establishment of some central development institution, in which rich and poor countries were represented within which all aid policies, including those of bilateral donors, could be discussed (in the way that they already are, somewhat ineffectually, in the Development Assistance Committee of the OECD).

One of the main functions of such a body would be to assess and compare the *quality* of the aid which is given. There has, as we have seen, been some improvement in this respect in recent years. Today 90 per cent of the aid coming from countries in the Development Assistance Committee takes the form of grants; repayment terms are easier; and debts have been rescheduled or cancelled. Perhaps the most important requirement now is a reduction in the 'tying' of aid to purchases in the donor countries. This remains a widely adopted but damaging practice (it has indeed increased somewhat in the last two or three years), which reduces significantly the value of the aid that is given. A new supervisory body for development should therefore demand pledges that the proportion of aid tied be progressively reduced. There is also a need for a larger proportion of aid to be in the form of programme lending, which can be used by the receiving country as it sees fit – for maintenance or for local costs – rather than being always allocated for new projects and

imported equipment. There should be much closer co-operation between donors in each country and between donors and recipients, to
ensure co-ordinated programmes, through more effective consortia.
There should be an increase in the proportion of aid channelled through
multilateral institutions: while for some smaller donors as much as 80
per cent goes in this way, for most of the major aid-givers the proportion
is far smaller (for France and Japan, for example, the proportion is only
20–25 per cent) and only 30 per cent of concessional aid overall goes
through multilateral bodies (much of the World Bank group's lending is
not concessional). In all these matters improvement is only likely to
come about if more effective international influence can be brought to
bear. A new international body for this purpose could scrutinise the
performance of individual donors and recommend changes in their
practice where necessary, mobilising international pressures on each
donor.

But the main purpose of such a body would be to ensure that aid went
where needs were greatest. This would require not only that a larger
proportion went to the poorest countries of all, but also that more went
to the poorest *groups* within the receiving countries. In other words, a
world development agency could make a deliberate choice to pursue the
distributionist strategy: seeking to focus development among the groups
and regions which need it most. That course would be necessary partly
to secure common justice: to each according to its needs. But it would be
dictated also by economic rationality. For it is often where productivity
and skills are lowest that a small injection of capital can increase them
most. And a growth in purchasing power among the most deprived
groups can also, as we saw in the Introduction, by promoting the
consumption of basic products which can be produced locally, such as
food, clothing and shelter, do most to spread work and wealth within the
same economy, rather than stimulating (as does much development
assistance) further demands for expensive imported goods, whether
capital equipment or consumer products.

Such a body could also help to bring about a more rational
distribution of the burden of aid *giving*. At present some of the countries
with the strongest economies and the highest income a head, such as the
United States, Japan and Austria, have the worst aid performances.
Countries of roughly similar income a head give in aid proportions of
GNP varying from 0.2 to over 1 per cent. On these grounds the Brandt
Report proposed a system of 'universal revenue mobilisation' under
which all countries would be assessed by some international body as to
their capacity to give or need to receive aid. The system would be applied

to all countries. Rich states (including most communist states) would be assessed on the amount they could be expected to provide in aid. The poorest would be assessed in terms of needs. Middle-income countries would be expected to give a little and receive a little.

The standard demanded could depend not only on income a head but also on rates of growth and perhaps the balance of payments position of each country. On this basis a timetable could be set, laying down the time within which each country should reach the immediate target of 0.7 per cent of national income for development assistance and the long-term target of 1 per cent. If the obligations expected of each country were sufficiently publicised, and international pressures brought to bear sufficiently powerfully, such a system might raise the aid performance of many countries. Each government could be systematically and publicly cross-examined to persuade it to improve its record. In this way the aid burden could be slowly adjusted so that it is distributed more equitably than it is today. Where governments were under pressure of this sort, they might find it easier to win the support of their legislative bodies for the programmes laid down. Alternatively, an annual 'pledging conference', at which pledges of aid for the following year were made simultaneously (on the lines of that which already takes place for the UNDP), might, if sufficiently publicised, serve to bring pressure on governments to come up each time with worthwhile pledges.

Because it is always likely to be difficult to secure reliable commitments from individual donors, there has been increasing interest in establishing some type of *automatic* revenues which could be used for development assistance. Under the proposed Treaty on the Law of the Sea, such revenues will be derived from licensing seabed production. Equally, the proposal for a 'link' between the issue of SDRs and development assistance (p. 105 below) would create a form of revenues available almost automatically. The Brandt Report discussed certain other ideas of this kind: taxes on international trade or travel, on international investment, on exhaustible minerals, or on the use of international 'commons', such as the oceans, space channels, telecommunications and radio frequencies, or offshore oil and gas. There would clearly be a huge advantage in securing revenues that were independent of the will of individual governments and were likely to expand automatically with increasing use. The report especially commended the idea of a tax on the arms trade, since there seems a certain natural justice in taxing all those countries which are heavily involved in either the purchase or sale of arms; while a tax on some of the other activities would bear particularly severely on individual countries which were especially dependent on them (some countries are more dependent than others on trade, for example). Whether or not, however, this is the particular type of levy chosen, the recurrent problems of bodies such as IDA would be transformed by the creation of automatic revenues of the kind proposed. Again, a new international body concerned with development assistance would have the task of making recommendations concerning the type, form and scale of the revenues to be established: perhaps for subsequent consideration by a wider body, such as the UN General Assembly.

But, however much development assistance may be increased in this way over the next decade, it will certainly remain inadequate to meet the needs of poor countries. For this reason private investment will remain, at least for the middle-income countries, a significant and perhaps the main source of external funds for the foreseeable future. All three of the main types of private investment in poor countries – direct investment by companies, bank loans and bonds issued by governments for purchase in capital markets elsewhere – are at present threatened because of the increasing debt burden of poor countries and doubts over their capacity to repay. As we saw, this has already caused many banks, and the governments which oversee them, to become cautious about adding to existing levels of indebtedness. New private investment is therefore only likely to have a major part to play in these countries if something is done to alleviate the debt burden. A certain amount of the government debt has already been cancelled, reduced or rescheduled. But there is some injustice involved in that method since this benefits most those who have borrowed most and have already benefited most in the past. It is a reduction in *future* obligations that is most required. The World Bank already today grants subsidies to reduce interest rates (through its 'third window'). But such action is likely to be required on a much larger scale in the future. The IMF is considering subsidising interest rates for very poor countries using one of its facilities.[22] Rescheduling to lengthen debt maturities will be necessary. Finally, guarantees by international bodies, to make it easier for poor countries to raise money in world markets, may be increasingly needed. Only if the present burden of debt is significantly relieved in this way are the majority of developing countries likely to be in a position to incur further obligations, whether to aid donors or private investors, in the future.

There is also need for new types of lending which can increase the total resources available. One new development in recent years has been the growth of 'co-financing': that is joint financing from private sources and from the World Bank for particular projects. The Bank provides the skilled evaluation of the project and often supervision during construction; and this then helps to create the necessary confidence within the private sector to inject capital. It thus enables the World Bank funds to stretch further. The Bank also now lend for 'structural adjustment', development which saves imports or boost exports. Conversely the IMF has created new 'facilities', raising the amounts members can borrow for particular purposes, and thus provides what is almost development assistance. The role of the private banks could be preserved if participation in bank loans was broadened to spread the risks. Banks may also be willing to lend more for specific projects, sometimes on an equity basis. Finally, technical advice to poor countries could make it easier for them to issue bonds on capital markets elsewhere, a procedure in which most of them are quite inexperienced.

If direct investment by *companies* is to continue to be a significant source of investment funds for poor countries, certain conditions will have to be fulfilled. The governments of poor countries need to be satisfied about the role which such companies will perform within their economies. For this the companies may need to give pledges concerning their willingness to transfer technology, the employment and promotion of local staff, the provision of information about their operations, levels of investment, pricing, export policies and other matters. The UN Commission on Transnational Corporations has discussed a set of guidelines setting out the conditions which such companies should be prepared to fulfil. Increasingly, however, poor countries are demanding more than this. The Andean Pact countries, for example, have introduced legislation providing for 'fade-out', or the progressive transfer of ownership in foreign companies to local shareholders over a period of some years. More co-operation of this kind among host countries may be needed: for, example, to control the use of transfer-pricing to reduce tax burdens. In other words, the international character of the *companies* may need to be matched by international co-operation among *governments*, if effective regulation is to be brought about.[23]

In return, however, if the companies are still to be willing to invest, they will need to be given undertakings in their turn. They will need reasonable assurances against expropriation without adequate compensation. They will need certainty that they will be able to continue remitting profits on a reasonable level to the home country. A system for insuring their risks is required. And some provision will need to be made for the international adjudication of disputes on such questions.[24]

For all the purposes we have described – for devising and maintaining a system for assessing the aid obligation of donors, for considering the distribution of development assistance between recipient states, for scrutinising and improving the quality of aid, for examining the development needs of particular sectors, particular regions and the world economy as a whole, and for overseeing the activities of transnational corporations and international banks – new institutions will be required. What is necessary is not a new aid-giving agency (as the Brandt Report proposed). If the aim is to establish an institution more democratically controlled than the Bank, a more sensible aim might be to reform the Bank itself (especially since this will anyway remain the main aid-giving institution for the foreseeable future). The Bank is today not quite so dominated by the United States or Western governments as is sometimes suggested. The US vote in the Executive Board has diminished steadily from 39 per cent in 1950 to 21 per cent today. The share of Western industrial countries as a whole (excluding the Scandinavians and others that are normally sympathetic with the aspirations of poor countries) has declined from nearly 80 per cent to 52 per cent (see Table 2.6). Moreover, votes are only very rarely taken, so most decisions are the result of consensus (though this itself may be influenced by the balance of ultimate voting power); and poor countries have a majority of *voices* on the Executive Board. It would not be feasible to create a development agency in which decisions were in the hands of the recipient countries. What is required is a rough *balance* in

TABLE 2.6   *World Bank: voting power in the Executive Board, 1950–80[a] (percentage of total votes)*

	1950	1960	1970	1980
United States	39	30	25	21
Other rich countries[b]	40	35	31	31
Intermediate[c]	9	13	15	16
Poor countries	12	22	29	32

[a] Most of the members of the Board represent groups of countries, usually from the same geographical area, and cast the votes of the whole group.
[b] Including groups wholly or mainly composed of rich countries.
[c] Including the Scandinavian group (often sympathetic with poor countries) and three groups which have a majority of poor countries but are represented by a rich country (usually having a majority of the group's votes).

SOURCE   World Bank, *Annual Reports.*

voting power between donors and recipients. It does not require, as Table 2.6 makes clear, a very large shift in the present distribution of votes to secure this. If the criteria on which votes are based were only marginally changed, something like an equilibrium between developed and developing states would be established.

But what is lacking at present and what, as we have seen, is so badly needed is not a new body that *administers* aid. It is one that would maintain a general *oversight* of the development process all over the world and of the transfer of resources, both bilateral and multilateral, taking place for that purpose. This would need to be a body (unlike the Executive Board of the World Bank) regularly attended by ministers. It could be the type of world economic council already suggested (pp. 27–8 above), responsible for examining the general management of the world economy. The establishment of such a council, in which governments were represented by senior ministers rather than officials (as is at present the case in the executive boards of the World Bank and the IMF), would assist effective decision-making in one of the principal areas of international economic management today: the development of a common world economy.

Such a body would not need to be concerned with particular projects or programmes within individual developing countries (any more than national governments need to concern themselves with individual projects being financed through their regional development programmes): that would continue to be the concern of agencies administering the programmes, such as the World Bank, UNDP and the specialised agencies. It would be concerned with the total availability of funds for international development, whether through aid programmes, bilateral and unilateral, through direct private investment, through bond issues or through the international banking system; with the general distribution of those funds, among regions, among countries and types of country (rich, poor and very poor); it would be concerned, perhaps increasingly, with distribution among sectors – energy and food production, manufacturing industries and extractive industry, steel and shipbuilding – to ensure that the volume in each was adjusted to the needs of each region and of the world economy as a whole. And it would be concerned with the constraints restricting the flow of funds to particular areas, with the factors affecting the availability of funds of particular kinds and with the problems of repayment. If it were not itself responsible for policy in the trade and monetary fields, it would need to work closely with those bodies that held such responsibility (pp. 90 and 122 below).

Its overall aim would be to bring about a world development process sufficiently balanced to secure adequate rates of growth even in regions of limited resources and skills; and growth sufficiently stable and sustained to bring about steadily increasing prosperity for the international economy as a whole. It would be both more acceptable and more effective than bilateral donors or multilateral agencies dominated by the rich in influencing (as the World Food Council has in the case of food policies – p. 184 below) the development policies of individual governments. It is these policies, as much as the scale or nature of external resources, which determine rates of development today. Each country in theory retains the right to determine its own policies and, if it wishes, to go to economic destruction in its own way. But in practice the growing importance of external investment has the effect that those policies become subject to increasing influence from outsiders, influence that debtor countries can never wholly escape. One of the main reasons for seeking to create better international institutions in this field is to provide a source of influence that could have more authority than individual commercial banks lending in rivalry with each other (which did not prevent or even anticipate the problems of the Mexican and other economies), and take a wider and longer view than short-term lending institutions such as the IMF. It could thus more effectively than those ensure that available investment funds were used in a way most likely to promote the wider interests of a common world economy.

3 Trade

3.1 THE PATTERN OF INTERNATIONAL TRADE

A century ago more than three-quarters of all international trade was undertaken by seven advanced states of Europe and North America. At the end of the 1870s almost a fifth of world trade was in the hands of one country, Britain. Britain sold an even higher proportion of world manufactures: nearly 40 per cent. The United States held about 11 per cent of world exports and Germany about 8 per cent.

Thirty-five years later, just before the First World War, 43 per cent of world trade was still in the hands of these three nations. By this time the share of Britain in world exports had declined to 15 per cent (her share of world manufactured exports was still 27 per cent), while Germany and the United States had 14 per cent each; France and the Netherlands came next with 8 and 7 per cent respectively[1]. Of third-world countries only India had a significant share: about 5 per cent (see Table 3.1).

TABLE 3.1   *Shares in world exports, 1913*
(per cent)

Britain	15
United States	14
Germany	14
France	8
Netherlands	8
India	5
Belgium	4
Canada	2.5
Australia	2
Brazil	2
Japan	2
Indonesia	1.6
Switzerland	1.5

SOURCE   P. L. Yates, *Forty Years of Foreign Trade* (London, 1959).

International trade at this time consisted primarily of the exchange of manufactures from the most developed countries, such as Britain, the United States and West Germany, for raw materials and food, mainly from the white-settled countries of temperate climate, Canada, Australia, New Zealand and Argentina. The latter countries imported almost all their manufactures; they exported almost exclusively primary produce. For most industrial countries the reverse was the case: Britain, for example, sold mainly textiles, iron and coal in exchange for food and raw materials. Only a few developed countries, the United States and France for example, were already then, as they are still today, exporters of agricultural produce as much as of manufactures (manufactures were less than 15 per cent of US exports in 1876 and still under 20 per cent at the end of the century).

The relationship between primary produce and manufactures in world trade remained fairly stable. Primary produce remained consistently rather over 60 per cent of all trade (a proportion which held good for many years to come). Within that total, as time went on, food became a declining proportion and industrial materials an increasing one. During the long depression from 1873 to 1895 (pp. 2–3 above), though agricultural prices declined, the *volume* of primary-produce exports held up reasonably well. From 1895 onwards, when the terms of trade were reversed and the prices of primary produce again rose in relation to manufactures, the proportions again did not alter much, so that the real income of the countries exporting primary produce increased significantly. Throughout this period the total volume of trade increased rapidly, especially in the last 15 years before the First World War. During the 35 years before 1913 trade increased at an annual rate of 3.4 per cent, a higher rate than ever before.

After the First World War the distribution of trade changed significantly. The US economy was little affected by the war and flourished for the first 10 years after it. This was reflected in the growth of US exports, especially of manufactures. Britain, on the other hand, was not only more severely affected by the war and in deep depression for most of the twenties; by adopting an overvalued rate for the pound in 1925 she also limited her capacity to export, so that her share of world trade declined. Germany had been even more damaged by the war but enjoyed a period of rapid recovery in the late twenties. As a result, by 1929 Britain's share of world exports had declined to 11 per cent, Germany's was 10 per cent and France's still only 6 per cent.[2] Against this, the share of the United States had risen sharply, to 17 per cent. There was also some increase in the share of the temperate producers of foodstuffs, Canada, Australia, New Zealand and Argentina, though the price of their exports was already low and was to sink still lower.

The depression changed this pattern again. The main effect was that the total volume of world trade dropped dramatically. Between 1929 and 1932 world trade in manufactures dropped by 40 per cent and in raw materials by 25 per cent. The distribution between countries and regions also changed. The share of the United States, which was most affected by the slump, declined to 14 per cent once more. Britain's share dropped to 9 per cent, Germany's to 9 per cent and France's to 3.6 per cent.[3] More dramatic was the effect on primary producers, whose exports were hit hardest of all, being affected not only by the reduction in volume, but still more by a disastrous fall in prices. The share of the whole world outside Europe and North America, representing by far the greatest part of the population of the world, thus dropped once more from 42 per cent in 1928 to 36 per cent in 1937.

Moreover, the depression caused governments to take action which contracted trade still further. Concerned at high levels of unemployment and the resulting social pressures, they introduced a series of restrictions on trade, designed to restore their trade balances and to protect employment (p. 73 below). The consequence was that, even when domestic production rose, the recovery in world trade was inhibited. Thus in 1939 its level had still barely returned to that of 10 years before. The increase in world trade during the whole period from 1913 had been less than 2 per cent a year.

During the Second World War the US economy once more was little affected, and, indeed, grew at an unprecedented rate. European economies on the other hand were all, to one degree or another, seriously damaged by the prolonged conflict. US foreign trade had always been a small proportion of her total national income (about 5 per cent), and after the war she was even more self-sufficient than before. But the European countries were, far more than before, dependent on imports from the United States, above all for capital goods but also for wheat, tobacco, films and other products. The US share of world exports now therefore increased dramatically for a time. This resulted partly from larger exports of agricultural and other raw materials and was more at the expense of third-world countries than of other developed states. The share of the world outside Europe and North America in world trade thus dropped once more: to 34 per cent in 1953. By that time, when the immediate effect of the war was beginning to wear off, and the European economies, with substantial assistance from the United States, were beginning to revive again, the pattern of trade (excluding Eastern Europe) was as shown in Table 3.2.

TABLE 3.2 *Shares in world trade, 1953*
(percentage of world exports)

United States	21
Britain	10
France	8
Netherlands	8
Canada	6
Australia	2.7
India	2.5
Japan	1.7
North America	27.4
Europe	38.9
Asia	11.9
Latin America	11.3
Africa	6.5
Oceania	4.0

SOURCE Yates, *Forty Years of Foreign Trade*, pp. 32, 166.

At this time, therefore, developing countries, though they had three-quarters of the world population, had well under a third of world trade. During the next thirty years that proportion, though small enough, was destined to fall still further.

During the next 25 years international trade grew faster than at any earlier period in history, roughly doubling in the fifties and more than doubling in the sixties. But this growth was concentrated primarily among developed countries. The distribution was affected by a major change in the composition of world trade which took place at this time. Previously, trade in primary produce had maintained a roughly constant proportion of total trade. That proportion (about 60 per cent) had changed little from the 1870s till the early 1950s. From this point, however, the share of primary products declined. This is turn caused some decline in their relative prices during the next twenty years. The main growth point in trade was in manufactures, especially in capital goods and sophisticated consumer products (cars, refrigerators, washing-machines and similar goods), aircraft, computers and chemicals – all products in which rich countries specialised. Their trade therefore grew far faster than that of poor countries.

Most of the increase in trade was in trade between the rich countries themselves, rather than trade between rich countries and poor, still less between poor countries and poor. While, therefore, the exports of North America, Western Europe and Japan doubled between 1948 and 1958, those of the rest of the world rose by only 52 per cent; and, while the exports of the former increased by 136 per cent in the following decade, the increase of the latter was only 92 per cent. As a result the share of developing countries in world exports declined steadily from around 30 per cent in 1950 to 17 per cent in 1975. Excluding oil-producing countries, their share was considerably smaller: dropping from 19 per cent in 1955 to 12 per cent in 1976. In the same period the share of developed Western countries rose: from 58 to 67 per cent. By the mid-seventies, therefore, poor countries, though representing four-fifths of the world population, only accounted for about one-eighth of total world trade. And their proportion of exports of manufactures, the most rapidly growing sector, was still smaller, only about 8 per cent, though rising slowly (it rose from 5 per cent in the mid-fifties to 9 per cent at the end of the seventies).

In any case, the dramatic increase in the volume of world trade which had been seen during the previous two decades now slowed sharply. The huge increase in the oil price in 1973, withdrawing substantial purchasing power from the rich countries and compelling them to introduce deflationary policies, reduced the rate of growth and so of trade. Trade growth dropped from about 8 per cent a year in the previous 25 years to about 4–5 per cent in the years after 1973. The proportion of energy, and therefore of raw materials generally, in total world trade began to increase once more. While the oil-producers thus increased their share of world trade substantially, the share of most other developing countries declined more than ever.

There was only one exception to this general trend: the NICs (p. 14 above). These not only, as we have seen, secured rapid industrial growth, but they also attained a substantial increase in their share of world trade. They followed the path of Japan 30 years earlier by quickly developing the technology for producing manufactures which, with their lower labour costs, they were able to sell far more cheaply than the rich countries themselves. As a result, despite the protection which most rich countries maintained for such products, they succeeded in securing a substantial penetration of their markets. Their trade in consequence expanded far more quickly than that of any other group of countries.[4] Their exports of manufactures rose by 10–15 per cent a year. Thus a very large proportion of the increase in the exports of manufactures from poor countries generally came from this small group.

There were a number of reasons why most other poor countries were not able to increase their share in world trade, despite the small proportion which they already possessed. They were not able to produce the type of goods in which trade was increasing fastest: manufactures, especially high-technology products. The products which they did export were those against which protection in the rich countries, where the main markets existed, was highest. While protection of most other kinds was being progressively reduced during this period, it was being maintained in precisely those areas of greatest interest to poor countries: agricultural goods, processed products and simple manufactures. Agriculture had from the beginning been omitted from the post-war liberalisation process. Originally this had been demanded by the United States, so that she could maintain her system of agricultural support: later, ironically, it was the United States herself which sought to remove that exclusion, because of the effect of agricultural protection, especially in Europe, on her own very competitive agricultural exports. But the EEC, having established an even more blatantly protectionist system of agricultural support – combining high agricultural support prices, heavy levies on imports and large subsidies for agricultural exports, the three most anti-social protectionist policies that can be devised – was now still more strongly opposed to liberalisation in this field. Few other rich countries provided much scope for agricultural imports. Products processed in developing countries from their own raw materials were similarly penalised, often hit by cumulative tariffs which bore heaviest on the higher stages of fabrication. Finally, simple manufactures – textiles, clothing, footwear, hardware and electrical appliances, for example – almost the only products which developing countries (and not all of them) were capable of exporting, were subjected to tariffs, and increasingly to quota restrictions, which severely limited their access to the markets of rich countries. In almost all the main areas where poor countries could compete, therefore, they found severe restrictions placed on their exports. And the special system of preferences introduced in their favour – the Generalised System of Preferences (GSP) – had little effect, as it covered only a small proportion of their trade: only 4 per cent of Japan's non-food imports were covered, 13 per cent of the United States', and 29 per cent of the EEC's.

A further difficulty they experienced arose from the fluctuations in prices of primary products on which many such countries still depended for most of their export earnings. On these grounds from the thirties onwards there were continual discussions about the establishment of commodity schemes to stabilise prices for producers (in much the same way as governments introduced agricultural support schemes within states to stabilise prices for farmers). Such schemes usually operated either by limiting the amount of produce entering into world trade, through quotas for each country; or by establishing buffer stocks which bought produce at times of overproduction and low prices, and sold them from the stock at times of shortage, so maintaining reasonable stability of price. Though a few such schemes were negotiated and operated for a time – for sugar, tin, coffee, cocoa and rubber, for example – all of them broke down with alarming regularity. And by 1981 virtually none of the agreements v hich had been painfully negotiated over the previous 30 years was still effectively in operation.[5]

During the seventies there were further difficulties affecting the trade of poor countries (see Table 3.3). Their import needs grew. Most were severely affected by the increase in the oil price in the early seventies. Though in absolute terms their consumption of oil was small compared with that of rich countries, in terms of their national income, and especially of their export earnings, their dependence was greater.[6] Thus the increased price of energy created even greater difficulties for them than for the rich. Their need for imported food also increased. And the price of the capital goods they imported from the West rose rapidly. But it was harder for them to bring about the rapid increases in export earnings thus required, given the limited range of their exports and the

TABLE 3.3   *Total merchandise exports, 1965–80 (US $ billion at constant 1978 prices)*

	1965	1970	1977	1978	1979[a]	Average annual growth rates (%) 1965–70	1970–80[b]
All developing countries	138	169	235	252	261	4.2	4.6
Low-income	13	16	24	27	26	4.2	5.5
Middle-income	125	154	211	226	235	4.2	4.5
Industrial countries	301	512	795	840	878	11.2	6.2
World[c]	542	821	1240	1307	1374	8.6	5.7
Oil-exporting developing countries	80	86	91	89	89	1.7	− 0.3
Oil-importing developing countries	58	83	145	163	173	7.3	8.1

[a] Preliminary.
[b] Estimate.
[c] Also includes countries having centrally planned economies and the capital-surplus oil-exporters.

SOURCE   World Bank, *Annual Report, 1981*, p. 26.

small demand for them among the oil-producers, the only countries in surplus. They were severely affected by the declining rate of growth of world production and trade, resulting from the oil-price increase. And they faced increasing protection within the developed world as a result of rising unemployment there. Trade *between* poor countries remained insignificant: only 5 per cent of world trade in manufactures and 8 per cent of primaries was between south and south.

The trade of rich countries was affected by another problem. This was increasing overcapacity in certain industries. In many fields production capacity, as a result of high investment, greatly exceeded the total market available even in times of high growth. Overproduction occurred successively in shipbuilding, steel, automobiles, oil-refining, chemicals and other industries. With markets now growing more slowly than in earlier decades, and with production from the NICs being superimposed on that of the developed world, a situation arose in which sufficient sales outlets no longer existed for the products of many of these industries. Technical changes reduced the labour required for each unit of output. Severe contractions in the labour force became necessary. This stimulated still stronger pressures for protection, usually particularly insistent when the imported products came from developing countries. There were widespread demands for import controls, 'orderly marketing arrangements', threshold prices, 'managed trade' or similar policies – all policies designed, under whatever name, to reduce imports.

These demands were the latest manifestation of the calls for government controls on trade to reduce competition which had been so insistently made for many years.

3.2   GOVERNMENTAL RESTRICTIONS ON TRADE

For centuries governments had interfered in international trading contacts to promote what they conceived to be national interests. National interests, however, were conceived in different ways in different periods.

During the Middle Ages, protection of native industries or merchants was not usually the main concern. The most universal desire of rulers was to maintain supplies of basic necessities, especially food, on which the population depended; this so-called 'policy of plenty' caused governments to *welcome* imports rather than to penalise them and to *ban* the exports of food and other products. Equally important was the concern to build up the military and naval power of the home state: this 'policy of power' caused governments to encourage the import of strategically vital products such as naval goods (timber, hemp, wax and so on), or to discourage their export (the export of horses, saltpetre, weapons and even iron was banned in many countries). Thirdly, trade was seen as the main source of revenue for governments: on these grounds they not only taxed incoming merchants and goods but would even tax their own country's main exports (as English kings, for example, taxed exports of wool). Finally, governments were concerned to attract trade to benefit their own merchants, to promote needed imports, and to provide a source of tax revenue; and for this purpose they established markets, fairs and 'staples', towns through which all traders were obliged to travel.

During the period of state-building which followed, a systematic attempt was made to build up native industries by excluding competing foreign products. Protection became the main motive of trade policy. Very high tariffs were imposed on many types of imports. Bounties and subsidies were provided to assist local industry. Monopolies were granted to particular companies and individuals. Draw-backs were given for products which were re-exported to markets abroad. Discrimination in the treatment granted to different countries was normal, whether for political or commercial reasons. With no agreed rules among governments, trade was distorted by increasingly heavy restrictions of this kind.

During the nineteenth century, with the growing influence of the manufacturing and commercial classes, there was a reaction against the widespread trade restrictions imposed in the previous era. Free trade principles won widespread support, especially in such countries as Britain which could hope to benefit most from them. Tariffs were reduced unilaterally (as by Britain in the 1820s and 1840s); or by agreement between two states (as between Britain and France in 1860). By the latter date most European countries had begun to reduce their tariffs. The 'most favoured nation' principle, under which governments agreed to accord each other the most favourable treatment they accorded to any other state applying the same principle, was widely accepted. So the general principle of non-discrimination in international trade for the first time began to be accepted. From the 1870s, with the onset of price depression in Europe, European governments (apart from Britain) again began to resort to protectionism, though now normally non-discriminatory except in colonies. American tariffs rose still higher than before. Though trade rose fast in the years before the First World

War, this was only despite the heavy protection imposed by most industrialised countries.

At the end of the First World War, governments proclaimed their desire to return to a more liberal trading system. International conferences, at Brussels in 1920, at Portorose in 1921 and at Genoa in 1922, all called for a reduction in tariffs and other such obstacles. Two conferences at Geneva in 1927 discussed the abolition of absolute prohibitions on particular exports (as still existed, especially for food, in some countries, particularly in Eastern Europe) and reductions in tariffs. The first produced a convention for abolishing export prohibitions; but this never secured enough ratifications to come into effect. The second produced recommendations for tariff reductions; but these too were never implemented and were indeed shortly followed by sharp increases in tariffs, especially in the United States. A world economic conference in 1933 produced many proposals for tariff reductions and other measures of liberalisation; but no agreement was reached.

In practice, governments at this time resorted to more blatant forms of protection than ever before. There was a widespread move to something approaching autarky. Tariffs were raised higher than ever; quantitative restrictions, in the form of quotas, were widely introduced; exchange controls were imposed; barter arrangements were made; and bilateral trade agreements of many kinds were undertaken. Governments everywhere were mainly concerned about restoring employment at home; and they believed that this could best be secured by excluding imports from abroad which competed with home products.

When the Second World War came to an end, there was a general desire to abandon the competitive restrictions of the inter-war period and to return to a more liberal trading system. This desire was felt to some extent by all developed countries at the time. But it was inevitably felt most strongly by the country with the strongest economy, which was likely to benefit most from the establishment of freer trading. Just as Britain, the strongest industrial power at the time, pressed hardest for free trade in the mid nineteenth century, now the United States played the leading part in promoting trade liberalisation. The first effort to establish an organisation for that purpose failed (p. 77 below). Though the GATT which finally came into existence was less ambitious in its aims, it reflected a commitment to progressive liberalisation new in world history. There had been once before – in the middle of the nineteenth century – a similar commitment for a time. But that period was brief (most of the agreements for tariff reductions were signed in the period between 1860 and 1875). And at that time the process was bilateral, spasmodic and *ad hoc*. Some governments liberalised far more than others; and some (for example, the United States) did not take part at all. Now most of the governments of the developed world pledged themselves to regular and systematic negotiations with a view to reducing tariff levels over as wide an area as possible and to the progressive elimination of all quotas which restricted imports by volume.

Over the next 15 years five rounds of negotiations took place (in 1947, 1949, 1951, 1956, and 1960–1). Governments negotiated bilaterally and item-by-item, one offering to reduce tariffs in one area against corresponding reductions by the other (though in both cases the reductions would have to be generally applied under the most-favoured-nation rule). These five rounds together brought average tariff levels among the countries participating down to an estimated average of around 15 per cent. Meanwhile within Western Europe ever more rapid liberalisation took place: first as a result of a process of organised pressures within the Organisation for European Economic Co-operation; and subsequently through the establishment of the EEC, which provided for the abolition of all trade barriers between its members. In the next round of GATT negotiations, the so-called Kennedy round, between 1964 and 1967, a more ambitious target was set. The aim was to bring about an average overall reduction of 50 per cent in tariffs. This was now to be done by across-the-board reductions, with exceptions where necessary, rather than by the horse-trading of previous procedures. In the final result, average reductions were about 37 per cent. At the end of the round, tariffs on non-agricultural products had been reduced to an average of 8.6 per cent in the EEC, 9.9 per cent in the United States, 10.7 per cent in Britain and 11 per cent in Japan. A few other measures of liberalisation were agreed: an anti-dumping code, a code on the taxation of cars, and rules for the valuation of chemicals for customs purposes (though the last of these, involving the abolition of the US 'American selling price', an artificial price designed to raise the tariff, was never implemented).

For a time after this it seemed as if the momentum of liberalisation had been exhausted. Pressures for protection arose in a number of states. But from 1973 a further round of multilateral negotiations took place: the so-called Tokyo round. This time the emphasis was not so much on the reduction of tariffs (though this was included) as on establishing codes of conduct to govern various other kinds of restriction which had become equally important in distorting trade flows: subsidies; discrimination in government procurement; countervailing duties (used where exports were alleged to be dumped – that is, sold below domestic prices); customs valuations; product standards (environmental, health and other regulations used as a means of excluding imports); import licensing; discrimination in trade in civil aircraft; and the 'safeguards' increasingly demanded by many governments to enable them to introduce restrictions where severe hardship was being caused to a local industry. The negotiations were not finally concluded until the spring of 1979. Apart from the question of safeguards, on which irreconcilable differences emerged (especially on the right to take discriminatory action against imports from a particular country), new or revised codes were agreed covering each topic. Equally important, machinery was established to supervise compliance with the new codes. There was agreement on a further 35 per cent reduction in tariff levels.

To some extent, therefore, the impetus towards liberalisation was maintained despite the strong pressures for protection now being felt in most rich countries. But, as with the Kennedy round, the benefits for poor countries were far less than those obtained by rich countries. And the types of protection that were most damaging to these, especially restrictions on agricultural exports, on processed products and on simple manufactures, were still little affected.[7] While, for example, the value of tariff reductions under the Tokyo round was on average about 35 per cent, it was only 25 per cent on those products which were mainly of interest to poor countries.

Moreover, many of the benefits of further liberalisation were reduced by a contrary trend. During the seventies new types of restriction began to be introduced, many of which especially affected the products of poor countries. Most were specifically intended to stem the flow of goods from poor countries to rich. First, there were so-called 'voluntary agreements' to restrain exports of particular kinds – in practice far from voluntary, since they were accepted only under the threat of more drastic action if they were refused: examples were the Cotton-Textile Agreement (later replaced by the Multi-Fibre Arrangement) restraining exports of textiles from poor countries, first negotiated in the early 1960s, and the various agreements to restrain exports of motor-cars from Japan. Then there were the 'countervailing duties', used not only for their original purpose against goods dumped below the domestic price, but also in any cases where imports were said to benefit from subsidies and to cause injury to a domestic industry (again, especially widely used against imports from poor countries). There was a revival of quotas, restricting the total volume of imported goods of particular kinds (used, for example, against imports of textiles, footwear, television sets and other electronic equipment). There were various kinds of 'non-tariff barrier' – national standards, pollution regulations, customs valuations and so on – carefully used to exclude inconvenient competition (widely used by Japan, for example, to restrain imports). There were 'trigger prices', minimum prices for imports, imposed to prevent unwelcome competition (as imposed for steel in the United States and the EEC). There were many new types of subsidy, including special assistance to industries or regions in difficulty, which in effect protected home industry against foreign competition. There were import surcharges, designed to raise the price of all imports in relation to home produced goods (as employed by Britain in 1964, by the United States in 1971 and by Italy on more than one occasion). And there were proposals for more general measures – 'orderly marketing arrangements', 'organised free trade', 'market sharing' – as a means of excluding unwanted imports from elsewhere.

The overall effect of these measures should not be exaggerated. They had far less effect in slowing imports than did deflationary policies in the industrialised countries. Even in the field of textiles, where the demands for protection were loudest, imports from developing countries continued to increase in all Western countries throughout the seventies. And the share of developing countries as a whole in world trade in manufactures continued to increase marginally. But such trade was concentrated, as we have seen, among a very small group of such countries: two-thirds was in the hands of only eight countries. The share of the poorest countries of all in world trade was minimal and continued to decline still further.

If a fairer trading system was to be established a better system for regulating permitted government interventions was clearly required.

3.3   INTERNATIONAL DISCUSSION OF TRADE QUESTIONS

Until fairly recently most international discussion of trade questions was on a bilateral basis. Governments negotiated separately with each other on trade agreements, tariff concessions, treaties of navigation and commerce and other questions. There were no general international agreements on such matters. A handful of customary conventions emerged concerning the obligation to assure 'national treatment' (that is, they accorded foreign traders rights similar to those granted to home nationals); rules of navigation; the settlement of commercial disputes; most-favoured-nation treatment for tariff purposes; and so on. But even these, though widely applied, were mainly granted by one nation to another through bilateral treaties rather than on the basis of multilateral Conventions.

It was only after the First World War that international discussion of economic questions began to be common. Within the League of Nations there was established an Economic and Financial Organisation, together with two committees (an economic and a financial committee) which were concerned with commercial and other economic relations between states. Sub-committees studied tariffs, exchange controls and commercial policy generally. All these bodies tried to reach agreement for the reduction of tariffs and other barriers, and the abandonment of nationalistic economic policies. A series of international conferences sought to lay down the principles that governments should follow in their economic relations with each other. But all these efforts were unsuccessful in deterring governments from adopting, especially after 1930, policies that were even more nationalistic, more autarkic and more indifferent to the welfare of other states than at any time in the past.

When the Second World War ended, therefore, there was a more determined attempt to establish new international institutions which might be able to bring a more effective regulation of trade relations between states. There was a widespread concern to prevent a return to the competitive nationalism of the inter-war period. The UN Charter itself committed all members of the organisation to join together 'to achieve international cooperation in solving international problems of an economic . . . character'. At first it seemed likely that a UN specialised agency would be established with responsibility for trade matters. The United States made proposals in 1945 for a new, more liberal international trading system. A conference at Havana in 1947 reached preliminary agreement on the establishment of an 'International Trade Organisation', which would oversee the operation of new rules governing tariffs, quotas, preferences, subsidies, commodity agreements, restrictive practices, state trading, and the whole field of trade between states. The proposal, however, ran into strong opposition, especially in the US Congress. As a result the charter of the organisation was never even submitted to Congress for ratification and the proposed body never came into existence.

The General Agreement on Tariffs and Trade (GATT), which emerged in its place, was undertaken first as an interim measure. It was far more limited in scope. It was not an organisation with specific functions, but merely an agreement to negotiate at regular intervals with the aim of reducing trade barriers. The parties committed themselves to enter into 'reciprocal and mutually advantageous arrangements directed to the substantial reduction of tariffs and other barriers to trade and to the elimination of discriminatory treatment in international commerce'. The organisation's concern was only with tariffs and other barriers to trade, not with the trading system as a whole. There were regular meetings of 'contracting parties' to look at particular problems and eventually a council; but no ongoing activities. It was, moreover, throughout its first 20 years dominated by rich Western states, and primarily concerned with their problems. For long, most poor countries did not bother to join, since it did not seem relevant to many of their needs (and many were, anyway, not anxious or willing to liberalise significantly). Only two or three East European countries – Poland, Czechoslovakia and Romania – became members. Only from the early seventies did a substantial number of poor countries begin to join, so that by the end of that decade its membership rose to 85. Even then the negotiations instituted under the agreement continued in practice, as we have seen, to be of far greater benefit to the rich countries than to the poor.

It was largely because of the feeling that the GATT was something of a rich man's club, and little concerned with many of the problems that were of greatest concern to poor states, that developing countries demanded, and finally secured, the establishment of another organisation that might be more responsive to their needs: the United Nations Conference on Trade and Development (UNCTAD). As its title implies, this, like GATT, was not an organisation in the strict sense. It was not a separate agency but part of the United Nations itself (though the relationship of its secretariat to the UN Secretariat has always been ambiguous and sometimes acrimonious). It was essentially a series of highly publicised conferences every three or four years about the major trade questions of the day, especially those of concern to poor countries (the word 'development' in its title was largely ignored, since there were other international bodies with a more direct responsibility in that field). Between conferences its board met regularly to discuss the same questions; and there were a number of important committees considering, for example, shipping, insurance, commodities and so on. It was, far more than GATT, a political body, designed for organised confrontation between rich countries and poor. Its procedures were established with this in view. The group system, which in most other UN bodies existed only on an informal basis, was here formalised and made an essential part of the structure. Negotiations took place between these groups: the group of 77 developing countries, originally Groups A

(Africa and Asia) and C (Latin America); Group B, developed free-market countries; and Group D, the communist bloc. UNCTAD was therefore above all the instrument through which the south could make demands for change in the international trading system. Sometimes the calls were without effect: as when it demanded drastic alterations in the terms of trade between commodity producers and other countries. Sometimes they produced at least some result: as with the demands for generalised preferences for poor countries, for debt relief and for a 'common fund' to finance commodity stocks. In each of these latter cases proposals at first rejected by most rich countries were discussed in detail in committees set up for the purpose and finally, at least in part, accepted (pp. 82–8 below).

There were one or two other bodies with responsibilities in the field of trade. It was recognised that there was a need for clarification and amplification of the law governing international trade questions. The United Nations Commission for International Trade Law (Uncitral) was therefore established, as a body of international lawyers, to discuss and draft new legal instruments on such questions. It considered such matters as the rules of arbitration for commercial disputes, the international sale of goods, negotiable instruments and commercial credits, conditions of sale, insurance and similar matters. On some of these new international conventions were drafted and signed.

This does not exhaust the roll-call of international bodies concerned with trade matters. The United Nations itself discussed such questions regularly: in Ecosoc, in the Assembly's Second Committee, various special assemblies, and in the Committee of the Whole (p. 26). They were discussed in a whole range of regional institutions, including the regional economic commissions of the United Nations and such bodies as the EEC, the Association of South-East Asian Nations, the Andean Pact and several African regions. Finally, they were considered in partial bodies such as the OECD and the Group of 77.

Thus a number of new institutions were established for discussing international trade questions in the years after 1945. But these efforts were dispersed among a wide range of separate institutions, each with their own responsibilities and having only marginal contacts with each other. It was widely felt that there was need for some more effective international institution in this field, or, at least, for a better division of labour among those which already existed.

3.4 CURRENT PROBLEMS OF INTERNATIONAL TRADE

If new machinery for considering international trade problems is required, what form should it take? In considering this we need to look in rather more detail at the trade difficulties which have emerged in recent years and how they might be overcome.

A major problem affecting the trade of many countries is its *instability*, either in prices or in total export earnings. This is experienced particularly by the producers of commodities – food and raw materials. The prices of these are highly sensitive to small variations in supply and demand. The main difficulty to be overcome is not the long-term decline in commodity prices in relation to those of manufactures.[8] Even if it could be shown that *average* commodity prices had risen less than the prices of manufactures, it is inconceivable that consumers would agree to arrangements which would reverse this trend by raising them artificially, or by maintaining some fixed parity with the price of manufactures. For this reason it is inevitable that commodity prices will eventually reflect overall market forces. And the right solution to the long-term problem is not to benefit a few producers at the expense of all consumers – the majority of them poor countries – by taking action that will permanently raise prices; but to try to reduce fluctuations and to help producers that are overdependent on commodities in other ways – by helping them diversify into other areas of production, for example.

The real source of concern, therefore, is *short-term* instability in prices. This can damage consumers as much as producers (as when many prices doubled in 1972–3). But producers are far worse affected. Since many producing countries depend on two or three, or even a single product, for most of their export earnings,[9] severe instabilities can have a catastrophic effect for them. Zambia, for example, almost entirely dependent on copper for its earnings of foreign exchange, saw the price of copper, and so its export earnings, halved in the course of a few months in 1974. Mauritius is almost entirely dependent on sugar exports to acquire foreign exchange; but the price of sugar can multiply in a few months and fall again as quickly at other times.

An obvious way to try to overcome this problem is through commodity agreements designed to lessen instabilities without altering the long-term trend. There have, as we have seen, been many attempts to negotiate such schemes from the thirties onwards. But there are formidable difficulties in reaching agreement on them.

First, there may be differences among producers themselves. Such schemes often require restrictions on export sales. Traditional producers may be reluctant to accord an adequate market share to new producers: as Latin American producers of coffee have been unwilling to accord African states quotas as big as the latter have demanded. Low-cost producers may be unwilling to accept a scheme which will limit their opportunity to win sales by competition. These problems alone may prevent the conclusion of a generally acceptable agreement.

But there is even greater difficulty in obtaining agreement between producers and consumers. In theory, consumers may benefit as much from stabilisation as producers; but only if the price at which stabilisation takes place is not significantly above market trends. Even if there is a general understanding (as consumers usually demand) that the prices should conform with 'long-term market trends', there can still be major differences about what this implies. Thus producers and consumers will differ on the required maximum and minimum prices. Whether the scheme operates on the basis of limiting exports, or of a buffer stock, some understanding on the acceptable price level is required. This is the question on which there has been most difficulty in negotiating agreements. And it is on this question that the agreements from time to time set up have mainly subsequently broken down (the tin, coffee and cocoa agreements have broken down on these grounds in the past two or three years). Especially where the price of a commodity, because of a sudden glut or shortage, falls well below the prices set in the agreement or climbs above it, there will be disagreement between producers and consumers on the appropriate action to take. It is generally accepted that a scheme providing for a buffer stock (provided the commodity is not, like rice or tea, so perishable as to preclude this) is better able to withstand the pressures of a changing market situation than one which provides for rigid quotas of production. But there are problems even here. It may be impossible with the funds available to buy sufficient to maintain the price; while, conversely, sales to depress it may exhaust the stock (each of these problems has confronted the tin agreement at different times). Consumers may begin to make purchases outside the scheme. Producers may demand the renegotiation of the agreement at a higher price level; or, if the price falls below the minimum provided for, may ask for renegotiation to limit sales in future. And there can be differences concerning non-commercial releases such as those from national buffer stocks: as has occurred several times when US commodity stocks have been released. Thus while it is easy to pronounce on the *desirability* of new commodity agreements, these are in practice by no means easy to secure. The innumerable breakdowns in such schemes over the last 50 years show only too clearly that it is unwise to place too much hope on them as a means of stabilisation. But at least there should exist, for each commodity (and not just a few as at present), a permanent council, representing the main producers and consumers, that can keep the problems of price and supply under permanent review; can supervise the operation of commodity markets; and propose appropriate stabilisation schemes if feasible.

From the early seventies there has been much discussion of a 'common fund' which would be used to help finance commodity schemes of this kind. Eventually, after much dispute, agreement was reached on a very modest scheme of this sort in 1978. This provided for only a small fund, of $400 million. Of this $150 million was to be contributed by governments, with the rest to be 'on call' from governments if absolutely needed. On this basis the Fund will be able to borrow in the markets. The Fund would also be able to receive cash deposits from the existing commodity schemes. The plan provided for another fund, a 'second window', to be financed partly by voluntary contributions and to support marketing, research and development. It is unlikely that in its present form the Common Fund will have any significant effect in stabilising prices, if only because the funds available are so small. Few states have ratified the agreement. In any case, the impact of the scheme depends absolutely on the existence of viable commodity agreements; and, as we have seen, almost none exist at present. The Fund is at best only the germ of a larger and more effective scheme in the future.

On these grounds many people today believe that there is a greater hope of success through schemes which seek to stabilise *earnings* rather than prices. Usually these schemes are designed to replace part or all of the loss of earnings which producers suffer because of a sudden fall in prices. There are two main schemes of this sort at present. The better is the EEC's Stabex scheme negotiated under the Lomé agreement. This provides for grants or loans to compensate producers (of some, but not all, commodities – most minerals are not covered) for losses in earnings. The other is the IMF Compensatory Financing Facility, set up in 1963 and since improved. This provides loans to producer countries where they have suffered a loss of export earnings from a drop in prices. Such schemes, because they interfere less with normal market forces and require no understandings concerning prices or levels of production, have obvious advantages over commodity schemes. Probably the most effective way of helping the countries which produce commodities without excessively penalising those which consume them (mainly poor countries) is, therefore, to seek to negotiate a more comprehensive and effective scheme of this kind. What is really required is a global Stabex covering (as the Stabex scheme at present does not) all products and all producing states (Latin America and South Asia are at present excluded).

A more fundamental problem in the international trading system stems from the various restrictions imposed by governments on normal trade. These are today imposed mainly against imports from developing countries. The abolition of such barriers is over the long term as much in the interests of rich countries as of poor. The ancient economic doctrine of comparative costs – that each nation can maximise its welfare by exchanging what it can produce most economically for the products that other nations produce most cheaply – which brought calls for the reduction of barriers among developed countries, demands today a similar opening of markets to the products of poor countries. The process of liberalisation which has already brought about such advantage to rich states, in terms of more rapid growth and a more efficient division of labour, might bring them further benefit if applied to the international economy as a whole.

Many who theoretically accept that premise add the qualification that, however necessary, this should not be done in a way which unduly threatens the livelihood of those who work within old-established industries in developed countries. These deeply felt apprehensions cannot be ignored. They certainly will not be by governments. A new programme of planned liberalisation is therefore only likely to be viable if it takes some account of these fears.

Many of the difficulties created for rich countries in removing restrictions result from the *speed* of liberalisation rather than from the fact that it takes place at all.[10] Improved access for imports from poor countries has clear long-term advantages for the rich countries. It makes available cheaper supplies of many important products. It allows manpower and capital resources to be diverted to areas where productivity, profits and export potential are higher. Above all, it allows poor countries to buy greater quantities of their own exports. Rich countries at present export four times the value of manufactures to poor countries that they import in return ($125 billion against $32 billion in 1978). They would export still more if the latter could afford to buy more (since within poor countries there is an insatiable demand for imports from the North). This means that increased access for imports from the south will normally be made good by the increased exports of other kinds it makes possible. The cost of liberalisation thus falls only on *particular* industries and *particular* regions: those which at present manufacture the products that would be replaced by imports. In other words, liberalisation brings long-term and broadly shared benefits against which must be set short-term costs for particular groups.

The best way of reconciling these two interests is to allow imports to grow but only on a gradual and controlled basis, with a systematic programme of adjustment assistance to reduce the cost to the particular groups and areas affected.[11]

An early (though unsatisfactory) example of controlled liberalisation of this kind was the Multi-Fibre Arrangement. This provided for a steady increase in the share of the market in rich countries to be accorded to textile imports from poor states. Originally that share was to grow by 6 per cent a year. It was later, however, so modified and hedged about by amendments that its original purpose was largely frustrated. Its effect on particular countries depends on bilateral negotiations in which all power lies with the importing country. In addition it was never applied against imports from developed countries. It is important, therefore, that any more general commitment to controlled liberalisation should be in a form that cannot be easily modified or retracted. The commitments should preferably be 'bound', in the same way that tariff reductions agreed in GATT are bound: that is, they should not be altered except in acute emergency. Even then, any modification should require international endorsement and not be possible by unilateral action.

One of the difficulties of this approach is the danger that concessions of this kind will overwhelmingly be taken up by a very small group of NICs. As we have seen, though there has been a substantial increase in the sales of manufactures from poor countries in the North over the last decade (they were growing by over 15 per cent a year during the seventies), these have come overwhelmingly from about half a dozen super-competitive states. A commitment by rich countries to concede a certain proportion of their markets to poor countries might therefore, unless proper arrangements were made, benefit only a small handful of countries and give little benefit to the great majority.[12] To apply the distributive strategy, markets would need to be deliberately offered on a discriminatory basis, with quotas allocated to particular regions or particular countries, to give better opportunities to the poorest countries of all. It would certainly need to be accompanied by a process of 'graduation', by which any special concessions granted to poor countries were gradually withdrawn from those which passed a certain level of development (measured perhaps by income a head or by the level of export growth). Finally, it is equally important to ensure equity among *rich* countries by establishing some objective measure of the degree of liberalisation already achieved there – measured perhaps as a percentage of the market accorded to imports from poor countries.

The complement of this policy would be a substantial programme of adjustment assistance to the rich countries which opened their markets. The greater the assistance of this kind available, the more willing such countries will be to liberalise. Such a programme would involve help in the retraining of workers, in assisting them to move to new areas where employment prospects were better, special redundancy and early retirement payments, assistance to firms – in tax credits, accelerated depreciation and subsidised loans – in switching to new forms of production, and regional programmes to assist entire areas affected by the decline of a traditional industry. A number of rich countries have already introduced national programmes for this purpose (for example, under the US Trade Expansion Act of 1962, West Germany's industrial modernisation programme, Japanese measures to assist the closure of shipyards and other industries, and the British measures in the early sixties designed to assist firms to move out of textile production). But there is need for international programmes too to assist this transition. The EEC gives grants under its social and regional policies which are sometimes used for the purpose. But what is required is a wider international programme of assistance for this purpose.

Liberalisation on these lines has been checked in recent years by the demand of rich countries for 'safeguards': the right in a critical situation to place restraints on imports for limited periods. These measures, either in the form of new quotas or 'countervailing duties', have been widely used and have been the cause of great controversy. Under Article 19 of GATT, parties are permitted to place such restraints where imports are causing 'serious injury' to a domestic industry. But there is no attempt in the article to define what injury is serious; and states so wishing have therefore been enabled to introduce such measures without authority, and even without presenting evidence to justify their actions. A number of attempts have been made in GATT to secure some definition but so far without success. The issue was the most bitterly contested during the Tokyo round and the only one on which agreement proved impossible.[13] It is thus now vitally necessary that some agreed criteria should be established about the circumstances in which safeguard measures (to be applied non-discriminately) are justified: perhaps related to the rate of growth of imports of a particular kind, or the speed of job loss as a result.[14] So long as no definition is agreed, rich countries will feel justified in resorting to such action whenever a local industry which is politically powerful demands assistance against foreign competition. Whatever criteria are devised, the important thing is that they should be applied not by each government acting individually according to its own interpretations, but only with the authority of an international body set up for the purpose (on the lines of the Textiles Surveillance Body set up to police the Multi-Fibre Agreement). Such a body, in receipt of an application for safeguard action, would investigate the circumstances, consulting the exporting country concerned, and decide whether the action proposed was justifiable and for how long (if necessary, only if the necessary adjustment assistance was introduced). Every government would be committed to abiding by those rulings.

This process of controlled liberalisation is most obviously needed in the areas where barriers remain highest: agricultural trade, processed goods and simple manufactures. It is towards liberalisation in these spheres that the next round of GATT negotiations should be mainly directed. The difficulties should not be underestimated. It is not by chance that protectionism among rich countries has been most stubborn in these fields. It is because it is here that liberalisation most threatens employment at home (all the industries affected are high employers of labour) and is least likely to lead to access to flourishing markets in return.[15]

To liberalise imports of simple manufactures, the first task is to abolish the discrimination under which, in some cases (textiles), imports from poor countries are controlled, but not those from rich countries. Secondly, some understanding about reciprocal liberalisation may need to be secured if there is not to be a net loss of jobs within rich countries. Finally, there is a need to improve the preferences enjoyed by poor countries. The idea of generalised preferences for the exports of poor countries was first discussed at the two UNCTAD meetings of 1964 and 1968. After negotiations lasting for several years, schemes to provide for such preferences were introduced by the EEC, Japan, the United States and other developed states during the early seventies. The value of the schemes introduced was limited, however, by the wholesale exclusion of some products and by the establishment in other cases of tariff quotas, i.e. limits to the volume of imports which benefit from the preferences. Moreover, as tariff reductions have taken place among the rich countries, the value of the preferences has been lessened (though the reductions of course still benefit poor countries in relation to home-country producers). Two things are now needed. The widespread exceptions and quota ceilings which at present reduce the value of the schemes (so that only a fraction of total imports are covered) should be eliminated. And consideration should be given to providing additional preferences for the poorest countries of all.

The second type of product for which liberalisation is especially necessary is processed goods. As we have seen, many rich countries impose tariffs which become higher the greater the degree of processing that has taken place. This has the effect that, while poor countries can continue to sell their raw materials freely, it becomes difficult for them to set up processing facilities that will be economic. While, for example, rice itself may be imported free of duty to the EEC and the United States, processed rice faces a tariff of 15 per cent in the United States and 13 per cent in the EEC. While crude palm oil can be imported into the EEC with only a 4 per cent tariff, when it is semi-refined the tariff is 12 per cent. When the rate of the tariff increases with the degree of processing, the effective degree of protection, as economists have often pointed out, is higher than the nominal rate. Freight rates are also often higher for the processed product than for the raw material.[16] On purely economic grounds it is obviously more sensible that processing facilities should be concentrated near where the raw materials are produced; and such processed goods are among the few types of product which many poor countries can hope to export successfully. Here too, therefore, rich countries need to agree gradually to transfer processing capacity to the countries where the materials are produced (as has been happening recently in the case of aluminium, for example).

The third area for which liberalisation is most required – agricultural products – is perhaps the most difficult of all. Here the root of the problem lies in the systems of agricultural support that have been established in many countries of the north. For many years most developed countries have been concerned, both on strategic and social grounds, to provide generous support for their agricultural population. These policies often involve the establishment of artificially high prices, the restriction of imports, in some cases the subsidisation of exports. Because large sections of their population are dependent on those policies for their livelihood, governments are less willing to abandon them than any other form of protection. Even so, there is perhaps now a better hope of securing some modification of the policies, or at least some type of understanding about the *type* of protection employed, than at any earlier time. Many in the rich states themselves are increasingly impatient at the high cost of food which results. The United States has for many years been irked by the barriers placed in the way of its agricultural exports by the EEC. Now many members of the EEC too are becoming deeply concerned at the high budgetary cost of its policies, as well as the effect on prices. Finally, many developing countries, whose exports are also severely restricted are increasingly vocal on the issue. There is thus a real hope that the next trade round will tackle this issue. International bodies could at least use their influence to promote the types of protection least harmful to outside producers (for example, the deficiency-payments system formerly used in Britain, which assures the farmer of a minimum income without protecting him altogether from the effect of market forces). And it should not be impossible to secure agreement on the abandonment of export subsidies, one of the most anti-social and indefensible of all forms of agricultural support (helping EEC beet sugar, for example, to displace cane sugar from poor countries in world markets).

Not all protection in the modern world, however, is against the exports of poor countries. Over recent times there has been a considerable increase in the use of restrictions by rich countries against other rich countries. As we have seen, this sometimes results from massive overinvestment in particular industries, such as automobiles, leading to strong pressures for the exclusion of imports. In many of these cases – shipbuilding, steel, computers and aircraft production – there had been huge government assistance to the industry concerned, which has often encouraged excess capacity in industries for which markets do not really exist: this leads to massive losses, pleas for further state assistance and eventually to widespread unemployment. That situation may result simply from a failure to estimate the market accurately. Often, however, it is the effect of inadequate co-ordination of investment decisions among the producer countries, in each of which the industry or government may underestimate the capacity available elsewhere and overestimate its own competitiveness. Sometimes the problem is intensified by competition from new producers, as with shipping (South Korea), automobiles (South Korea and Brazil) and petrochemicals (most of the oil-producing states). Clearly, what is necessary here is far greater international co-ordination of production and investment plans – at the very least, greater exchanges of information – so that overinvestment can be avoided. Here once more problems of trade policy are intimately connected with the problems of investment and growth which we considered in the last two chapters.

Another form of protection is that which results from *political* discrimination. The communist countries in general seek to slant their trade towards each other, through the mechanism of Comecon. Western countries sometimes ban trade with certain communist states altogether; and the United States for long banned all trade with China and Cuba, and now bans trade with Vietnam. Or they refuse to grant them equivalent trading conditions: thus the United States today continues to withhold most-favoured-nation trading rights from the Soviet Union and other East European countries, refusing to grant them any tariff cuts made since 1934 (thus still applying the Smoot–Hawley tariff of 1930, the highest in US history). Such forms of discrimination are rooted in political problems and can probably only be solved through political solutions: detente at the political level is likely to be followed by detente at the commercial level too. But at least international trade bodies can attempt to define the principles – for example, the applicability of the most-favoured-nation rule – which would reduce the seriousness of these political factors.

We have looked at only the more important problems which make a better system of international trade regulation necessary. There are other areas in which undertakings are increasingly required. These include, for example, restrictive business practices at the international level, including market sharing arrangement;[17] intra-firm trading and pricing; export subsidies, including those involved in support for ailing industries; rights of establishment and access to distribution networks (the restriction of which is a form of concealed protection in certain countries); discrimination in services, for example in shipping and insurance; and regional development policies, with their effect in subsidising manufacture. All of these represent practices, whether employed by governments or companies, through which normal trading patterns can be distorted. All therefore are likely to require increasing attention at the international level over the coming years.

If such problems are to be adequately tackled, far better international machinery will be required for that purpose than exists today. The most obvious step would be to replace the proliferation of bodies that now exists with a general International Trade Organisation, as envisaged immediately after the Second World War. This would take over a general responsibility in the field of trade and would therefore assume most, if not all, the present functions of GATT and UNCTAD. This has been often suggested (most recently in the Brandt Report). It is manifestly the tidiest and most logical answer, which would make possible a more co-ordinated international approach to world trading problems.

There are, however, two major difficulties which may prevent it from being accomplished. The first is political. Though the problems which prevented the original proposal from coming to fruition (doubts in the US Congress about the purposes of the proposed organisation[18]) are now less likely to arise, at least in the same form, there would be new objections on quite different grounds. Many governments of developed countries, which attach importance to the businesslike and non-political character of GATT negotiations, would be unwilling to see that organisation abandoned in favour of a new body which would probably be more political in its approach and which would certainly have a built-in third-world majority. Though certain kinds of safeguard might be devised to reduce the risk of railroading by that majority, it is not certain that these would prove effective (similar safeguards in UNCTAD have not prevented it from appearing to be dominated by its third-world majority). Conversely, poor countries might be reluctant to see UNCTAD, which they see as their own special forum, sacrificed for a new organisation which, if it was to be acceptable to the north, might need to operate in a quite different way. Secondly, and perhaps more fundamentally, the functions performed by GATT and UNCTAD – on the one hand negotiating the fine print of detailed agreements for tariff and other trade arrangements, on the other the mobilisation of organised pressure to bring about changes in the whole trading system – are each necessary but are quite distinct. And each requires a different organisational framework if it is to be performed effectively. Whatever new system is adopted, the appropriate procedures for each would be needed, so that the final outcome might not prove so very different from what exists today.

Probably a better alternative, therefore, is to bring GATT and UNCTAD into a much closer relationship than exists between them today. At present almost the only thing that brings them together is their joint management of the International Trade Centre in Geneva (which provides technical assistance to poor countries in the business of trade promotion). Apart from this, relations between the two are somewhat frigid. This separation is damaging and unnecessary. What is required is perhaps a new joint supervising council, in which both bodies would be represented. This would survey their common problems, set up new joint committees or activities where appropriate, reduce overlap (at present there are a number of questions considered in both) and seek to bring about an appropriate co-operation between the two. Such a council should also perhaps supervise the work of Uncitral, which, though highly specialised in function, is concerned with the same broad field of activity. The basic functions at present performed by UNCTAD and GATT, which reflect fundamental needs, are unlikely to be changed drastically under this or any other arrangement. But a closer co-ordination of their many activities might make the work of each of them better focussed and more effective.

The new structure would be concerned above all with maintaining the momentum of the liberalisation programme set in motion over the last 35 years. The continuation of that process is required, as much on the grounds of economic rationality – securing a better division of labour between states – as it is on grounds of equity – achieving a more just balance in the opportunities for trade enjoyed by different nations and groups. There have been many and justified fears, over the past decade, of a new bout of protectionism. So far the movement towards liberalisation has held up better than might have been feared, given the pressures in the opposite direction. The central task of international bodies operating in this field is to ensure that the commitment is maintained. To do this they would need to establish a clear measure of the degree of liberalisation attained, adjusted to levels of economic development.[19] This would include not only tariff levels but also, for example, the volume of trade diverted by quotas, the value of export subsidies and non-tariff barriers. Finally, it would be the task of any new supervisory body to publicise the relative performances of states in achieving liberalisation and bring the necessary pressure for improvement.

All these problems would need to be considered in conjunction with other aspects of international economic policy. Trade policy and monetary questions are intimately interconnected (it was for this reason that the original International Trade Organisation was supposed to be closely linked to the IMF), and it is important that both should be considered together. Trade and development matters likewise are closely linked (as was recognised when UNCTAD was established): trade has always been seen as a vital engine of growth, so that the development of a poor country may depend on its securing adequate trade expansion. It is thus important that trade matters should be considered not only by a specialised body with responsibilities confined to that field, but also by some organisation with a wider perspective. They must therefore fall within the purview of the type of international economic council which we considered in the last two chapters (p. 27 above). The problems of rising protectionism, the difficulties of agricultural trade generally, imbalances in the trading system, the difficulties of access to markets and the corresponding problem of access to supply (for example, to essential raw materials) – all of these would need to be considered on a continuing basis, in conjunction with all the other economic problems of the day, by any body concerned with the management of the international economy as a whole.

Those questions are not purely technical but often highly political. Every country has a political stake in their resolution and all therefore need to be represented, if not directly at least indirectly, in the body that attempts this. 'Economic summits', in which only developed countries are represented, clearly cannot perform the task required. Nor can institutions with low-grade representation, such as the present Ecosoc or Committee of the Whole to which few governments pay regard. Only a body sufficiently representative to win the confidence of all states, and sufficiently high-powered to exercise genuine influence, can perform the task of regulation that is now increasingly required. Trading opportunity at present, like productive capacity and investment, is seriously maldistributed. That maldistribution results partly from deliberate policies of differential protectionism. It will be adjusted only by deliberate policies to reverse that differential protectionism and improve opportunities for the countries that now most lack them. In this way it may be possible to establish not only a freer but also a fairer trading system than exists today.

4 Money

4.1 THE EMERGENCE OF THE CURRENT MONETARY SYSTEM

Another area of conflict in economic relations between states is the international monetary system.

There have always been problems in making payments between one nation and another. Wherever trade takes place there is always a need, if barter is unacceptable to either party, for some currency which both will accept. For centuries the most widely used such currencies were gold and silver, both highly prized in most countries. When national coinages based on such metals developed, there was need of money-changers who would, taking account of the metal content of each coin, as well as of supply and demand, exchange the currency of one country for another. But the varying relationship between the value attributed to the two different metals in different countries (a relationship usually laid down by the arbitrary decision of rulers) produced many difficulties. In time some governments began to move towards the adoption of a single metal standard. Britain abandoned the silver standard in 1819 and based her currency on gold alone. Later, in the early 1870s, most of the other major states followed suit. So an international gold standard was established.

Under that system all currencies were valued at a fixed parity in terms of gold, and so at a fixed rate in relation to each other (exchange-rates could not fluctuate more than the cost of shipping gold from one centre to another). The parity adopted for each was that thought likely to balance trade in normal conditions. Any imbalance that arose was supposed to be adjusted automatically. If a country fell into deficit, that implied a rise in its price level in relation to that of other countries. The deficit would make necessary the export of gold (and the higher price level encourage it). By reducing the money supply at home this would lower demand and so reduce the general price level. Credit policy would be adjusted accordingly: interest rates would be raised in the deficit country to lower activity and attract funds from abroad. Conversely, the excess gold arriving in a surplus country, and the lowering of interest rates which resulted, would raise demand and the price level there, attracting more imports. So in both cases the imbalance should in time be remedied.

It is doubtful if the system ever worked so smoothly as this theoretical description implies. Wage levels, and therefore prices, did not always fall obediently in response to the lowering of demand caused by a loss of gold or a raising of interest rates. Price levels were affected by other factors: the size of harvests, improvements in technology and productivity, and market conditions generally. Even if the system did operate eventually so as to adjust imbalances, it worked only slowly and stickily and at the cost of severe deflation in deficit countries. Despite these problems the system did serve for fifty years to sustain a generally high level of economic activity and a rapid growth of trade between states, without changes in parity, without significant inflation and without any sustained period of depression for any country.

With the coming of the First World War, the need to protect reserves caused governments to give up converting their currencies to gold and to ban gold exports. So the gold-standard system was abandoned and was never to be fully restored. When that war was over, a new variation of the system, the gold-exchange standard, was substituted. With the economies of many countries disrupted, a deficiency in gold supplies and an imbalance in the reserves available to individual states, the use of gold reserves came to be supplemented by the use of currencies, mainly pounds and dollars. These were held by central banks mainly in the form of short-term investments in the money markets of each reserve currency. Four-fifths of the currency used at first was sterling. The total amount of these sterling holdings, which were of course liable to be disposed of at any time of crisis, was four or five times the size of Britain's gold reserves. Between 1925 and 1928 the major currencies were on this basis gradually relinked with gold. But this was sometimes done at inappropriate parities. Sterling was fixed at its pre-war rate of exchange, now much too high, so that Britain found it impossible to balance her external accounts without severe deflation and very high unemployment. The franc, on the other hand, was deliberately undervalued, making French exports very competitive and attracting large quantities of gold to Paris.

The new, small countries of Eastern and Central Europe possessed inadequate reserves to sustain their overseas trade except by resort to strict controls. The additional strain of the depression led to the collapse of the structure of credit in Austria, and the defaulting of the largest bank there. This, in turn, brought a crisis of confidence in other countries and eventually a withdrawal of funds from London. The Bank of England found it impossible to maintain the commitment to exchange pounds for gold and in September 1931 Britain therefore abandoned the gold standard and allowed the pound to float sharply downwards. This was followed in 1933 by the devaluation of the dollar, which was allowed to sink to \$35 an ounce, at which point the price was fixed and convertibility to gold restored. The franc was now seriously overvalued and this placed the French economy in serious difficulties till the franc too was devalued in 1936. At this point the United States, Britain and France signed an agreement under which they undertook to co-operate to maintain stability in exchange rates: the first agreement among governments committing them to co-operate in currency policy.

These currency problems were superimposed on the severe difficulties resulting from the worldwide depression. This created, in addition to the loss of production and employment, problems for many countries in maintaining an external balance. Suffering from unemployment on a major scale, most governments were now unwilling to resort to further deflation, as under the previous system, as a means of restoring equilibrium. They chose the easier way of insulating their own economy. Instead of seeking adjustment through changes at home – higher interest rates and a slowing of activity – they sought to place the burden on other countries: through higher tariffs, import restrictions, foreign-exchange controls, bilateral trade agreements and even direct barter deals. Parities were maintained by open market operations – the buying and selling of currencies – rather than interest-rate changes. A series of separate currency blocs came into existence: a sterling area, comprising the British Commonwealth and a few other countries; a gold bloc linking France, Italy, the Netherlands, Belgium and Switzerland; and a mark zone comprising Germany and most of Central and Eastern Europe. The United States, by undertaking numerous trade agreements with Latin American countries, established a comparable bloc in the Western hemisphere. For a time the international economy disintegrated into a series of almost disconnected regional and national economies.

But there was widespread concern to avoid the instabilities and uncertainties of such a system. At the end of the Second World War, a wholly new international monetary system was therefore established, designed to avoid the main disadvantages of both the previous ones. It would avoid the prolonged deflation which the gold standard was thought to have involved: by providing temporary assistance to a country in balance of payments difficulties so that it could maintain reasonably expansionary policies while the necessary corrective action to balance its payments was undertaken. And it would avoid the trade-destructive protectionism, as well as the instability and uncertainty, of the inter-war years: by establishing a liberal trading and payments system, with generally fixed parities and convertible currencies.

Exchange rates would be neither as rigid as under the gold standard, nor as unstable as between the wars: they would be 'fixed but adjustable'. Each government would fix a parity in terms of gold (and therefore of the dollar, which remained linked to gold); and would undertake to maintain the parity (through sales and purchases in the exchange market) within 1 per cent either side of the level set. This parity would only be changed in the case of a 'fundamental disequilibrium' and then only with the authority of the supervisory body to be established. In less serious cases this new authority would provide temporary financial assistance to help the government concerned to overcome its difficulties without recourse to severe deflation and so damaging the trade of other countries. For this purpose each member would contribute to the new International Monetary Fund (IMF) a 'quota', based on its share in international trade, GNP and so on: a quarter in gold[1] and the rest in its own currency. A member could draw its gold contribution relatively freely. But, with each subsequent 'tranche' of credit, the Fund might impose stricter conditions: conditions that would satisfy the Fund that the necessary domestic measures were being undertaken to reduce the deficit.

Responsibility for 'adjustment' was thus placed entirely on the nation in deficit. The British, in negotiating the agreement, attempted to ensure that an equal responsibility was placed on nations in surplus: the obligation to reduce the surplus by additional imports or by revaluation, for example. This might have brought adjustment of the imbalance with less overall deflation and less loss of employment. The proposal was turned down by the US negotiators (a decision their successors may have regretted 30 years later, when they themselves sought to see sanctions imposed against surplus countries). All that remained was a weak 'scarce currency' clause under which, if a country was so much in surplus that its currency became scarce, other nations would be allowed to impose restrictions on imports from it: a provision that was never brought into effect.

The essential feature of the new system was that it would be above all a *multilateral* system, jointly agreed and jointly operated. Governments would not only undertake to maintain an open economic system with mutually convertible currencies; they would also abandon some of the traditional prerogatives of government in relation to their own currencies, by according substantial authority to the international body. To avoid the disruption caused by unilaterally determined competitive devaluation, decisions concerning parities, changes in exchange rates, exchange controls and other restrictions on payments would now only be taken in consultation with, or even with the consent of, the new Fund. Above all, that body would keep the working of the entire system under continuous multilateral surveillance.

It was always recognised that many nations would find it difficult to commit themselves to operate such a system immediately. While the US economy had grown immensely stronger during the course of the war, the European economies had been shattered by it. The result was that, if controls were removed, the latter would immediately incur huge deficits, which the new system could not cope with effectively (even with controls, the total European deficit was about $15 billion in 1946–7). For this reason it was always intended that there should be an 'interim period' of five years before the new system came into effect. In fact, because of the 'dollar gap' – the insatiable demand in Europe for US goods at that time – the interim period lasted for 16. Britain, in securing a long-term loan from the United States, rashly undertook to introduce convertibility of currencies within a year. But, when she attempted this in 1947, the demand for dollars was so overwhelming that the attempt had to be abandoned within a few weeks – an experience that deterred others from following the same example. Among themselves the European states were able to bring about a limited convertibility. They established a European Payments Union under which a surplus with one country could be balanced against a deficit with another: a country in overall deficit was granted credit up to a certain sum and the balance had to be paid in gold. But their trade with the United States remained in serious deficit. Only gradually, during the course of the fifties, was the overall deficit reduced through the revival of European economies, through large payments of Marshall Aid and through growing US military expenditure and investment in Europe.

The new monetary system at first played little part in restoring normality. The Fund decided not to grant drawings for reconstruction purposes or for countries in receipt of Marshall Aid. Serious balance of payments crises were prevented mainly by domestic controls and by devaluation: like that of the pound and other currencies (without any effective consultation with the Fund) in 1949. Only after the Suez affair in 1956, when Britain and other countries experienced serious financial difficulties, did the Fund begin to provide credit on a significant scale.

Towards the end of the fifties the United States (which had earned a surplus of $10 billion in 1947) began to fall into overall deficit: by 1958 this reached $3 billion. Though her trade was normally in surplus this was more than offset by outflows for investment, aid and military spending. Because the US reserves were large and because she was anxious to assist the recovery of Europe and Japan, for political as well as for economic reasons, the United States was for a time willing to undergo this drain of dollars. But she was also anxious to see the liberal monetary system agreed in 1944 introduced as soon as possible. By 1958 the recovery of the European states was such that they were willing to put the new system into effect and so accept convertibility. Britain and 13 other countries introduced convertibility for non-resident currency in that year. The 'interim period' formally came to an end in 1961.

Only now did the new system devised in 1945 come into effect. It was to last exactly a decade. The system soon ran into trouble. Already by 1960 the total foreign holdings of dollars which were created by the US deficit were greater than the US gold reserve, now significantly declining. This introduced the first faint doubt whether the US commitment to convertibility of the dollar could be maintained. In November the price of gold in the London market increased above the US official price of $35 an ounce. Though the increase was marginal – to about $40 – it aroused considerable concern among central bankers. It made clear that the dollar was no longer as good as gold. If speculation in favour of gold had continued, it could have threatened the stability of the whole system. In consequence the chief central banks of the Western World (meeting monthly at the Bank of International Settlements in Basle) agreed to the creation of a 'gold pool', from which sales would be made in the free market to reduce and so stabilise the price of gold.

This did not, however, overcome the problem of speculation between currencies or even between currencies and gold. The major problem, which was not anticipated at the time the new system was created, was that there now existed huge amounts of internationally mobile capital, on a scale never before experienced. Companies using foreign exchange for legitimate trading purposes, international banks, large transnational corporations, as well as central banks themselves, were all concerned to protect themselves against exchange losses resulting from a change in exchange rates (the first significant change in parity, a revaluation of the mark, took place in 1961). At any moment of crisis, or any serious deterioration in a country's balance of payments, large volumes of funds were liable to be transferred from one currency to another, or to be sold for gold. Since governments maintained their parities by sales and purchases in the exchange market, huge sums would then need to be expended to maintain exchange rates at the official levels.

A number of *ad hoc* measures were undertaken to ease the problem. Central banks agreed to make 'swaps' of foreign exchange to assist currencies in difficulty. They undertook, under the Basle agreement of 1961, to give multilateral support to a country engaged in defending its exchange rate (a support that was given several times in the next few years, mainly to assist the pound and the lira). They entered into the General Agreement to Borrow, under which the Group of Ten chief industrialised states agreed to provide $6 billion to supplement the resources available to the IMF in particular cases, subject to their own consent. All of these measures were designed to make it easier for a government to defend existing parities. They reflected the concern of the bankers at this time that exchange rates should be more fixed than adjustable. It was widely believed that the problem they confronted was speculation, or short-term lack of confidence, rather than an underlying imbalance of price levels. And they were unwilling to believe that the former might often only reflect the latter.

In any case, these various measures, even together, did not overcome the instabilities of the system. Currency crises recurred regularly. The two reserve currencies, the pound and the dollar, were particulary vulnerable. In the case of the pound the weakness caused great problems for Britain and the sterling area, and led eventually to a further devaluation of the pound in 1967. But it was not fatal to the monetary system as a whole. The lack of confidence in the dollar was more serious. The US overall balance of payment continued to deteriorate throughout the decade. The deficit was met only by the willingness of most European central banks to hold dollars without seeking to convert them into gold (except for a period between 1965 and 1968 when France, not averse to causing problems for the United States, insisted on selling the dollars she acquired for gold, so adding to the dollar's weakness). The US government introduced a series of controls over the use of foreign exchange, especially for foreign investment (which at this time was huge): an 'equalisation tax' introduced in 1963 to increase the cost of foreign borrowing; voluntary restraints on foreign investment in 1965; mandatory restraints on such investment, together with restrictions on tourism and the tying of foreign aid, in 1968. None of these measures proved effective for long. In 1968 there was renewed speculation in gold. The Group of Ten thereupon imposed a two-tier gold price: only the official transactions of central banks continued to be undertaken at the official price of $35 an ounce, while for other purposes a free market for gold was introduced.

Meanwhile, in an effort to reduce the difficulties, international negotiations had been conducted over several years to establish a new type of international reserve unit to supplement, and if possible eventually to replace, the traditional reserve currencies. There were two main difficulties to be overcome. One was that encountered by the existing reserve currencies, primarily the dollar and the pound, resulting from their double function. The fact that they were so widely used as reserves made them especially vulnerable to widespread selling at the first sign of weakness; for central banks themselves then wished to sell. The need to forestall this possibility made it necessary for the governments of the countries concerned to be especially cautious in the management of their own economies and often to maintain them in a more depressed state than would otherwise be the case. Certainly Britain and the United States, whether or not for this reason, had the slowest growth of all Western countries. The second difficulty was the general shortage of international liquidity – gold and reserve currencies – widely believed to exist at the time. New gold production nowhere near matched the increase in world trade. This did not matter so long as the United States continued to run a large deficit and so long as central banks were willing to hold the dollars they so earned, since reserves were sustained by those dollars. But if the deficit was eliminated, as was widely hoped, or if central banks ceased to be willing to hold dollars, as many feared, there would be an urgent need for some alternative type of reserve unit to replace them.

Eventually, in 1968, it was agreed to create a new reserve unit, to be known as 'special drawing rights' (SDRs). These were additional drawing rights within the IMF, to be allocated to all members in proportion to their existing quotas. Since they were freely usable by the country concerned for central-bank settlements, they were in effect net additions to their total reserves. The SDR was a credit entry in a new special account of the Fund (a special account was necessary since members were not obliged to join the scheme). Over the first three years there were to be annual allocations of SDRs to a total of $9.5 billion. The rights would be transferred from one account to another on request, the borrower receiving convertible currency in return for the SDRs transferred. The creditor country would be obliged to accept such transfers up to a certain limit. In this way surplus countries would automatically give temporary credit to deficit countries in the way that

Keynes had envisaged when the IMF was first established.

Even this new arrangement, however, while it marginally increased the volume of liquidity, did not help to save the dollar, which was now more than ever under attack. The US balance of payments continued to deteriorate. A revaluation of the mark, following a devaluation of the franc in August 1969, did not improve the US position. Only a change in the US exchange rate, it was increasingly believed, could remedy the position. The United States would have preferred other countries to revalue: this would have left the dollar price of gold unchanged and need not alter the basis of the Bretton Woods system (including the privileged position of the dollar within it). The European governments, however, believed that the US deficits resulted in part from the domestic policies of the United States (at the time involved in heavy military expenditure in Vietnam) and felt that there was no reason why that country alone should be protected, through their own willingness to hold dollars in their reserves, against the normal requirement to 'adjust' counter inflation.

In 1971 these problems came to a head. The US deficit became worse than ever. Now, for the first time since 1893, she experienced a deficit in her visible trade as well as in her overall balance of payments. The outflow of investment, which had been heavy throughout the sixties, now became greater than ever: in part a direct reflection of the overvalued dollar and the lack of confidence of US businessmen in their own economy. By this time US currency held abroad (which could be cashed for gold at any time) amounted to $80 billion, against US gold reserves of little more than $10 billion. US liabilities, like Britain's 40 years earlier, greatly exceeded her assets. It was increasingly clear that only drastic measures could save the situation.

The crisis erupted in August 1971. The United States then took unilateral steps to remedy her position. She abandoned her long-standing commitment, which she had been the last government to maintain, to exchange her currency for gold. She introduced an import surcharge of 10 per cent. At home she imposed strict wage and price controls. The dollar exchange rate was not immediately altered, either with other currencies or with gold; but the US government proceeded to undertake vigorous negotiations with other countries to induce them to agree to a revaluation of their own currencies. Eventually, at the end of the year, under the so-called Smithsonian agreement, a major realignment of currencies took place. The dollar was devalued by an average of 10 per cent; the dollar price of gold was raised to $38; and the mark and yen were revalued. In addition it was agreed that from this point currencies would be held by their governments within 2½ per cent of the precise parity, instead of 1 per cent as before. Only in return for these changes did the United States abandon her 10 per cent surcharge.

Despite all these steps, however, confidence was not restored. In January 1973 a further devaluation of the dollar took place. This too was not enough. Already in June of the previous year Britain had decided to allow the pound to float freely (effectively ending the sterling area, since those countries which had previously linked their currency to sterling now ceased to do so). From March 1973 other major currencies, including the dollar, were also floated. So were the currencies of the EEC, most of them already linked together in the so-called 'snake'. By this time, with the abandonment of dollar convertibility and of fixed exchange rates, little was left of the system established at Bretton Woods.

The adoption of floating rates for the major currencies was originally seen by many as a temporary step.[2] But it fairly soon began to appear more permanent. One effect was that the disruption caused by the large volume of internationally mobile funds was now reduced. The periodic rises created by systematic speculation against an overvalued currency were replaced by more gradual changes in response to market sentiment. But new problems replaced the old ones. Floating was not often genuinely free. Governments intervened in the markets, either to support the exchange rate of their currency or to depress it. Even if the rate was set entirely by the foreign-exchange markets, it was not necessarily a rate which would balance a country's external payments. An extreme example was that of Britain, which because of her possession of North Sea oil, found her currency held at a level which, while it reduced inflation at home, made it virtually impossible for her to sell competitively abroad. The Japanese yen declined against the dollar in 1981–2 at a time of astonishing Japanese surpluses. The market thus reflected relative interest rates and other factors, rather than balance of payments prospects. To deter interventions, the IMF in 1974 sought to formulate rules for floating, but these were so vague that they committed governments to nothing very much, and foreign-exchange markets remained highly unstable.

Steps were taken to reduce the role of gold and enhance that of SDRs within the monetary system. In July 1974 the SDR was revalued in terms of a basket of currencies, instead of gold. In 1975 the official price of gold was abandoned (and in time most countries revalued their gold reserves at the much higher market price, unstable though this proved to be). The Fund ceased to undertake to make and receive payments in gold.

Transactions between central banks in gold virtually ceased. And in 1976 the Fund agreed to sell a third of its gold stocks, returning half of the proceeds to member states, while the other half were used for the benefit of developing countries. The Group of 10 undertook not to increase the total stock of gold they held through purchases, nor to peg the price of gold. The Fund's articles were amended to declare the SDR the principal reserve asset of the system. Finally the SDR was increasingly used as the numeraire for the measurement of all currencies. But, while in theory the SDR was given a larger role, its real importance remained limited. By the early eighties it still accounted for less than 2 per cent of all reserves (against 8 per cent 10 years earlier).

The international payments system was again transformed by the dramatic increase in the price of oil which occurred in 1973. This brought about a radical redistribution of the world's reserves. The oil-producers became the major creditor countries, acquiring surpluses they were quite unable to spend on imports. At the same time the major industralised countries, even those that had been in chronic surplus, such as West Germany and Japan, together with the majority of developed countries, were thrown into serious deficit. It was clear that some means needed to be found for transferring the unused surpluses of the oil-producers to the deficit countries, so that they could maintain their imports. Without this world deflation on a catastrophic scale would occur. The IMF introduced a relatively small special 'facility' to assist the worst-hit countries (the United States had proposed a more ambitious safety net, but this never materialised). For the most part, however, the role of redistributing the petro-dollars within the international economy was undertaken by the private international banking system. This relent the funds deposited by the producers: both to developed and to developing countries (which thereby fell increasingly into debt). The number of poor countries which benefited was small. But in general recycling was achieved at this time more successfully than many had feared.[3]

Poor countries, however, remained dissatisfied with the way the monetary system worked. In their eyes the IMF acted as a harsh creditor. It allowed drawings only in return for undertakings on policy which they regarded as inappropriate and excessively severe. Over the years the Fund had slightly relaxed some of its conditions. In 1952 it had introduced 'stand-by' credits through which a country could, in return for certain assurances, secure the promise of support without necessarily making a formal drawing. In 1958 access to the first credit tranche (the first beyond the gold tranche) was made easier. Later, a series of 'facilities' were introduced mainly for the benefit of poor countries, with varying degrees of conditionality attached: one for compensatory financing (for countries suffering from falls in export earnings – see p. 82 above); another to finance contributions to internationally controlled commodity stocks; one for supplementary financing, intended to provide special assistance for countries which had small quotas in relation to their needs (using funds specially lent for the purpose by developed and oil-producing countries); another to help those countries most seriously affected by the oil-price rise; a trust fund, set up from the proceeds of gold sales, to assist developing countries; the extended Fund facility to provide credit for longer periods (up to 10 years) and in larger amounts than would be possible under the Fund's normal criteria; and, most recently, a cereals facility to help poor countries hit by crop failure or higher prices of imported cereals. By the second half of the seventies, considerably more borrowing took place under these various facilities than under the normal credit procedures (see Figure 4.1). For some facilities borrowing conditions were relaxed.

Poor countries continued to feel, however, that the Fund demanded unduly harsh terms for a drawing, usually entailing severe deflation,

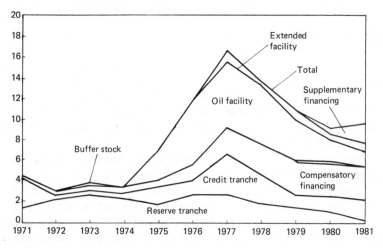

Source   IMF, *Annual Report, 1981*, p. 83.

Figure 4.1   *Types of borrowing from the IMF: use of the Fund's resources at 30 April 1971–81 (SDRs billions)*

reductions in public spending, high interest rates, credit restrictions and sometimes devaluation. They therefore wanted a reduction in this 'conditionality'. And they sought in particular the creation of a 'link' between monetary support and development assistance: that is, they wanted to see SDRs distributed specifically to developing countries to help them to import more freely.

By the end of the seventies, the international monetary system had become something wholly different from that which had been planned in 1945. The system had indeed never operated as was originally intended. It had never been genuinely multilateral: all exchange-rate changes, as well as the major abandonment of convertibility by the United States in 1971 and the adoption of floating rates in the following two years, were undertaken by individual governments acting unilaterally. Drawing rights were not granted liberally by the Fund, as once proposed, to avoid deflation: on the contrary, the Fund normally *demanded* deflation as a condition for its help. Exchange rates had never been 'fixed but adjustable': before 1972–3 they had been fixed but rarely adjusted; while after that they had been perpetually adjusted but never fixed. The central role of gold in the system had been abandoned; and that of the dollar had considerably declined. Finally, a wholly new reserve unit had been created, undreamed-of at the Fund's creation, in theory designed to become the dominant reserve asset but in practice only marginal in effect.

For all these changes, instability in the system had not been removed. New and serious problems were arising which it was still not well equipped to confront.

4.2 INTERNATIONAL MONETARY INSTITUTIONS

During the nineteenth century there were no world monetary institutions. The whole beauty of the gold standard was that it was supposed to operate automatically. No international body was required to supervise its working. There were rarely even meetings of central bankers to discuss its operation.

After the First World War there was more intensive discussion between governments on monetary matters. The League's Financial Committee was supposed to keep such questions under review, and made various recommendations about them. The Bank of International Settlements (BIS), linking major central banks, was established in 1930, originally to supervise the transfer of German reparations and other war-debt payments. The series of international conferences which took place in the twenties and early thirties (p. 73 above) examined monetary problems among others and made recommendations to governments. The early post-war conferences, for example, advocated an early return to the gold standard, though with an increased use of currencies for reserves. Even when such conferences were able to reach agreed decisions, however, their recommendations were little heeded. The World Economic Conference of 1933, which it was hoped might restore monetary stability once more, was pre-empted by President Roosevelt's decision at its beginning to devalue the dollar, and finally came to nothing. There were some attempts at bilateral co-operation: especially, for example, between the US and British central banks. But attempts to establish a co-operative international monetary system at this time failed. Even the tripartite agreement of 1936 between the United States, Britain and France, in which they each committed themselves to co-operate in maintaining stability in exchange rates, did not affect the policy of Germany and other important countries; and in any case was quickly overtaken by the Second World War.

The establishment of the IMF in 1944 appeared therefore to represent a fundamental advance. For the first time a large number of governments joined in creating a permanent organisation to supervise the world's payments system. The new organisation was intended to be as fully representative as possible. Most members of the international community joined at its foundation; and membership increased steadily to more than 130 by 1980. The Soviet Union, though participating in the founding conference, refused to join the Fund, mainly because of her unwillingness to provide statistics on the level of her reserves and other matters, though partly because of her contention that it was a capitalist-dominated organisation. Czechoslovakia, which had been a member at the Fund's foundation, withdrew in 1954. Other communist countries, however – Yugoslavia, Romania, Hungary, China, Vietnam and Laos – are all members.[4]

Final authority within the IMF rests with the Governing Body, the only organ to which all members belong. This meets once a year, at the same time as the Governing Body of the World Bank, always seen as a closely related body (membership of the bank is conditional on membership of the IMF). The meeting is attended normally by ministers of finance. It is the occasion for wide-ranging surveys of the international monetary situation, as well as for many bilateral consultations. There are occasional decisions, as on formal amendments to the Articles of Association. But it is essentially an occasion for consultation. The

Governing Body is too large and unwieldy to be an effective decision-making body on anything but the major lines of policy.

Thus day-to-day decision-making rests in the hands of the Executive Board. This consists of six 'appointed' members (at present the United States, West Germany, France, Britain, Japan and Saudi Arabia, a major creditor); 15 other members, each representing a constituency of generally like-minded states, and wielding the votes of that group; and China, as a major power, a permanent member unelected by a group. It is this body which oversees, and in effect seeks to manage, the world monetary system. Unlike almost any other council within the UN system it is a genuine executive body. It meets as frequently as required, often twice a week, and in private. It does not merely endorse proposals put to it by officials. In effect it determines the policy of the Fund as a whole.

Finally, there exists the Managing Director (the Fund uses the terminology of the business world) and his staff. The Managing Director (traditionally a West European) chairs the Executive Board and has a casting vote. The staff are of high calibre, requiring first-class economic qualifications. They also enjoy considerable power, especially in relation to individual requests for assistance. Despite attempts at diversification, the staff continues at present to consist predominantly of North Americans and West Europeans.

From the time the Fund was founded, power within it was supposed to be related to financial and economic strength. Voting power, in both the Executive Board and the Governing Body, is distributed according to the initial quotas granted to each member; and these quotas are themselves related to shares in world trade, size of reserves, and similar factors. This means that the large and rich states inevitably hold many times more votes than poor countries. As new members joined, and the developing countries acquired a larger share in world trade and production, this balance changed a little. At the time when the Fund was created, the United States, for example, held 31 per cent of the votes; today it has 20. In 1976, with the big increase in the financial strength of the OPEC countries, their quotas were doubled (to about 10 per cent); other developing countries (now including mainland China) have increased their share of votes slightly from just over 20 per cent in 1945 to about 28 per cent in 1980.

As a result, during the Fund's life the balance of power has shifted a little. But it is still the case that non-oil developing countries, representing three-quarters of the world's population, still hold under 30 per cent of the votes. Moreover, within the Executive Board (see Table 4.1),

TABLE 4.1 *IMF: voting power in the Executive Board, 1950–81 (percentage of total votes)*

	1950	1960	1970	1981[d]
United States	31	26	23	20
Other rich countries	40	37	34	28
Intermediate groups	3[a]	11[b]	12[b]	16[b]
Developing countries	26	26	31	34[c]

[a] Including East European countries.
[b] Including groups having a majority of poor countries but represented in the Board by a rich country usually holding a majority of the votes.
[c] Including Saudi Arabia.
[d] The total does not add up to 100 per cent because four countries holding 1.8 per cent of the vote did not participate in the elections to the Executive Board.
Note: Most Members of the Executive Board represent groups of countries, usually from the same region, and wield the votes of the entire group.

SOURCE IMF, *Annual Reports*.

where most of the important decisions are taken, poor countries in practice have a smaller proportion of votes and places (four groups with a majority of poor countries are represented by rich countries there). And, because any major change in the system now requires an 85 per cent majority, relatively small groups (even the United States alone) hold a veto power. In fact votes are almost never taken. Decisions are reached essentially by consensus, so, as in the World Bank, the balance of *voices* may sometimes count as much as the balance of votes: and here the developing countries are actually in a majority, always in the Governing Body and sometimes in the Executive Board. But in practice decisions are still influenced by the known balance of voting power. And certainly no decision can be taken that is unacceptable to two or three chief contributors.

The balance of power in monetary matters depends, in any case, on other factors than voting strength. Many important decisions in this field are discussed in other bodies. The principal developed countries meet, for example, in the BIS, the organisation of central bankers from such states which meets once a month in Basle. The Group of Ten, comprising the ten most financially powerful countries of the Western world, meets regularly to reach decisions on monetary questions: it is this body which decided on the General Agreement on Borrowing and undertook all the preliminary discussions of the SDR scheme. In recent times the Group of Five, the five Western permanent members of the

Executive Board, representing the world's most powerful financial states, also meet together separately to formulate agreed policies on many questions. Working Party Three of the OECD, where discussion of monetary questions takes place among Western industrialised countries, also plays an important role in discussing such questions. Finally, the Western economic 'summits' of heads of state reach understandings on all economic matters independently of discussion in the IMF. Thus major issues concerning the monetary system are often discussed first among Western countries in other fora. And these discussions may predetermine the decisions which are subsequently taken in the institutions of the IMF.

In response developing countries too have evolved fora of their own where such issues are raised: the group of 77, UNCTAD and various regional groups. Within the IMF representatives of developing countries now meet regularly in the Group of 24 to co-ordinate tactics and issue statements of their position. Monetary questions have been aired following special sessions of the General Assembly on north–south problems. And proposals for a new international economic order (NIEO) have included proposals in that area.

There have been some changes in the structure of the Fund within the last decade. In 1972 a Committee of 20 was established, attended by ministers of finance, to examine the future development of the monetary system. This was not able to arrive at agreed conclusions. But in 1974, when it completed its report, it was kept in being, renamed the Interim Committee and given a general responsibility for keeping the working of the monetary system under review. At about the same time a Development Committee, also representing finance ministers, was set up under the aegis of the IMF and the World Bank, to ensure that the development implications of monetary decisions were well borne in mind. Finally, there have been proposals, first put forward by the Committee of 20 and endorsed in the second amendment of the Fund's Articles of Agreement, to establish a Council of Governors which would acquire some permanent responsibility for policy-making within the Fund. Each of these developments has reflected a concern that the voice of developing countries should be better represented in the decision-making bodies of the organisation.

Yet these steps have not altered the fundamental balance of power within the Fund. The rich countries still dominate monetary decisions. This does not result only from the voting system within the Fund. It stems as much from the fact that they are the states (with the largest oil-producers) which are most powerful, and therefore most independent, on all financial questions. Though in a formal sense some degree of consensus is now necessary for major decisions within the IMF, any such consensus is at present weighted in favour of the views and interests of developed states. If decisions are to be reached which are more widely acceptable, a new decision-making system may be necessary, reflecting more closely the balance of interests among the different states and regions of the world.

4.3 PROBLEMS OF THE CURRENT MONETARY SYSTEM

Before considering if and how these institutions might be reformed, let us consider what are the main problems confronted in the current monetary system.

The first question concerns the type of *exchange-rate regime* to be applied. As we have seen, there are many who still favour a return to a system of fixed rates. The Committee of 20, for example, proposed the establishment of a system in which rates would be 'stable but adjustable', though floating rates would be allowed in particular circumstances. There should be clear indicators, such as the movement of reserves, which would be used to stimulate exchange-rate changes. Many other observers have favoured a return to more stable rates; perhaps a system of rates changed only at regular intervals, as under the so-called 'crawling peg' system (providing for adjustments once a quarter or once a month). But major governments today show no signs of wishing to pursue these proposals. It is likely, therefore, that for the foreseeable future floating rates will continue.

This system has certain clear advantages: far greater flexibility, an easier and more gradual adjustment process, and a reduction in the most destabilising types of speculation. But it also creates considerable difficulties. The most obvious is the inconvenience to traders, investors, bankers and others which results when rates cannot be accurately predicted in advance. Fluctuations between rates may be extreme, even in the short term: as was seen, for example, in 1973–5 (when there were fluctuations of 20 per cent between major currencies in a few months) and again in 1977–80 (when the dollar first fell hard and subsequently rapidly recovered). In 1981 alone the dollar fluctuated by over 40 per cent against other currencies. Such fluctuations are self-magnifying, since they promote more intensive efforts to protect against exchange loss by the switching of funds. They are heavily influenced by short-term factors, such as changes in relative interest rates, which are often independent of underlying competitiveness. As a result it may be impossible to raise interest rates (to withstand inflationary pressures) without raising the exchange rate as well; or to reduce interest rates without devaluing the currency. The rates are also still influenced by 'dirty floating'. The attempts by the Fund to establish rules for floating have so far proved both vague and unenforceable. Finally, as already noted, even if there were no 'dirty floating' at all, the rate set by the market would not necessarily be the one likely to balance external accounts over the long term.

Related to this problem is a second concerning the *adjustment process*. In theory, floating rates should bring an automatic adjustment: over the long term a deficit should weaken the parity, lowering export prices and raising import prices, and so lead to an improvement in the balance. But because of the other factors just described – relative interest rates, dirty floating, speculative pressures, differing resource endowment (such as Britain's North Sea oil), propensity to import and export, capital flows, and so on – they will not always do so. Countries with rising exchange rates, such as West Germany and Japan, have continued to export more, while those with falling rates, such as the United States and Britain, continue to export less. A downward movement in rates is a less compelling alarm signal to most governments than were large deficits or large movements of hot money under a fixed-rate system: so inadequate adjustment takes place and instability continues. The prevalence of unemployment and inflation and the determination of many governments to resist them influence policies more than currency imbalances. Deficit countries are reluctant to adopt deflationary policies to balance their accounts, since this will make their unemployment still worse, while surplus countries are reluctant, by reflating, to risk aggravating inflation. The IMF system itself (because the scarce-currency clause was never implemented) provides no sanctions against surplus countries. The only sanctions available are those of bilateral pressures. But, since these come mainly from countries in a position of economic weakness, they often prove ineffective. In practice each country decides unilaterally what adjustment measures it wishes to undertake. And collectively these do not add up to a total which will restore a healthy monetary system.

A third problem concerns the *reserve assets* to be used within the system. In the seventies, as we have seen, there were three main types of asset in use: gold, foreign exchange (principally dollars) and SDRs. After 1971, with the end of dollar convertibility and the increasing weakness of the currency, it might have been expected that the reserve use of dollars would decline. The flow of dollars to the central banks of

Western Europe had long been unwelcome to the Europeans, who resented the 'exorbitant privilege' the United States enjoyed in having her deficits absorbed in this way. In practice, however, far from declining, dollars became a far larger element in world currency reserves, the proportion rising to nearly 80 per cent by 1980. The effect of this was to create a large 'overhang' of dollars. If maintained, this could in theory be released onto the market at any time should confidence finally collapse. If, on the other hand, the US deficit were to be reversed, the availability of liquidity from this source would disappear. There was some attempt to make use of other currencies, such as the mark and the yen, in the reserve role;[5] but this was a solution which the countries responsible for those currencies, fully aware of the liabilities suffered by reserve-currency states, generally resisted. There was thus increasing discussion of another solution: the substitution of SDRs for at least a proportion of the dollars held in reserves. Though the most obvious solution, however, it was by no means easy to accomplish (pp. 117–18 below).

This raised the related problem: *the role of the SDR*. In theory, as we saw earlier, there was agreement that this should become the 'principal reserve asset'. This would make it possible for the volume of international liquidity, and even its distribution, to be determined by a deliberate act of the international monetary authorities, rather than depending, as now, on the size of the US deficit, on decisions in two or three countries concerning the production of gold, or the vagaries of the gold price. But this decision of principle has never been fulfilled. To some extent the SDR was made a more attractive asset for central banks to hold: its interest rate was raised to market rates and it was made more freely usable in central-bank transactions. It was made unnecessary for a government wishing to use SDRs to secure the authority of the IMF or to prove a balance of payments need. But their use was still restricted (it was confined to dealings among central banks and international institutions, so that the scope for using them remains far smaller than that for other reserve assets). Finally, their total volume remains tiny. New allocations are spasmodic, disputed and inadequate. Instead of becoming the substantial factor once proposed, therefore, SDRs have remained only an insignificant element in the world monetary system.

Related to this again is the continued use of *gold* within that system. In theory, decisions of the seventies were supposed to reduce the role of gold. In fact, some have had the opposite effect. The abolition of the official price has in practice, by raising the price, made gold more, not less, attractive as a reserve asset and has increased the total proportion of reserves which gold represents. The sales of gold undertaken by the

Fund had no impact in reducing the price: indeed, they were quickly followed by an astronomical rise in the price of gold in 1978–9. These changes have affected official attitudes. Countries holding gold in their reserves, and even the poor countries which benefit from IMF sales, have an interest in the gold price remaining high and so value its role in the system. Despite the long-standing doubts about the continued use of this 'barbarous relic', therefore, something like half of world reserves continue to consist of a commodity which is widely used for other purposes, whose production is uncertain and controlled by only two or three countries, whose present distribution is uneven, and whose price is highly unstable.

Another problem concerns the *recycling* of the huge surpluses enjoyed by the oil-producing countries to reduce the crippling deficits for other states, both rich and poor, that are their counterpart. Though, as we have seen, the IMF took limited steps to meet this problem when it first materialised in the early seventies, these were fairly marginal in their effect. The oil-producing countries were relatively generous with aid (giving for a time well over 2 per cent of their national income for this purpose, compared with 0.35 per cent given by developed countries). But this redistributed only a fraction of the funds. It was the private banking system, especially the large US banks operating internationally, which were mainly responsible for relending the surpluses to deficit countries, including to many poor countries. The funds went, however, predominantly to a handful of countries. Their distribution bore no relationship to development or balance of payments needs. Finally, the redistribution was achieved only at the expense of creating a huge burden of debt for the receiving states: 40 per cent of the total debt of developing countries (over $500 billion by 1981) was to commercial banks.[6] And partly because of these debts the commercial banks became increasingly reluctant to lend further to countries whose credit-worthiness seemed exhausted.

Next, the very success of the private banking system in operations of this kind created problems of its own. The establishment of the *Euro-currency markets* – that is, markets engaged in the reinvestment of currencies held in banks outside the country of origin – had contributed to the enormous volume of funds that were now used internationally and had thus intensified international monetary difficulties. The volume of this lending increased many times, until by the beginning of the eighties, it was believed, well over $1000 billion was invested in this way (including inter-bank transactions). The volume increased at the phenomenal rate of 25 per cent a year. The market was a highly competitive one, in which tiny margins might be decisive. There were increasing fears that imprudent loans might be made which could imperil the entire structure of credit. The collapse of one or two major banks in Europe – especially the West German Herstatt bank – intensified these fears. Yet this market was almost entirely unsupervised, either by national or by international monetary authorities. Without some such supervision there was a danger of defaulting by one or more borrowing countries, leading to a financial crash of disastrous proportions.

A more general problem concerned the operations of *the IMF* itself. It was widely felt that it had not adjusted sufficiently to the type of problem now existing. There was increasing resentment at the type of de-flationary policies it demanded in return for credit. Developed countries, originally expected to be the main users, had for long resisted turning to the Fund for that reason. Only very occasionally did a rich country, if in serious enough trouble, seek substantial assistance from the Fund and in consequence have to accept the terms it imposed: as Britain did in 1967 and 1976, and Italy did on a number of occasions.[7] The United States, though in frequent deficit (and though its policies had greater impact on the international monetary system than those of any other country) never had to subject itself to IMF disciplines. Most other rich countries sought by all possible means to avoid recourse to the Fund. Sometimes they were able to secure bilateral assistance from a friendly country on less favourable terms: as Italy did from West Germany on more than one occasion, and as West Germany herself did from Saudi Arabia. Or they were able to make arrangements for mutual central-bank support which enabled them to avoid recourse to the Fund.

It is not surprising, therefore, that poor countries were also increasingly averse to undergoing the severe discipline to which they were subjected in return for credits. During the seventies such countries preferred to turn to the loans offered by the commercial banks, loans which, whatever their financial provisions, did not involve the onerous undertakings concerning economic policy which the IMF required. For that reason, in the last years of the seventies, despite all the acute monetary problems of the day, the Fund was little used, repayments actually exceeding new drawings. By 1980, however, the private banks began to feel that the credit-worthiness of most poor countries was exhausted. Many hesitated to lend further. From that point it became apparent that, if such countries were to avoid bankruptcy with serious repercussions for the world's financial system, the IMF would need to play a far more significant role. In 1979–80 drawings were somewhat liberalised: in the periods of loans, in the amounts lent, and above all in the conditions imposed. The maximum that can be drawn was then raised to 600 per cent of the recipient's quota over three years.[8] Credit was made available for at least three years; and, under the extended Fund facility, for 10. Some wanted these limits raised still further; or even abolished altogether. But others, especially in the richest countries, were demanding a further tightening of the conditions of credit.

So some changes were taking place in the way the IMF operated. But given the nature of the strains being experienced by the world's financial system it was likely that its central institution would require more radical reform if it were to be in a position to meet these problems adequately.

4.4 THE FUTURE OF THE INTERNATIONAL MONETARY SYSTEM

Perhaps the most basic problem is that at present liquidity (like income, investment and trade) is maldistributed. And here too a deliberate strategy would be needed to redistribute it to correspond more closely with needs. What kind of changes would be needed to establish a more satisfactory system?

Let us look in turn at each of the difficulties we have noted and consider what type of adjustments would be necessary to overcome them.

The first problem we looked at concerned the exchange-rate system. There are many who believe that a more stable system will never be established without a return to fixed parities, even if provision has to be made for more flexibility in rates than existed before 1973. Others hold equally firmly that, because of the character of modern monetary relations, especially the volume of internationally mobile capital that now exists, such a system could never again be made to work effectively. But both parties might accept that the system requires exchange rates that are *more flexible* than before 1973 but *less unstable* than have existed since that time. This middle course could include either rates that are fixed but can be rapidly changed, as under the so-called 'crawling peg' system (where the rates are changed at regular and frequent intervals); or a more stable form of floating. The higher rates of inflation which prevail today, and the greater variations between those rates, as well as the vulnerability of all currencies to sudden movements of confidence, make necessary a system that is highly responsive to rapid market changes; and any system that is sufficiently responsive will be close to a floating regime. It therefore seems likely that the solution will be closer to a more stable kind of floating than to a more flexible type of fixed rate.

More stable floating will require a greater degree of international influence on the intervention policies of central banks than exists today. A degree of international influence over exchange rates was supposed to have been achieved under the Bretton Woods system, through the arrangements for 'consultation' on changes. Even before 1973 this never operated effectively. There was no real consultation with the IMF about exchange-rate changes: governments in practice undertook these changes as and when they chose, merely notifying the IMF a few hours in advance. Since 1973 that influence has been even less. Governments now determine their own rates through 'dirty floating' and interest-rate decisions. Exchange-rate policy is thus returned to national hands once more, and is influenced almost entirely by national considerations. It was for this reason that the attempt was made by the IMF to lay down rules for floating. Those rules were contained in guidelines issued by the Fund in 1974, as well as in the second amendment to the Articles of Association of 1976 (implementing decisions reached in Jamaica that year). The latter provided that central banks were to 'avoid manipulating exchange rates or the international monetary system in order to prevent effective balance of payment adjustment or to gain an unfair competitive advantage'. But rules in such general terms are unlikely to have much effect. When they buy and sell currency, governments persuade themselves that they are merely attempting to stabilise their own parity around the proper level and will never accept that they are seeking an 'unfair competitive advantage'. It is almost impossible to distinguish clearly between fluctuations in rates that are 'erratic' (which the rules allow to be corrected) and those that reflect 'underlying economic and financial conditions' (which they do not).

The need therefore is to establish objective criteria to govern such open market policies. The ideal ultimate solution would be for the task of intervention to be transferred from central banks to some international authority or at least to be shared with it. Rates would then be established in accordance with a less subjective assessment of economic needs. But it is unlikely that at the present time governments would accept such a radical sharing of sovereignty. This leaves two alternatives. Either clear indicators should be established – perhaps based on trade flows or movements of reserves – which central banks would be supposed to follow in undertaking their own intervention policies. [9] The other, and perhaps more probable, solution is that national authorities should be subjected to far closer and more continuous influence, both from the IMF and from other governments, concerning the rates they seek to maintain at any moment. In either of these ways the multilateralisation of exchange-rate policy, which was supposed to have been introduced in 1944, would be restored.

This leads to our second problem: what kind of reserve assets should mainly be used and how should new liquidity be created? One of the main tasks of an international monetary authority, as has often been pointed out, is to ensure, as do monetary authorities within states, that the supply of money within the system (in this case reserve assets) is sufficient to sustain international transactions without fuelling inflation. It is thus illogical that the total volume of reserve assets should, as at present, remain so dependent on chance factors: the size of US deficits, the decisions of governments concerning gold production and sales, and the eccentricities of the gold market. The creation of SDRs gave the IMF an instrument through which in theory it could control the total size of reserves; and the decisions over the last decade to enhance the role of SDRs appeared to be designed to increase that power. But in practice that power has not been used: the proportion of SDRs in reserves is so small that a new issue scarcely affects the total. They have not been increased to offset the effect of falling gold prices. Nor are SDRs as yet, despite technical changes to make them more acceptable, as freely usable as gold or dollars. Recent decisions to raise the interest rate to market levels and to base the SDR on five major currencies, rather than on 16 as before, may increase its attractiveness. But it should be made possible for SDRs to be acquired by a wider range of financial institutions:[10] this would lessen the need for currency hedging and reduce instability. They should increasingly be used as the intervention currency in maintaining exchange rates, so eliminating the problems which the use of the dollar for this purpose causes at present.[11] Most important of all, new SDRs need to be created on a regular annual basis, so that they genuinely become the 'principal reserve asset', and the main source of new liquidity.

Such changes would make possible a corresponding reduction in the role of the dollar. The most feasible way of achieving this is by the proposal to create a 'substitution account' through which dollars could be exchanged for SDRs. The difficulties which remain over this proposal are political rather than technical. The technical difficulties could easily be solved. It should, for example, be possible to safeguard governments converting dollars (which would be invested in US treasury bills) to SDRs against exchange loss: the element of subsidy required for this purpose could be found either through gold sales or from subscriptions from governments (the United States would no doubt be the main contributor). Poor countries could be given assurances that normal allocations of SDRs would continue. More difficult are the political problems: especially the hostility of the West German and to some extent the US governments (still ambivalent about the resulting loss of its 'exorbitant privilege'). SDRs are still distrusted by some as 'funny money', which they fear might, if a change of control in the Fund were to take place, be used in an irresponsible and inflationary manner. These difficulties are not insuperable and there is no reason why serious negotiations, to establish more precisely the principles that would govern the creation and distribution of the units, should not overcome them.

However, it is not only the role of dollars but also that of gold which must, if a more rational and deliberate process of liquidity creation is to be established, be progressively reduced. Some recent steps have been taken in that direction.[12] But the efforts to reduce gold's role have not been wholly successful. Some are only cosmetic. Gold still represents over half the world's reserves.[13] It is thus important that the IMF should continue the progressive demonetisation of gold on which it has already embarked. It could, for example, dispose of its remaining gold by sales for the benefit of developing countries (perhaps using the proceeds, as the Brandt Report proposed, to create an interest subsidy for loans to poor countries). And ultimately it could refuse altogether to deal in gold or to accept gold as part of IMF subscriptions.

If the SDR were to become in this way the main, instead of only a minor, reserve asset, both the supply and the distribution of international liquidity could be adjusted to the needs of the international economy. At the same time, there is no reason why SDRs should, as at present, always be distributed to all members in proportion to quotas. Distribution could and should be varied according to economic criteria and needs. Less, for example, could be allocated to countries that remain in persistent surplus, which clearly both need and deserve them less. On the other hand, more could be allocated to the very poor countries whose need is greatest (and which contribute little to world inflation), or to other poor countries in difficulties which could be shown to be exercising a responsible monetary policy. In this way countries suffering from balance of payments problems through no fault of their own – for example, because of big increases in the price of oil or capital goods, because of recession in the developed world, or because of declines in the prices of their own exports – would be enabled to maintain their total volume of purchasing. At the same time the *total* volume of liquidity created would not necessarily be increased. It could be adjusted in line with increases in the total volume of trade (or, more accurately, average imbalances of trade). It could be expanded most when the world economy was most in need of revival, and least when inflationary pressures were greatest.

An equally important need is for more effective international control over the operations of the international banking system (which creates far more credit than the IMF). As we have seen, there has been a fear in recent times that the private banks may become overcommitted in their lending policies, and may experience defaults leading to major crises in the system. At present most of their operations abroad are beyond even national control.[14] On these grounds a better system of control has been demanded. National bank regulations are being introduced in some countries, requiring greater disclosure of international banking operations. But it is better *international* supervision that is mainly required. The BIS has a standing committee on the Euro-markets which has examined the problems. In 1980 the central bankers of the Group of 10 proposed that this should report twice a year on the situation on these markets; and that banks should produce consolidated accounts to include the dealings of their overseas banks. What may be finally required are internationally established reserve requirements placing a limit on the amount of foreign lending a bank may undertake in relation to its deposits.

The next problem we considered was the difficulty which the IMF has at present in bringing about the necessary adjustment policies, whether by countries in deficit or in surplus. At present it is only when countries need to make substantial drawings (at least to the second credit tranche) that the Fund is in a position to influence economic policies. The problem is not so acute in the case of deficit countries, since pressures on reserves, or on exchange rates, or both, are usually sufficient eventually (with or without Fund pressure) to bring about adjustment. Indeed, the Fund may need to be more liberal, rather than more restrictive, in dealing with such countries: in a world in which unemployment has steadily increased over recent years, it is more than ever necessary that the Fund should return to its original philosophy of helping countries to overcome balance of payments problems *without* adopting the severely deflationary policies that contract world trade. But the need for adjustment is at least as great among surplus countries; and it is here that the Fund is most powerless. One possibility would be to revive the 'scarce currency' clause in some form, so as to legalise discriminatory trade measures against countries in persistent surplus which are making no efforts to reduce the surplus. Another would be (as the Committee of 20 suggested) to raise interest charges on excessive reserve holdings amongst such countries. But perhaps most needed is the use of sustained pressures by the organs of the IMF, especially the Executive Board, on countries in chronic surplus: perhaps through the procedure which proved so effective in the early fifties in pressuring governments towards trade liberalisation – persistent and organised confrontation to produce a change in policy.

The next problem we noted is that of recycling: transferring the surpluses still acquired by some oil-producing countries to the deficit countries that need them. Because of the increasing debts of poor countries, leading to loss of credit-worthiness, it is doubtful if the private banking system will undertake this as effectively in the next decade as it did during the seventies. The Fund itself may therefore need to play a larger role in the recycling process. The Fund has, partly for this reason, sought additional funds to lend to countries in need. It has raised quotas. It has secured a large loan from Saudi Arabia. It has discussed raising funds from the world's capital markets. Already its rate of lending has increased dramatically: it multiplied by six between 1979 and 1981. It has acquired a still larger indirect role. The Fund today often provides, even if its own loan is small, a 'good housekeeping' seal (a reassurance on the policy likely to be pursued in the receiving country) which alone encourages private banks to lend.

That role for the Fund is likely to increase. For the most serious problem of the international monetary system in the coming years will continue to be the growing deficits of poor countries. Even in good times non-oil developing countries can rarely escape balance of payments deficits. They must import almost all capital goods; some consumer goods; some raw materials; energy; and also, increasingly, food. Their export capacity is usually limited. Today these problems are exacerbated by external factors outside their control: higher oil prices, high interest rates, world recession, protectionism, low prices for their own exports, high prices for their imports. Poor countries, therefore, have much greater need than rich to call on the assistance of the IMF.

For this reason many have demanded more liberal lending policies by the Fund. Fund credit will of course never be 'automatic'. The Fund will continue, like other lenders, to demand conditions for its loans. The real question is not whether it demands conditions: it is what *type* of conditions it is sensible and relevant for it to demand. This will depend on the causes of the deficit. There may still be cases where deficits can clearly be shown to result mainly from irresponsible domestic policies. In such cases reductions in public spending and tighter monetary policy may still be appropriate remedies to demand. But, where the deficit results from external causes outside the control of the country in deficit – higher oil prices, inflation in the West (raising the price of imports), world recession (reducing exports and export prices) and very high interest rates (increasing the debt burden) – those remedies may be irrelevant to the real problem.[15] Even if credit and demand are squeezed, deficits may remain. Incomes policies and improvements on the supply side – the development of new exports – are then the main need. Liberalisation of trade may be a particularly inappropriate condition for the IMF to impose in such conditions. Far from bringing about the adjustment required, the freeing of trade may lead (as it has in some South American countries) to huge increases in imports of expensive consumer goods for the wealthy classes and the destruction of local industry. It may therefore intensify rather than reduce balance of payments problems. On these grounds a more appropriate condition for the IMF to demand would arguably be policies to redistribute income: for the effect of these is to *reduce* imports of expensive consumer goods and to *promote* local production by increasing demand for food and simple consumer goods. The distributionist strategy in this case could help to promote the IMF's traditional objectives.

Whatever the conditions, the IMF will need to lend more. There are a number of steps the Fund could take to increase the volume of credit it can provide. The size of quotas should be increased. In 1945 they equalled about 16 per cent of world trade; in 1965, 12 per cent; now they amount to only 4 per cent. They should be increased once again; and this time proportions adjusted so that poor countries get a better share.[16] Secondly, whether or not quotas are raised, the allocation of SDRs could be increased; and a larger allocation given to those countries who need them most (again often the poorest). Finally, there could be a move towards the 'link': the distribution of SDRs to poor countries alone to help them meet their development needs. All three of these proposals have been opposed by some rich countries on the grounds that they could be inflationary in effect. But, as has been pointed out, the allocation of SDRs in accordance with need does not have to involve creating any *more* SDRs than would anyway be necessary; it is the distribution and not the total that would be altered by proposals of this kind. By increasing the capacity to import where it is at present most constrained, such moves would not only reduce the maldistribution of purchasing power: they could help revive the world economy and restore the rates of growth achieved before the oil-price rise.

If these ends are to be secured, the most fundmental need is for changes in the structure and operation of the IMF. It was intended, as we have seen, to be an instrument for multilateral surveillance. But if multilateral surveillance is to be effective it must be genuinely multilateral: that is, the body that undertakes it should be seen as genuinely representative of the international community. This would require some change in the current voting system. This need not be dramatic (indeed there is danger that, if the change were too radical, the rich countries would listen less than ever to what the Fund has to say and concentrate their attention still more on such bodies as the BIS, the Group of 10 and the economic summits). It would be sufficient to make the Fund appear more representative if something like equality between the rich countries and poor were secured: so that every decision depended on consensus. This could be achieved most simply by increasing the quotas, and so the votes, of poor countries:[17] a relatively simple reform. At the same time the 85 per cent vote required for certain decisions – including changes in quotas and new allocations of SDRs – should be reduced so that the United States alone can no longer veto such decisions.

But a change in the IMF's structure is less important than an increase in its effective influence. At present the surveillance which the Fund undertakes is sporadic and ineffectual. Over countries which have made substantial drawings the Fund has considerable, perhaps excessive, influence; over most other countries, including the surplus countries, its influence is negligible. It has never been able to influence US policy, for example, though this has a greater influence over the international monetary system than has that of any other country. It is equally unable to influence a member state determined not to reflate, or refusing to allow its currency to depreciate.[18] If effective influence is to be exerted on the policy of governments, a new way may be needed to mobilise international pressures.

The Interim Committee, which meets only twice a year, issues only general statements about the monetary system and makes little attempt to influence individual countries. The Committee of 20 in 1974, therefore, proposed the creation of a Council of Governors which was to be given 'the necessary decision-making powers to supervise the management and adaptation of the monetary system'. Provision was made for this in the second amendment to the Articles of Association. Yet this has not so far been implemented. There is a strong case for arguing that this proposal should be revived; or that the Interim Committee itself should be transformed into such a body. This could then become the forum for high-level negotiations and decision-making about the system: especially on the long-term problems the Executive Board has little time to confront. And it could be above all the instrument for the organised confrontation with and pressure on individual states – surplus as well as deficit countries, rich countries as well as poor – that is most required if the world's monetary system is to be made to work better than it does today.

Better regulation of the world's disorganised monetary system is an essential condition of bringing about a better management of the world economy generally. Just as the management of the monetary system within a state is a central task of economic management generally, so the running of the world's monetary system is likely to be central to world economic management. But that task has to be seen in the context of the long-term needs of the world economy, not the immediate crises of particular states. There needs to be thus a much closer relationship between the IMF and other economic bodies: especially with any new international body set up to look after the world economy more generally – such as the council of economic management proposed above (p. 27). By its control of the issue of SDRs and its credit policy generally, it might then become responsible for influencing the level of economic activity in the world economy generally. The multilateral surveillance which is supposed to be its role could then become a reality.

5 Resources

5.1 THE AVAILABILITY OF WORLD RESOURCES

Any system for managing the world's economy would need to be concerned with the husbanding of the earth's remaining natural resources.

Until recently few people thought in terms of a *world* problem concerning resources. There was concern about the problems facing individual *nations* in that respect: deficiencies in the availability of important materials – tin or timber, coal or iron ore – on which a country's security or prosperity might depend. But it was accepted that no country could be fully self-sufficient; and that (in peace-time at least) it could make good any shortage that existed through imports from another. Some countries might, to safeguard supplies, promote investment in the development of resources elsewhere: as Britain did in the last century and the United States has done in this. Occasionally they might even be tempted to make war to procure resources: as Japan made war, at least in part for the sake of coal and iron in China and oil in South-East Asia, in 1931–45, and as colonial powers are said to have done, partly for similar reasons, at an earlier period. In other words, attention was focused on the resource needs of individual nations; not on those of the world as a whole.

That concern was reflected in the development of the conservation movement in the United States in the early years of this century. Supporters of that movement – Theodore Roosevelt and Gifford Pinchot, for example – felt that there was a danger that the resources of the country, vast as they were, were in danger of being exhausted through the rapid pace of industrialisation. They believed that the wasteful use of resources was producing growing scarcities which would rapidly increase their real cost, so that output would decline and all would become poorer. They therefore stimulated efforts to measure, for the first time, the extent of the natural resources available within the United States and to promote policies to conserve them.

124

Governments everywhere became increasingly affected by such thinking. There was concern that, if resources were used too quickly, or if there was insufficient investment in exploring and developing new reserves, a nation's economic growth could be inhibited. After the Second World War these concerns were intensified. In the United States, the Korean War revealed shortages and pressure on prices. As a result the Paley Commission was appointed to examine the availability of resources in the United States, to consider the rate of depletion and the needs of replacement, and to recommend policy to the government. It estimated that demand for minerals in the United States would double in the next 25 years. Already, instead of producing 15 per cent more materials than it consumed, as at the beginning of the century, the United States was consuming 10 per cent more than it produced. For the moment the deficiencies could be made good from imports. But world demand was rising rapidly, and for some minerals – especially lead, zinc and tin – shortages would soon develop. In consequence the Department of the Interior and the Bureau of Mines were given greater responsibility for monitoring the situation, stimulating exploration and maintaining stockpiles where necessary. But concern over the issue persisted, especially after the oil shock of 1972–3. And in that decade two further US commissions were established, on materials policy (1973) and on supplies and shortages (1976), to look at the problems once again.

Other governments have manifested similar concerns. Today, however, it is increasingly felt that such difficulties are not national but world problems. Fears have been aroused that rapid industrialisation, in rich countries and poor alike, will bring the rapid depletion of the world's remaining stock of materials. Total demand for some of these has increased many times over the last 30 years. If demand were to grow at the same rate in the future, or even increase still faster as developing countries industrialised, there could be a real risk, some have held, that irreplaceable mineral supplies would be exhausted altogether.

Some of the forecasts of this kind that were made a decade or so ago are now generally felt to have been sensational and oversimplified.[1] Often, in assessing total available resources, they used figures of existing *proved* reserves, only a fraction of the reserves that are likely to be ultimately available; or they multiplied these by an arbitrary figure (say 5)[2] to indicate the maximum future figure that could reasonably be expected. They made little or no allowance for the effect of technical advance either in discovering new resources, devising new materials altogether, reducing the cost of exploitation or economising on the use of materials. They assumed not only that overall rates of economic growth would continue at the maximum rates achieved during the fifties and sixties, but also that demand for resources within industrialised countries would continue to grow at a similar rate, despite the continuing decline of manufacturing as a proportion of economic activity. They took little account of the possibility of substitution of one resource for another. Finally, they did not allow for the effect of rising prices, as availability declined, in promoting conservation, or substitution, or both.

Others have on these grounds tended to belittle the problem. They have taken it for granted that technical advances would be able to overcome any future shortages, or that any shortages which could develop would be automatically adjusted by the price mechanism so that, as some materials became more expensive, further exploration or substitution would be stimulated. Man's inventiveness, it has been assumed, could be relied on to conquer whatever difficulties might arise. Sometimes the problems have been minimised for other reasons. Developing countries were inclined to consider the problems those only of richer countries, where most materials were consumed. And they have been understandably suspicious of theories advocating policies of no growth, while they themselves remain in an extreme stage of under-development. Others again have preferred not to bother their heads about the matter at all.

Where does reality lie between these positions? The best estimates seem to indicate that (except possibly in the case of oil) there is no reason for concern about *overall* availability of any of the materials at present in most common use. These are present in the earth's crust in abundance, sometimes up to depths of several thousand metres. According to one estimate,

> There can be no reasonable doubt that the earth's crust contains more of the chief elements used in the production of materials than could be used for millennia to come. At present consumption rates the top kilometre of the land surface contains over 10,000 million years' worth of aluminium, a hundred million years' worth of iron and over ten million years of – amongst other things – lead, zinc, chromium and mercury. Sea water and the ocean floors, especially manganese nodules, also contain equally gigantic quantities of various elements . . . .[3]

Much of this, however, is not likely to be available for human use at any time in the foreseeable future, either because of inaccessibility (for example, depth beneath the earth's surface), or because the minerals do not exist in concentrations that would make exploitation economic. The relevant question is not whether particular materials exist at all, but whether (taking account of advancing technology) they can be exploited at a cost that is economic in relation to the proposed uses.[4]

That question cannot be answered categorically without making certain assumptions: about the rate of discovery of new deposits, about the development of new technology affecting exploration, exploitation and use; future patterns of consumption; changes in life-style; and so on. Most observers, however, taking account of such factors, have concluded that there is no reason for undue alarm about the rate at which most materials are being used and are likely to be used in the future. A UN study published in 1977, taking what it called a very 'cautious and conservative' view of existing reserves, concluded that 'mineral resource endowment is generally adequate to support world economic development at relatively high rates but that these resources will most probably become more expensive to extract as the century moves towards its conclusion'.[5] The authors of another UN study stated that they could 'in no way concur with the views of the pessimists' (preoccupied with future limits to growth) – save in respect of fresh-water resources. The UN experts were 'inclined to be optimistic in view of recent surveys, progress in exploration, development and processing, the use of low-grade ores and above all the almost daily discovery of new deposits'.[6]

No estimates of this kind can be conclusive, but there are a number of reasons for thinking that the most alarmist views may prove unfounded.

First, in the case of most minerals new reserves are continually being discovered. There are still large areas of the world that have been comparatively little explored (though by now most of the more favourable areas probably have been surveyed). Over recent years new proved reserves have constantly increased faster than consumption. Between 1950 and 1970, for example, known reserves of tin increased by 10 times, of chromite by 675 times, of iron by 1221 times, of potash by 2360 times and of phosphate by 4430 times.[7] In addition, in the case of some important minerals, there are vast resources available beneath the seas which have not yet been explored, let alone exploited.

Secondly, though newly discovered reserves are often less favourable, and therefore more costly to exploit than those discovered in the past, this is more than offset by improvements in the technology of extraction. Thus in the case of copper, for example, while in the 1880s the average ore grades being exploited were of 3 per cent, today the average percentage is about 0.5. Yet the real cost of copper today is no higher than then; while the total volume of known copper reserves has been increasing (partly *because* lower ore grades are now exploitable) by 7 per cent or so a year. It is because of continual technical improvements of this kind that over the last 30 years the real cost of most minerals has not increased, despite rapidly rising demand, and in some cases has declined.

Thirdly, there is a continuing process of substitution. As one material becomes scarce or more expensive, it is replaced by others that are more abundant. So, for example, over 80 years the use of aluminium, of which the raw material (bauxite) is widely available, has increasingly replaced that of copper and steel for a number of purposes. So plastics and other synthetics, widely available today, have replaced minerals for many purposes. New processes (such as the production of oil from coal and petrol substitutes from sugar) allow existing minerals to go further or replace them altogether. Even if, therefore, a mineral now in use were finally to become scarce, it is likely that the rising price would stimulate the development of alternatives which can be produced more cheaply.

Fourthly, increasing scarcity, if it were to occur, would give rise to far more intensive efforts at conservation in the use of existing materials. The striking reduction in the use of energy in general and of oil in particular over the last decade is an indication of the process that would take place. The greater the scarcity that develops for any one material, and the higher its price, the greater is the incentive for technological advances which will reduce its use.[8]

Finally, as pressure on existing resources increases, so the incentive for recycling of used materials is increased. Already today, where the price of the mineral is sufficient (as in the case of lead and copper), substantial proportions of used minerals (50 per cent and 40 per cent respectively in those two cases) are collected and recycled. If the price of other minerals justified it, increased quantities could be obtained through a similar process. Moreover, as prices increased there would be greater incentive for technological advances which might increase the amount of recycling that was undertaken (reducing energy consumption at the same time, since less energy is used for recycling than for primary extraction).

All this does not mean that there is no reason for concern about the availability of resources. It remains the case that mineral resources are finite. These facts mean that the date of their ultimate exhaustion may be further in the future than is sometimes suggested: not that it will never occur. The very fact that there appears to be no great cause for alarm today may, as was the case for oil before 1973, allow prices to be established at levels which take little account of long-term scarcity and encourage rapid depletion. Poor countries may find their own development eventually inhibited because, by the time they are in a position to require resources on a substantial scale, they will already have become scarcer and more expensive.

Thus, if the long-term interests of the world economy are to be safeguarded, decisions at the international level as well as the national may be required. And such decisions will need to be concerned not only with the overall volume of resources which are available but with the factors affecting their supply as well.

5.2 THE SUPPLY OF WORLD RESOURCES

For the fact that resources exist at all is no indication that they will be available on world markets. There are other constraints on availability deriving from different causes.

First, supply may be deliberately restricted by those who control it. This may result, for example, from action among producer governments seeking to enhance the price of the material concerned, or to restrict its supply for political or other reasons. The success of OPEC in increasing the price of oil, and so the revenues obtained for it, created among some the belief that producers of other minerals might achieve a comparable success by similar methods. The governments of those countries producing bauxite, for example, joined in a co-operative effort to demand higher revenues from the operating companies. They were, however, far less able than the oil-producers to secure their ends. Because bauxite is more widely available than oil, the effect was to drive companies to seek deposits in countries making less exorbitant demands, including developed countries such as Australia. The copper-producing countries established a similar organisation. But they too were unable to secure any firm control over the production and export of copper, and this remained in practice subject to the normal fluctuations of the market. But there remains the possibility, especially in the case of rare minerals found only in a few countries,[9] that producer governments might successfully, by export restrictions, win control of the market and raise the selling price. Effective management of the world's economy therefore requires means of dealing successfully with supply problems of that kind.

But similar restrictions may, secondly, be imposed by private companies engaged in the production of particular minerals. A substantial proportion of the companies involved in the production of uranium succeeded for a number of years, by agreement among themselves, in maintaining the price at a level far above what would otherwise have been obtained in world markets. Much of the world production of tin, copper, bauxite and lead–zinc is in the hands of a relatively small number of major international companies, which have a strong incentive to use their market power to raise prices. International shipping companies, including those responsible for the transport of many minerals which are traded internationally, have for years engaged in monopolistic agreements to restrict competition in freight charges and maintain the price of their services. Any restrictive arrangements of this kind make necessary international action to establish fair trading conditions. Just as national governments have for many years sought to regulate restrictive arrangements and monopoly practices among producers within their own territory to protect consumers, so international authorities may increasingly need to control their operations at the international level for the same purpose.

Thirdly, the availability of materials may be restricted by political factors. Investment in the development of new resources may be deterred by the attitudes, believed or real, of the governments in the producing states. Political instability in such countries, concern about the possibility of nationalisation or heavy tax burdens (in addition to doubts about future growth rates in the world economy) may discourage the expenditure of large sums in identifying new resources, sinking mines, and developing the necessary transport and other facilities which successful exploitation requires. The producing countries themselves may find difficulty in raising, whether from private or public resources, the huge sums required – sometimes $2 – 3 billion today – for a major mining venture. Nor, even if they had the funds, would they necessarily be able to procure the necessary mining technology. Conversely, governments of importing countries may on security grounds deter investment in overseas territories where the resources mainly exist. Whatever the reasons for the lack of investment, the effects may be that the availability of minerals in the world economy as a whole is reduced. This is another threat to supplies that must be of concern to those responsible for the welfare of the world economy.

Fourthly, even if investment funds were available, the development of mineral supplies may be discouraged by the instability of commodity prices. Since a long period is required for developing new resources – 10–15 years in some cases – and since the level of prices at the end of such a period is difficult to predict, large commercial organisations may be reluctant to commit substantial resources to an enterprise whose profitability may be threatened by uncertain or unstable prices. Even if there is no long-term deterioration in real prices, there can be considerable variability in prices over a period, and on these grounds alone companies can doubt whether the investment is justifiable. There have been many attempts over the last 50 years, as we saw earlier (p. 80 above), to overcome variations of this sort through commodity agreements, designed to stabilise prices and therefore earnings. There are, however, as we saw in our earlier discussion, huge difficulties in reaching agreement on such arrangements – differences of interest both between producers and consumers and between different producers – and no such arrangements have operated for long successfully. In a few cases (for example, that of copper) producer companies themselves have for a time unilaterally operated schemes designed to adjust prices in such a way as to reduce instability. But these too have not operated successfully for long. Here is yet another factor affecting the market in minerals, and so their availability, which could adversely affect the successful operation of the world economy.

Finally, there may be technical constraints on the development of mineral supplies for the future. In many cases the production of minerals is highly energy-intensive, so that large increases in the price of energy (such as have occurred over the last few years), or overall energy shortages, can affect its feasibility. Similarly, an essential precondition for the development of some minerals is the availability of ample water supplies; and here too threats to these, because of increasing demands for water for many other uses, can affect the practicability of a particular mining investment. Or the appropriate technology may be the monopoly of particular mining companies which are not regarded as acceptable partners by the government which controls the resources. For all these reasons, resources that are known to be available may none the less fail to be developed.

There are therefore a number of factors, over and above the overall availability of resources, which can inhibit their supply to the world economy. All are problems, it may increasingly be felt, which require the consideration, and if necessary the intervention, of public authorities to promote the public interest of the world community as a whole.

5.3 THE DEVELOPMENT OF INTERNATIONAL ACTION CONCERNING WORLD RESOURCES

International action to conserve world resources is a relatively recent development.

The economic bodies of the League of Nations never showed any significant interest in this topic. But soon after the UN was founded, there was a demand for joint action in this field. In 1947 Ecosoc decided to call a conference on the conservation and utilisation of resources. When this took place in 1949 it produced a call for more comprehensive surveys of the world's resources and for greater help for developing countries in undertaking these. As a result, in 1951 the Secretary-General was asked by Ecosoc to produce plans for a systematic survey and inventory of resources to help reach decisions on what might need to be done to assist poor countries in carrying out the survey within their own territories. From this time technical assistance began to be provided, through the United Nations' Technical Assistance Programme and Special Fund, for resource surveys in individual countries. In the following years this programme was progressively expanded. And from 1962 the Secretary-General reported regularly every two years on the way it was progressing.

During the 1960s international efforts to assist in the exploration of resources were intensified. The UN Development Programme, after it was founded in 1965, gave a substantial proportion of its assistance for work of this kind: altogether it spent about $100 million for that purpose during the sixties. In 1966 Ecosoc agreed on a five-year plan for the development of the resources of developing countries, intended as an element in the UN Development Decade. Groups of experts were established to advise on the organisation of surveys of minerals, water resources, and energy. An Ad Hoc Committee was set up to supervise the execution of these plans; and in 1967, on the basis of this advice, a programme of exploration was drawn up, to be financed by the UNDP and other funds.

In 1972 the United Nations agreed to the establishment of a Revolving Fund for Natural Resources Exploration. This was formally established by the Assembly in December 1973 and its administration placed in the hands of the UNDP (as have many of the small trust funds which provide contributions earmarked for particular purposes). The Fund was to be financed by voluntary contributions from governments. But, as in the case of a number of similar funds, the amounts contributed proved to be very small (only $5 million was contributed in the first four years). The Fund therefore cannot be said to have made any significant contribution to the development of mineral resources in poor countries.

Much of the emphasis at this time, therefore, was on the need of *individual* countries for better knowledge of their own resources: the role of international bodies was mainly in providing assistance in helping them to do so. But developing countries sought UN help in another way. Many, on reaching independence, found that a substantial part of their mineral resources were effectively controlled by foreign companies, often operating on the basis of concessions granted them many years before their independence. While nationalisation was possible, the payment of the necessary compensation (essential if they were ever to hope for further investment in the future) was extremely costly; and in any case they did not possess the technical capacity to exploit the resources themselves. While they might therefore refrain from nationalisation, they wanted at least an unequivocal reassertion by an international authority of their ultimate ownership of the resources within their territories and their right to reasonable royalties or other payments from those who exploited them. This demand for 'permanent sovereignty over natural resources' was first raised at the United Nations in 1952. In 1958 the United Nations established a Commission on Permanent Sovereignty over National Resources to press the issue. In 1962 the Assembly adopted a declaration affirming the right of nations and people to 'permanent sovereignty' over the natural wealth and resources within their territory and their ability to dispose of these as they felt necessary and desirable. Foreign investment agreements should be observed in good faith; but nationalisation, expropriation or requisitioning were none the less legitimate steps if taken on grounds of public utility, security or the national interest. If there were disputes on such questions they would be settled in national courts in the first place, or through arbitration and international adjudication if both parties agreed. This implied that, if the nationalising government did not agree, the question would be settled on the basis of its own legislation, a conclusion strongly contested by many rich countries.

There was also considerable activity on resources questions at the regional level. Each of the United Nations' regional economic commissions were concerned about the problem. The Economic and Social Commission for Asia and the Pacific (formerly the Economic Commission for Asia and the Far East), has been particularly concerned with the resources problem in that area. It has undertaken a systematic inventory of the mineral deposits of the region, published a map of mineral distribution, promoted regional and sub-regional projects for mineral exploration, established a tin research and development centre for South-East Asia, and organised technical assistance for discovering and developing mineral resources in the whole region. The Economic Commission for Europe (which brings together representatives of both Western and Eastern Europe) has had a number of committees concerned with particular resources or materials – for example, steel, coal, gas, electric power, and water. In 1969 it produced a study on the world market in iron ores, which examined reserves, production and trade in iron all over the world, but with special reference to the problems faced in Europe. The Economic Commission for Latin America has been particularly concerned with surveying water and energy resources in the region but has also given help in exploring and developing mineral reserves. The Economic Commission for Africa has tried to assemble basic information about the mineral resources of Africa, has published a coal map of Africa, advised governments on the organisation of their geological research, collected materials on mining legislation and agreements, set up centres for training in aerial surveying, and undertaken research and given advice on the management of natural resources.

A number of other UN bodies acquired responsibility for particular aspects of the problem. UNCTAD, for example, has been concerned with commodity prices, commodity trade and the effect of these on the earnings and therefore on the development prospects of poor countries. The International Atomic Energy Agency is concerned with the supply of uranium. The World Bank has provided substantial loans for mineral development in particular countries, though this has never represented a large proportion of World Bank loans, perhaps because the Bank has felt that, once deposits have been identified (through pre-investment work mainly financed by the UNDP), their development can normally be left to commercial arrangements through the major mining companies.[10] Above all, the United Nations itself, especially through its Centre for Natural Resources, Energy and Transport, a section of the Secretariat, has had a continuing responsibility in this area. The Centre normally acts as the executing agency for UNDP projects in the natural resources field. It provides technical assistance in exploring and developing resources, in strengthening local survey, laboratory and administrative services, in the training of local experts, in marketing methods and mining legislation. Its activities are said to have resulted, for example, in the discovery of deposits of copper in Mexico, Ecuador, Peru, Malaysia and Iran, of uranium in Somalia, coal in Pakistan, bauxite in the Solomons, among others. It has helped to set up geological and mining institutes and provided assistance in cartography. It also maintains a general oversight of the world resources situation. It calls many meetings of experts on specialised subjects and it has tried to standardise terminology and conventions – for example, on the important question of the criteria used for defining 'proved reserves'.

Apart from these wider international bodies, there are a number of more limited organisations concerned with particular minerals and other resources. There have been a small number of commodity organisations, operating full-scale commodity agreements designed to stabilise prices or trade: for example, for tin and rubber. There are also less formal 'study groups' and committees, usually representing both producers and consumers, which meet to consider the problems affecting particular materials (for example, for lead–zinc and tungsten). Then there are producer associations, bringing together the governments of producer countries, which seek to promote common action to maintain or boost prices: such as those for bauxite and copper already mentioned. Finally, there are non-governmental organisations, bringing together private companies operating in a particular field (for example, the International Iron and Steel Institute).

Over the last decade or so there has been an increasing desire for international action concerned not with the needs of particular countries or areas, nor the problems of particular commodities, but with the resource needs of the world as a whole. On these grounds, in 1970 the United Nations decided to set up a permanent Committee on Natural Resources. This was established with a membership of 38 countries and meets every two years.

It started by considering the availability of world resources and the policies required for their development. The UN Secretariat undertook or commissioned studies providing the best state of knowledge about water resources, energy and minerals. These suggested that there was some reason for concern about the world's water resources, which could not be increased but which would have to meet the needs of a rapidly rising world population and growing demands for irrigation and other purposes. In the case of energy, the variety of possible energy sources and the development of new technologies would probably prevent the emergence of any acute shortages, but there would be need for adjustment to take account of the increasing depletion of natural gas and oil over the next two or three decades. The report on other minerals found that, contrary to the alarm being expressed at the period by some environmentalists (it appeared immediately after the publication of *The Limits to Growth*), there was little cause for immediate concern. New technical advances had made possible both the discovery of large new reserves and exploitation of lower-grade ores. The resources which were being consumed fastest – for example, iron ore, bauxite and copper – had proved to be considerably more extensive than had been believed. Large parts of the world still had not been properly explored, whilst seabed exploitation would make available another vast new store. But the report emphasised the need for better surveys than existed at present, especially in developing countries, to show the extent and accessibility of available resources, if possible using airborne methods and infra-red photography; and demanded a new programme for training in such work. It suggested that regular surveys of the supply and demand situation in the principal minerals were needed, together with more detailed studies of the situation affecting particular minerals when necessary.

Some of these recommendations were implemented. The Committee on Natural Resources decided to keep the supply and demand situation for the main resources permanently under review. The Secretariat now undertakes regular studies of the long-term position affecting all minerals every two years (that is, before each meeting of the Committee). It has undertaken detailed examinations of the problems of financing mineral development. It undertakes regular studies of the supply and demand situation affecting particular minerals. It publishes a quarterly journal, the *Natural Resources Forum*, as well as a natural resources and energy newsletter, concerned with questions of supply, demand and price. It has established a number of *ad hoc* groups of experts to consider particular technical subjects: for example, methods of exploiting low-grade ores, advanced mining technology, exploration in developing countries, and so on.

International bodies are therefore no longer exclusively concerned with ways of helping national governments. They are now more and more involved with general international purposes: the conservation and monitoring of the world's remaining natural resources. It cannot, however, be said that any broad international policy has yet been evolved for that purpose; and we must now consider what such a policy might involve.

5.4   AN INTERNATIONAL POLICY FOR NATURAL RESOURCES

What would a more effective policy for managing the world's natural resources require?

The first need is for more adequate institutions to confront the problem. The existing UN Committee on Natural Resources is too low-grade in calibre and amateurish in composition (it consists mainly of relatively junior diplomats) to undertake the task effectively, or to command respect. What is needed is a body of high-level *experts*, acknowledged specialists in this field, appointed by governments but not directly employed by them, balanced by nationality and regions like all international bodies, but essentially unpolitical in its approach, to keep a permanent watch over the world's natural resources. It would thus become a new international Commission on Natural Resources. It would need to be served by an expert staff, including economists as well as geologists. It would undertake a series of studies about the likely future supply and demand situation for particular resources, over the short and the long term, as well as about more general problems relating to the discovery, production and marketing of minerals.

This expert body would report, in the first place, to a new inter-governmental Council on Natural Resources (comparable to the World Food Council). This council should be more high-grade than the existing Committee (consisting perhaps of the appropriate ministers of governments) and would meet every six months or so. It would report to Ecosoc in the first place, and ultimately to the General Assembly.

If an international policy in this field is to emerge, the first need is for full and accurate information to be available about the present situation concerning the world's resources (the somewhat discursive biannual surveys undertaken at present by the UN Secretariat are not adequate for this purpose). A major task of the new expert Commission would therefore be to ensure that an adequate basis of authoritative inform-ation was available to the Council. One type of information required would be that concerning *existing* production and exploitation plans. This would be needed to prevent overinvestment in particular minerals, as well as to guard against short-term shortages. Estimates would have to be made of likely future availability and costs of replacement. Many optimistic analyses of the reserve situation have assumed that in the long run the price mechanism can be relied on to match supply and demand (as has ultimately occurred in the case of oil). But, as that example shows, that method of balancing supply and demand involves very heavy costs, over both the short and the long term, and it is costs of this kind that a more rational anticipation of future supply shortages may be able to avoid.

There are a number of reasons why reliance on market forces alone may fail to provide adequately against shortages and so against very high prices in the future. The first and most obvious is that the mining companies, to whom the task of achieving a balance at present falls, do not have any very clear interest in succeeding in that task. An acute shortage of, say, cobalt or molybdenum or uranium is no more likely to be disadvantageous to those companies than the sudden shortage of oil which occurred in 1970–1, 1973–4 and 1979–80 proved to be to the oil companies: on the contrary, it is those who control secure sources of supply who usually prove to be the main beneficiaries in that situation. Secondly, the decisions of mining companies concerning development are heavily influenced, inevitably, by political factors. Fear of nationalisation, or of demand for 'participation', or of political disorder in the producing countries, causes such companies to restrict their investment programmes, and so may reduce production in the future. Thirdly, such companies may in any case be overcautious in their assessment of the future growth of the world economy and so of the capacity that may be required at some time in the future (and, again, may gain substantially from such overcaution, while, with investment costs of $1–3 billion for a major project, they may suffer heavily from being overoptimistic). Fourthly, they may make assumptions about alternative sources of supply which in the event prove unjustified: at present, for example, the expectation of substantial mining production on the seabed may serve to deter investment in land resources of minerals, yet may ultimately prove unfounded; or companies may assume production within developing countries will increase faster than in fact proves to be the case. Finally, such companies may make their calculations on the assumption that normal conditions will prevail, and fail to allow for sudden interruptions in supply (such as the brief outbreaks of fighting in Zaire that have twice caused huge increases in the price of cobalt, or strikes among miners in Bolivia, Canada or Zambia affecting the price of tin, aluminium or copper), in just the same way that the oil companies failed to foresee the successive interruptions in oil supply which caused the price increases of 1970, 1973 and 1978–9 (pp. 151–6 below).

It is thus unreliable and dangerous in seeking to safeguard supplies for the future to depend on the judgement of self-interested private companies. It is on these grounds that national governments have, for many years, sought to make their own judgements of long-term national requirements. Internationally precisely the same need arises. Indeed, because most national governments cannot influence the supply situation which will affect them (because the resources are not produced on their territory), an international policy on such matters is far more relevant to national needs. Only international action is in the long run likely to be able to match future demand and supply effectively. When it seems likely that a deficiency may emerge in a decade or two, an international body can draw attention to the problem; it can urge national governments to encourage investment or reduce consumption;

it can encourage private companies to invest in the necessary capacity (in the knowledge that other companies will do so if they do not) and it can propose action by international bodies, such as the World Bank, to help develop the production capacity that will finally be required. International action might be particularly important in the case of the rarer minerals – such as cobalt, lithium, titanium, barium, vanadium and tungsten – which have an important place in modern industrial processes and for which at present the international community may be dependent on one or two countries only (not necessarily always reliable sources of supply), such as South Africa, the Soviet Union and China.

Such a body may also be able to help avoid *short-term* supply deficiencies. It may find a need, as in the case of oil and food grains, for ensuring that there are adequate stocks which could be used to meet immediate needs when crises occur, whether from rapidly expanding demand or deficient supply. The Commission would not necessarily itself be responsible for financing and managing such stocks (a very costly operation). It might, however, seek to ensure (as the World Food Council does in the case of grain) that national governments in different parts of the world maintain stocks at levels that could be used to overcome temporary shortages. Conversely, however, the Commission might need to control or at least influence the operation of *national* stockpiles, to avoid disruption of world markets. At present, when no such regulation exists, sudden releases of tin or other minerals from the US stockpile, for example, can have a dramatic effect on prices and serious consequences for the countries producing the minerals released.

Because it would be concerned with the development of future resources, the Commission would need close relations with other international organisations – such as the World Bank – engaged in financing mineral development in various parts of the world. One feature of the present situation is the *imbalance* in the amount of exploration, and therefore of exploitation, undertaken in different parts of the world: an imbalance that is not necessarily closely related to natural endowments. As many studies have pointed out, the territories of rich countries have been far more intensively explored than those of most developing countries. The former have better geological surveys, higher technological capacity, and above all far larger available capital resources for that purpose. The result is that today 85 per cent of all exploration work still takes place in rich countries; and about 60 per cent of all the world's mineral production is still concentrated in only five countries (the United States, the Soviet Union, Canada, Australia and

South Africa), which comprise only 37 per cent of the world's land area.[11]

The imbalance in the present distribution of capacity is thus another question which an international Council on Natural Resources might be expected to examine. It might wish to encourage new exploration in developing countries; and new development of resources already discovered. For that purpose new sources of financial support would be needed. According to a World Bank estimate, more than $100 billion will be needed in investment in mineral resources during 1981–5, at least half in developing countries. On these grounds the United States at one time proposed the creation of an international resources bank to facilitate the flow of private capital for the development of minerals in poor countries (partly by guaranteeing private investment against non-commercial risks). There is a strong case for establishing an affiliate of the World Bank specifically to help finance the development of minerals, on the lines of that proposed for energy.[12] The availability of the funds for this purpose, even for international institutions, might prove to depend on the conclusion of agreements for the guarantee of investments by the receiving countries: to provide safeguards for the repayment of the funds invested and, where private capital is involved, for compensation against appropriation, together with arbitration in disputes. Multilateral insurance schemes, it has been suggested, could also help to strengthen safeguards of this kind, though there have been considerable difficulties in negotiating such arrangements so far.

International bodies may have a role to play in encouraging arrangements of this kind and generally influencing relationships between producer governments and exploiting companies.[13] Over recent years a number of new types of relationship have been developed. Host governments have sought to win for themselves a greater share of the benefits from their own resources. In many cases they have passed legislation modifying the original concessions. Sometimes the new arrangements have provided the governments with an equity share – whether a minority or majority holding – in the mining undertaking; sometimes they have given the government or a national company the right to a share in the output; sometimes they provide the government with some element of control or veto over production decisions; sometimes they provide a share in operations and a proportion of management jobs for local nationals; sometimes they provide for a joint venture, with participation and control equally shared between the foreign company and the local undertaking; or they may provide for a management or service contract, under which the undertaking is fully nationalised but in practice the foreign company continues to operate it under an agreement for that purpose, sharing in the output and securing repayment of its operating costs. Other conditions are sometimes attached under such agreements: that the company will maintain a certain rate of exploration or exploitation, will fulfil certain import and export requirements, will employ a certain proportion of senior staff from the host country, will transmit information of particular kinds, will reinvest at a particular rate, and so on. Sometimes there is a 'fade-out' arrangement, by which the equity in the company is progressively transferred into local hands. Any of these agreements can give rise to disputes. While there is often legal machinery established for arbitrating over such questions (as well as the World Bank special arbitration service for those countries which have accepted it), some of the problems are political rather than legal. An international resources commission could play an important part in studying such problems and proposing solutions.

One of the problems which has arisen between companies and governments concerns processing operations. Developing countries often complain that foreign companies are very willing to exploit and to export their raw materials, but are much less willing to set up facilities for processing in the country of origin. Of the main minerals mined only tin and lead are at present largely processed in the producing country. Iron ore, nickel, copper and zinc are more often exported in raw form for fabricating in rich countries. Most rich countries maintain protection against refined products but allow the import of raw materials free, so creating a substantial deterrent to the building of processing facilities in the place of origin. This practice can have a huge effect on the value of exports from the producing country. Copper wire and cable, for example, has a value seven to nine times greater than that of a unit of copper at the mine; pig-iron is three times more valuable than iron ore; aluminium ingots are 10 times more valuable than the bauxite from which they are made; steel pipes and tube are 18 times, and steel-wire products 30 times, the value of the original iron ore. It is true that, with foreign processing, the final product is often much closer to the principal markets, while in the host country there will only be a very small market, often too small to justify large-scale production of refined products. Even so, there is undoubtedly room for a greater degree of processing in the country of origin. And an international commission might be in a position to help resolve disputes on this subject too.

Finally, in considering the long-term needs of the international community, the Commission would require to consider whether more needed to be done to encourage conservation and the recycling of materials. How far these take place at present depends largely on the level of *current* prices. But current prices, like oil prices in the fifties and sixties, do not always adequately reflect long-term scarcities. Here is another way in which the market does not necessarily provide the signals needed, from the point of view of long-term welfare, to promote the action required. Sometimes only action by a public authority, reflecting the long-term international interest, may be able to do this. For example, research on new methods of conservation, substitution and recycling may be needed because there is no private interest which, on the basis of current prices, has a sufficient interest in so doing: indeed, mining companies, the main bodies with the necessary technology and funds, may have a directly contrary interest. The international community as a whole, however, producers as much as consumers, has an interest in ensuring that resources which are by nature finite can be made to last as long as possible. Such steps also conserve scarce world energy resources (because less energy is needed to produce a given value of mineral by recycling than by primary production); and can also reduce pollution and environmental damage (because, again, less is caused through recycling techniques). Poor countries could be said to have a special interest in such processes, because they could be saved the expenditure of scarce capital resources and scarce foreign exchange; and because without them they might find that raw materials have become scarcer and more expensive at the time when they themselves become major consumers. They therefore have a special reason for promoting international action in this field.

These are only a few of the more obvious functions which a new international resources commission might need to perform. Certainly, if shortages are to be avoided, over the short and long term, if exploration and production are to be more widely distributed, if the necessary actions for conservation are to be undertaken, there is a need for a body which can inject into discussion of the use and development of the world's remaining resources a concern for the public as well as the private interest: the international as well as the national advantage.

6 Oil

6.1 THE DOMINANCE OF THE COMPANIES

Oil has probably played a more significant part than any other single resource in economic relations among states.

This importance is relatively new. Though bitumen was known in Mesopotamia in ancient times and oil of a kind was produced in Japan in the ninth century and in Burma in the fourteenth, it was only in the mid-nineteenth century, after the development of drilling techniques to bring it to the surface, that oil came to be widely used and traded. Even then, before the internal combustion engine, its importance was far less than today. The oil products mainly in demand were kerosene for heating, industrial fuel and lubricants.

The main centres of production at first were the eastern parts of the United States and the Caucasus in Russia. A number of companies emerged to engage in the production, refining and distribution of the oil. In the United States, the Standard Oil Trust, formed with the support of Rockefeller and other financial interests, quickly acquired a dominant control of pipelines and refineries; later of production; and finally of marketing facilities in other parts of the world, especially in Asia and Latin America. In Europe, companies backed by Rothschild's, Nobel and other interests emerged to undertake the refining and distribution of Russian oil.

By the end of the century, with the development of the motor-car, petrol had become by far the most important refined product. The total market for oil began to expand and the search for crude supplies became more intensive. New deposits were found: in the Dutch East Indies, Burma, Persia and Venezuela. Companies at that time were able to secure concessions which usually covered the entire territory of the producing country.

A few large companies increasingly dominated the industry. By far the largest was still the Standard Oil Company. But the dominance it acquired, both in the United States and abroad, led to charges of monopoly. In 1911 an anti-trust suit was brought against it. As a result it was broken up into its 30-odd component parts, each based in an individual US state. The largest of these were Jersey Standard (forerunner of Esso and Exxon), the original holding company, which, though it inherited few production facilities, acquired a widespread marketing network and soon again became and remained the largest company in the world; Standard Oil of California (Socal), which disposed of plentiful supplies of oil from that state, but had few marketing outlets; the Standard Oil Company of New York (Socony), which, conversely, had a good marketing infrastructure but at first small supplies of oil, Standard Oil of Indiana, which was originally smaller but eventually became larger than several of the majors; and Standard Oil of Ohio, a substantial company eventually acquired by British Petroleum (BP). Other large US companies included the Texas Oil Company (Texaco) and Gulf Oil, both originally selling oil produced in the south of the United States, though later acquiring substantial supplies elsewhere. The main non-US companies before 1914 were Burma Oil, producing mainly in Burma, and acquiring, with the help of the British government, a dominant marketing position in India; Royal Dutch, closely linked from 1907 with Shell, mainly dependent at first on supplies of oil from the Dutch East Indies; and the Anglo-Persian (subsequently the Anglo-Iranian) Oil Company, established early in the century to exploit the deposits discovered in Persia.

Governments of the major industrialised countries became increasingly conscious of the strategic and political importance of oil. They often gave diplomatic and other help to their own companies in the search for concessions. European governments particularly, having no supplies of crude at home, were especially concerned to help their companies win access to supplies abroad. The British government helped to bring the Anglo-Persian Oil Company into being; soon took a 51 per cent control of it; and gave it strong diplomatic backing in its dealings with the Persian and other governments. The French government established the Compagnie Française de Petroles, with a substantial government holding, in order to promote French interests in this field. Smaller European countries established similar companies. After the First World War, the US government too, concerned that the influence which European powers possessed as colonial powers might give them dominant access to supplies outside the United States, began to exert strong diplomatic pressure on behalf of US companies; and managed, in 1928, to bring about the admission of US companies to the Iraq Petroleum Company (IPC), the consortium of foreign companies which acquired exploiting rights in the mandated territory of Iraq (in succession to the pre-war Turkish Petroleum Company).

The governments of the producing countries, on the other hand, were at this time both politically and militarily weak and totally unsophisticated in their knowledge of the oil industry. They were therefore often willing to make agreements for the exploitation of their oil resources, which they were quite unable to develop themselves, on terms that were relatively favourable to the companies. These normally provided for royalty payments based on the volume of production. Since the level of production, and therefore their own revenues, increased fairly steadily, the governments remained for the moment relatively satisfied.

In this way, from the First World War onwards a few great companies began to acquire control over the greater part of production and trade in oil all over the world. Pre-eminent among them were the seven 'majors' (sometimes called the seven sisters); in order of size at that time: Jersey Standard, Shell, Anglo-Iranian (later BP), Socony (later Mobil), Socal, Texaco and Gulf. All these companies were, to one degree or another, integrated companies: that is, they engaged not only in the production but also in the refining and marketing of oil. Some had greater supplies of crude at their disposal than they needed for refining and marketing: they were, that is, 'crude-long': Gulf (which had ample supplies in the United States, Mexico, Venezuela and later in Kuwait and Nigeria) and Socal (with supplies in California, Bahrain and eventually Saudi Arabia) were in this position. Others were crude-short: that is, they needed to buy crude oil, often from other companies, to meet their needs for refining and marketing: for example, Jersey Standard, Shell and Socony.

As the market for oil rapidly increased, these companies became engaged in an intensive search for new supplies of crude oil wherever they could be found. The crude-short companies were able in this way gradually to improve their position. Jersey Standard acquired new supplies in Venezuela, Sumatra, Iraq and eventually Saudi Arabia; Shell acquired new sources in Iraq, Iran (after 1953), Abu Dhabi, Nigeria and Oman; Socony linked with Vacuum and later with Mobil to win from them more secure supplies than she previously had available. There was increasing interest, as time went on, in the deposits of the Middle East. Oil production had taken place in Iran from the early years of the century and in Iraq from the early thirties. In the next two decades new discoveries were successively made in Bahrain, Kuwait, Saudi Arabia, Qatar, Abu Dhabi and Oman; later still new supplies were found in African countries – Libya, Algeria, Nigeria and Egypt. Middle East supplies became the most valuable to acquire, not only because of their size, but also because of the very low costs of production: in the early fifties a barrel of oil cost 10 cents to produce in the Middle East against 30–40 cents in Venezuela, and $1.40 in the United States.

Because few companies were engaged and all had similar interests, a considerable degree of collusion developed between them. There was little price competition. What competition there was took place almost exclusively in winning access to supplies. Even then the companies had an interest in not overbidding each other in the terms they offered to host governments. Occasionally during the inter-war years major companies engaged in brief price wars, normally designed to put smaller companies out of business altogether. But, because the market was tight and demand relatively inelastic, such wars were extremely expensive to the companies and competition in prices was thus avoided where possible. There was indeed little real market in crude oil. Most was sold for refining within the same companies; and the rest sold between companies on the basis of long-term contracts. For products (such as petrol) where a market often did exist, there was usually a form of price leadership, under which a price change by one company was quickly followed by a similar change by others. The major companies were able to reach understandings on other matters affecting competition. Under the so-called 'Red Line' agreement of 1928, the five majors involved in the IPC undertook not to seek concessions in other parts of the former Ottoman Empire. And under the so-called 'as-is' agreement of the same year, the three largest companies, Jersey, Shell and the Anglo-Iranian Oil Company (AIOC), agreed to abide by certain principles for pricing and market-sharing between them.

This co-operation extended to shared production arrangements. The system of joint concessions, adopted in Iraq in 1928, was increasingly followed in other areas. Thus Gulf and the AIOC joined to share the rights to production in Kuwait. Five US companies joined in establishing Aramco to develop the huge resources of Saudi Arabia. A similar arrangement was made after 1953 for Iran, where a number of companies took over the concession formerly held exclusively by the AIOC. Later Shell and BP shared production rights in Nigeria. Shell and Exxon entered into an arrangement for co-operation in exploration in Europe. There were also joint marketing arrangements: such as that between Socal and Texaco which set up Caltex to sell the former's oil to the latter's markets east of Suez; or that between Standard Oil and Vacuum which set up Stanvac to market Jersey's oil in Socony's markets in the Far East.

The dominance of the major companies reached its peak in the period just after the Second World War. For a time they exercised almost total power within the market for oil. By 1950 the seven majors controlled between them 75 per cent of production outside the United States and the communist world, 70 per cent of refinery capacity, 55 per cent of the tanker fleet, and 50 per cent of marketing outlets. Since they controlled most known sources of supply, and to develop new sources was hugely expensive, they were under little immediate competition from other producing companies or countries. For the same reason they were able to share markets between them on an agreed basis and so to avoid significant price competition.

Because every major company controlled supplies in a number of countries, they could, by adjusting levels of production in each, deter excessive demands by any host government: for example, after the nationalisation of the AIOC in Iran in 1951, and after the threatened expropriation of the IPC in Iraq in 1958, they were able to avoid the need for concessions by sharing supplies and increasing production elsewhere. Above all, they were able to control *overall* production levels; and so could ensure that this was just sufficient to meet existing levels of demand without exerting a downward pressure on prices. Not surprisingly, in this relatively favourable situation, with rapidly rising demand for oil, the profits of the companies were large and increased rapidly. Between 1950 and 1970, total company profits roughly quadrupled (from $800 million to $3.3 billion).

Against this, the power of the producing countries remained at first limited. They were militarily and politically weak. They became in many cases ever-dependent on their oil revenues (which at that time they were still able, and needed, to spend). Above all, they still negotiated separately with the various producing companies (who themselves were in close communication with each other), so that their bargaining strength was weakened.

The companies were thus able to ensure that their revenues steadily increased. Soon after the Second World War a new system of payment was introduced. Until that time the payments made by the companies had been mainly in the form of fixed payments (royalties) for every barrel of oil produced. Though total revenues, with increasing production, went up all the time, they did not rise as fast as the host countries wished: nor always as fast as the profits of the companies. Increasingly the governments began to demand payments which matched those profits. In 1948 the companies concerned agreed with Venezuela, and in 1950 with Saudi Arabia, to introduce the so-called 50–50 system. Under this the profits were shared: the host government secured tax payments equal to the notional profits of the companies on the production of crude oil (excluding, that is, the profits on refining and marketing). This system was by no means unwelcome to the companies, since under US tax law they could offset tax payments of this kind against their US tax liability. In effect, therefore, the cost of the new and higher payments was met not by the companies but by the governments of their home countries.

The new system did, however, enable them to keep the host governments happy for a time. The revenues of the five main producing countries rose from $570 million dollars in 1950 to 2.2 billion in 1960. Even so, the producing governments began to be restless. They became increasingly aware that they remained totally without influence over the decisions that affected their most precious natural resource: especially those concerning the rate at which it was produced (and therefore depleted) and the price at which it was sold. Moreover, even their revenues were not assured: since the companies determined the price, and so the profits acquired on crude production, they could unilaterally reach decisions which radically affected the revenues obtained by each country. The host countries therefore gradually began to demand a greater control over the use of their most valuable assets.

6.2   THE TAKE-OVER BY THE GOVERNMENTS

Before the end of the fifties the dominant position that had been enjoyed by the major companies began to be threatened by a number of developments.

First, their control over the sources of crude oil declined. New competition from a number of directions began to emerge. An increasing number of 'independents', smaller oil companies, mainly of US origin, came into being. These were able to negotiate agreements with producing countries, especially in the Middle East, which gave them access to substantial quantities of crude: for example, in Libya, Algeria, Abu Dhabi and elsewhere. New producer countries such as these were no longer willing to offer concessions for all their territory to a single company or consortium. Old producers too welcomed the chance to deal with alternative concessionaires; in a number of countries, majors were compelled to relinquish to independents the areas where they were not producing: by 1963 the principal con-cessionaires in Saudi Arabia, Kuwait, Iraq and Qatar had all been obliged to give up areas in this way. Independents secured access to the consortium operating in Iran in 1954; won concessions in Libya in 1955; in Algeria in 1965; and in an increasing number of offshore contracts. At the same time national companies were set up by some producing governments which, though at first they took little part in production, took a share of the oil and began to dispose of significant quantities of oil independently of the majors. Governments of consumer countries too were concerned to win access to crude supplies that was independent of the majors. Several set up state companies, which reached their own arrangements with producing countries: ERAP (France), ENI and AGIP (Italy), the Arabian Oil Company (Japan), Hispanic Oil (Spain) and so on. Finally, increasing quantities of oil were being sold on Western markets by the Soviet Union. Thus the semi-monopoly position which the companies had enjoyed for so long was increasingly threatened.

Secondly, increasing supplies of oil, partly from new sources, caused a downward pressure on prices. Huge new reserves had been discovered in the Middle East, which provided crude at very low prices. The companies, as a result of the new competition, no longer enjoyed the control over overall production levels which had previously enabled them to sustain prices. The new producing companies, in order to win access to markets previously controlled by the majors, were willing to offer substantial discounts. The majors themselves began, in retaliation, to offer discounts, both in the sales they made to each other and on those to outside distributors. Controls on imports into the United States, introduced in 1958 to protect US domestic producers and to avoid, for strategic reasons, excessive dependence on outside supplies (which had ultimately precisely the opposite effect, causing unnecessary depletion of US oil when prices were low and so *hastening* ultimate dependence on outside supplies), increased the volume of oil available for sale elsewhere. Producer countries were not yet aware of the importance of limiting production to maintain prices: on the contrary, they competed for 'offtake' of their own oil. Though demand still rose steadily – by about 7–8 per cent a year – the market could still not withstand this dramatic increase in overall supply.

Thirdly, however, and perhaps most important of all, the governments of the producer countries became increasingly self-confident in their dealings with the companies. Their knowledge of oil operations and economic sophistication steadily improved. Nationalist pressures among their population increased. The demands placed on the companies were thus gradually raised. The first manifestation of this was the nationalisation of the AIOC by the Mossadeq government in Iran in 1951. Though eventually, because of the refusal of other major companies (partly under threat of legal action by the AIOC but mainly because of collective self-interest) to market Iranian oil, the company was allowed back into Iran, the nationalisation was not formally reversed and BP's dominance was weakened, since she was forced to share production with a consortium which included other foreign companies, including independents. Iraq, in 1958, demanded the renegotiation of all existing agreements, an increase in her share of the profits, the relinquishment of areas not worked by the companies, and participation by the government in the equity of the consortium: in 1961 she expropriated 99 per cent of the concession areas; and in 1967 entered into a new agreement under which France was given access to Iraqi oil on terms far less favourable than the companies had previously enjoyed. As a result of these moves, by infection, the demands of all producer countries were raised.

It was above all the gradual erosion of prices which stimulated the increasing assertiveness of the producer countries. The companies had adopted, from about 1950, the practice of publishing 'posted prices', on which their tax payments were based. The posted price had at first approximated to the prices at which the oil was actually sold, both in sales to outside companies and in their internal transactions. But, with the increasing pressure of new supplies on the market and the large discounts which were increasingly widely offered, a growing gap between the realised prices and the posted price began to appear. Under US tax law it had suited the companies to show relatively high profits on their crude-oil sales, made abroad, rather than on their other operations; and they had been willing for a time to maintain the posted price above the realised price. But, as the true price dropped, this became increasingly expensive for them. In 1959 and 1960 the companies, acting unilaterally, introduced two successive reductions in the 'posted price', so of course causing a corresponding reduction in the revenues acquired by the producing countries.

This brought a sharp reaction amongst the governments of those countries. It showed them that, so long as the companies alone determined price, the 50–50 system would not necessarily assure them ever-rising revenues. The move was particularly damaging to Venezuela, the most expensive producer, since price competition would inevitably increasingly squeeze her own share of production. It was therefore Venezuela which took the lead in proposing the establishment of a new body, the Organisation of Petroleum Exporting Countries (OPEC), whose purpose would be above all to seek to prevent the companies from again reducing prices unilaterally.

The new organisation correctly recognised that it was likely to be able to influence prices only by limiting production. But this could be done, it was then believed, only if a formal system for allocating production levels among the producing states could be introduced. In the mid-sixties there were prolonged discussions about such a system, but it was not possible to reach agreement on the way it should be operated. The organisation was able to bring about some modest changes in the basis on which oil revenues were paid. Members got the companies to treat the royalties they paid to them as 'expenses', to be paid over and above the tax payment due on the profits which remained.[1] And they forced the companies to accept a reduction in the allowance they had previously been able to claim for marketing expenses.

They were not at this time, however, able to secure larger benefits, because competition among the countries remained, despite the creation of OPEC, greater than competition among the companies. The former had still not sufficiently recognised that self-discipline in levels of production was the essential condition of raising prices. There was continued pressure from some among them, notably Iran, for increased offtake of their own supplies. The result was that, while the price of oil in the market was relatively high in relation to the cost of production (in the Middle East at least), it failed to reflect its real value in terms of the high and inelastic demand which existed for it and the constant depletion of finite supplies. By 1970 it had become 25 per cent cheaper in relation to other goods than it had been in 1955. As a result it was increasingly displacing other forms of energy. Coal-mines were being everywhere closed down. Nuclear power was made to appear un-economic. Little investment was undertaken in alternative renewable sources. And there was virtually no incentive for conservation of energy of any kind.

In the following decade this situation changed radically. The first major advance in oil prices resulted from events in Libya. In 1969 Qadafi's revolution displaced the old monarchist government there. Soon afterwards the new government opened negotiations with the oil companies. All the bargaining power lay in the hands of the Libyan government. About half the production was held by independent companies, some of them totally relying on Libya for their oil supplies. The closure of the Suez canal three years before had hugely raised the demand for Libyan oil, which (besides being relatively sulphur-free) could be transported to European markets without using the long sea route. This demand rose much higher during 1970, since Tapline, the pipeline across Syria, was cut that spring. Libya was already unable to spend all her revenues, and therefore easily in a position to forgo some part of them, if necessary, to exert her will on the companies. Realising that the majors, with resources elsewhere, were better placed to resist its demands, the government concentrated on the independents, isolating one in particular, Occidental, which was totally dependent on Libyan oil. It imposed a drastic limitation on its permitted production level, which was cut by nearly 50 per cent. Occidental was thus compelled to concede both a substantial rise in the posted price (of 30 cents); and an increase in the government's tax rate, to 55 per cent. Similar increases were reluctantly accepted by other companies operating in Libya. And eventually they were conceded by those operating elsewhere as well.

During the next two years there were further increases. At the end of 1970 the OPEC countries, recognising how far all had benefited as a result of Libya's negotiating strength, determined that in future they would negotiate jointly. The companies for a time hoped to show a similar unity. Having just been picked off one by one, they now decided, led by Shell, that they would negotiate jointly (and were released from anti-trust liability by the US government for the purpose). But they agreed, pressed by their governments, to negotiate separately with the Gulf producers; and, since only some of them were involved in the Gulf operations, their unity was quickly destroyed. Despite the fact that the agreements reached a few months earlier had been supposed to last for five years, OPEC quickly put forward new and higher demands. A meeting in Tehran in January–February 1971 led to a further increase in prices and in the government take. Further increases followed over the next two years. Between the beginning of 1971 and the middle of 1973 revenues per barrel roughly doubled (from $0.98 to $1.82 a barrel for Saudi Arabia Crude, for example).

Towards the end of 1973 a still more dramatic rise took place. During the previous year an unprecedented boom had been taking place throughout the developed world. Imports of oil into the United States had increased by a third in 1972 alone. This rapid increase in demand inevitably led to a rapid increase in realised prices. Prices in the spot market rose substantially above the official posted prices. When the October war between Israel and the Arab states broke out in 1973, these market pressures became stronger than ever. The Arab producers imposed an embargo on exports to the United States and the Netherlands, as well as general cut-backs in production of 25 per cent. This further increased shortages and so provoked panic buying. Because

oil production at this time was increasingly concentrated in the Middle
East (Saudi Arabia, Iran and Libya alone were responsible for around
half of all world trade in oil) there was little spare capacity elsewhere on
which the companies could draw. Spot prices rose to $15 a barrel. In this
situation Middle East countries had strong economic as well as political
reasons for raising the price. In September Algeria had already
demanded a posted price of $5 a barrel. A month later, after the
outbreak of the war, Arab producers announced a 60 per cent increase in
price. In December they imposed a further increase of 100 per cent,
raising the price of 'marker' crude to $11.65 (compared with little more
than $2 the previous June). In two or three months a price revolution
had occurred.

As we have seen in earlier chapters, these increases had calamitous
effects for the consumer countries as a whole, especially the poorest,
causing huge balance of payments deficits and deflation in the entire
world economy. They were not, however, particularly damaging to the
oil companies. In general their profits rose as the price rose. Already
between 1971 and 1973 their profits had increased from 30 cents to 90
cents a barrel. Because of the strong and inelastic demand for oil
products, they were able to pass on the increased price of crude by
raising the prices of their products. Increasingly, therefore, there
developed a common interest between producing countries and the
companies. Both equally benefited from higher prices.

There was, however, a major shift in the balance of power between the
two. Control over posted prices had now shifted almost entirely to the
producer governments: at first acting individually (as did Libya in 1970
and Algeria in 1973) but later deciding prices collectively within OPEC.
Even more important, they had won control over supply (on which the
price ultimately depended). They were increasingly well aware (as only
Venezuela, Kuwait and Libya had been before) that their ability to
maintain prices depended entirely on their also assuming control over
production levels. For the first time now, the governments of the
principal producers, Iran, Saudi Arabia, Abu Dhabi and Nigeria,
refrained from pressing for higher offtake. This control, however, was
exercised not collectively, as they had once hoped, but individually.
OPEC, despite much discussion of the question, never acquired control
over production levels.[2] But because each individual government was
increasingly aware of the important effect of such levels, they were
usually able at this time, even when acting separately, to maintain by
self-restraint the prices they demanded.

But producer governments were not only winning control over levels of production and prices. Increasingly they were directly taking over production facilities.[3] Iraq, as we have seen, had already taken over part of the oil installations in that country in 1961; and in 1972 it nationalised the IPC's main operations in Kirkuk. In 1971 Algeria nationalised pipelines and gas-fields, and 51 per cent of French oil concessions. In the following year Venezuela introduced a progressive take-over of all hydrocarbons, to be completed in 1983. In the same year Saudi Arabia, Kuwait, Qatar and Abu Dhabi demanded 'participation' – that is, a direct government share in the production of crude oil in their own territory; and in October of that year reached agreement with the companies for a progressive transfer of ownership by the companies, to reach 51 per cent in 1982: a figure that was later raised to 60 per cent, and finally to 100 per cent. In June 1973 the Shah of Iran announced that the companies which operated in that country were to turn over their assets to Iran, in return for an agreement assuring them of long-term supplies. In the same month Nigeria acquired 35 per cent participation in the Shell–BP concession, rising to 55 per cent in the following year. In September of the same year, Libya announced 50 per cent nationalis-ation of most of the companies operating there. In 1975 Venezuela, Kuwait and Iraq reached agreement with the companies for full nationalisation. By the end of 1975, therefore, producer governments throughout the Middle East and North Africa owned at least 50 per cent, and sometimes 100 per cent, of the oil operations in their countries.[4]

Governments in most cases acquired an agreed share of all the oil produced, and sold part to the companies at a special price and part to outside purchasers, again at a specified price. At about the same time the artificial 'posted' price was abandoned and OPEC adopted the far simpler system of agreeing on a level of government return per barrel (the return for Saudi and marker crude had risen to just over \$10 in 1975 against only about \$1 in early 1971). Something like 96 per cent of revenues from production of crude oil now went to the governments and only about 2 per cent to company profits. Even so, the price of products such as petrol was raised mainly by consumer governments. Even at the end of the seventies the governments of consumer countries in many cases took a larger share of the final price of petrol in tax than did producer governments.

In time the interest of the governments moved even further downstream: that is, from crude production to refining, petrochemicals and even distribution (Saudi Arabia offered at one time to guarantee the supply of oil to the United States in return for permission to invest in downstream operations). They were not entirely successful in their penetration of these activities. Petrochemical operations, using subsidised oil, were sometimes highly successful. But most marketing remained under the control of the companies. And, though large, and excessive, refinery capacity was built, there was not always a market for the products these new refineries supplied.[5]

While the producer countries had increased their power in these various ways by common action, the consumers remained totally disunited. Even over the short-term crisis which the 1973 embargo created they had not shown a common front. Fellow members of the EEC had been unwilling to take any steps to assist the Netherlands, a victim of the embargo; and only the action of oil companies in reallocating supplies prevented the embargoed states from suffering acute difficulties. Each consumer country introduced, individually not collectively, various measures to restrain consumption: controls over heating and lighting, restrictions on the use of motor-cars, speed limits and even petrol rationing. Some placed restrictions on the export of various refined products. The European countries and Japan made political statements of various kinds, designed to conciliate the Arab countries and so secure supplies. Some entered into special agreements for that prupose. Discussion began on more long-term measures of protection. The United States proposed an oil-sharing scheme for use in subsequent emergencies (as well as a 'safety net', a $25 billion fund, which would provide help in overcoming the large oil deficits of the consumer countries). Finally, in November 1974, a new organisation of industrial countries, the International Energy Agency, was set up in Paris to co-ordinate action among those countries in the same way that OPEC did for the producers.

The bargaining power of the consumers, however, was raised not so much by these measures as by the serious deflationary effect of the oil-price increase. This brought for a short time, as we have seen, an actual reduction in GNP in the rich countries and a substantial slowing of growth rates for the following years. The demand for oil, and therefore the bargaining power of OPEC, were thus reduced. In the next five years the *real* price of oil actually declined. While the price per barrel rose from $9 in early 1974 to $13 in early 1979, this was far less than the increase which had taken place in the price of manufactured goods imported by the oil-producers.

From the beginning of 1979 this situation changed again. With the partial revival of the world economy which had taken place by that time, and with the continuing high level of oil consumption in the United

States (where petrol prices, for political reasons, had been kept artificially low), demand began to rise again. The Iranian revolution, and the sharp reduction in Iranian oil exports which followed, once more increased the pressure on supplies and so on prices. The outbreak of the Gulf war between Iraq and Iran in September of the following year, by reducing their exports, accentuated this pressure. Prices in the spot market shot up again: to over $40 a barrel. As a result OPEC was able to secure substantial further increases during those two years. The price of oil virtually tripled once more, rising from $13 a barrel at the beginning of 1979 to $39 a barrel at the end of 1980 (with additional premia for higher-grade oil or favourable location). While world recession, and the pressure of Saudi Arabia, compelled some reduction in 1981, it seemed not unlikely that prices would begin to climb again as world economic activity revived.

During this period, therefore, control of the production and price of oil had been transferred almost completely from the producing companies to the producing countries. Essential decisions thus remained in the hands of a relatively small group who, mainly by determining their own levels of production, were able to fix the price which consumers had to pay for their oil. Yet this was not, any more than before, a closely knit cartel, jointly fixing the amounts produced in particular countries or the prices obtained. Each individual producer government made its own decisions concerning the level of production it would allow. But each took its decisions always in the clear knowledge of the effect they would have on the level of prices secured. Governments, especially the dominant government, that of Saudi Arabia, sought to ensure that production levels were such as to maintain the price agreed. In times of recession, when competition for markets was greater, this was not always easy to achieve: at such times (in 1981 for example) prices could be progressively eroded by competitive discounts. In the long run revenues depended on the economic prosperity of the West. As this recognition was increasingly forced on the producers partly by the market and partly by the actions of Saudi Arabia, their pricing policies became more cautious.

The oil companies, though their independence was reduced, in no way suffered from the new system. On the contrary, they secured hugely increased profits as a result. It was the consumers who paid the price. And those who were worst affected of all were the poorer countries, who now found themselves obliged to pay huge proportions of their foreign-exchange earnings to pay for their imports of oil. Rich countries were little less badly hurt. Inflation was intensified; very large deficits were suffered; and the overall rate of growth was substantially lowered.

The oil revolution had transformed not only the wealth and power of the producing countries. It had transformed the international economy as a whole.

6.3 INTERNATIONAL INSTITUTIONS CONCERNED WITH OIL

All the international institutions that operate in the field of energy at present are partial in character. Either they represent only particular interest groups, such as producers or consumers; or they are only regional in scope.

The governments of the producing states, as we have seen, for many years dealt with the oil companies individually. Only slowly did they begin to recognise the possible advantages of co-operating with each other. The lead in this was taken by Venezuela (which had most reason to fear competition, because her own production costs were high). Already in the late 1940s, at the time when Iran was seeking to renegotiate the terms of the AIOC's concession (which had been affected by legislation restricting dividends in Britain), Venezuela was offering advice on tactics. In 1949–51, because of her concern at the increase in sales of Middle East oil that was cheaper to the companies than her own, she organised more widespread consultations with Middle East producer governments.

Middle East countries created their own machinery for consultation. The Arab League set up a Committee of Oil Experts, which first met in June 1952. And in 1954 it established a Permanent Petroleum Bureau (later renamed the Department of Oil Affairs). Besides organising periodic Arab congresses to promote knowledge and expertise about oil questions, this proposed various ambitious joint projects, such as an Arab oil-pipeline company, an Arab oil-tanker company, a petroleum research institute and even an Arab oil-producing company. All of these, however, (like many proposed inter-Arab projects at this time) were dreams which came to nothing as a result of rivalry among the various Arab states.

In 1959 at a meeting of the Arab Petroleum Congress, the Venezuelan Minister of Mines and Hydrocarbons proposed the establishment of an Oil Consultative Commission, in which the oil-producers could discuss common problems. Such a commission was briefly established and included most of the major oil-producing countries. It recommended the stabilisation of posted prices, a guarantee by the companies that they would consult about prices, and an increase in the 50 per cent level of taxation at that time prevailing (Venezuela especially favoured this because, the higher the level of taxation, the less the competitive advantage enjoyed by the low-cost Middle East producers). However, because of the hostility of Iraq and Iran to the dominant role played by the United Arab Republic (in whose territory it operated), the Commission was short-lived.

In the following year the Organisation of Petroleum Exporting Countries (OPEC) was established in its place. Its creation was stimulated by the two successive reductions in the posted price (on which tax revenues were calculated) which the oil companies introduced, without consultation with producer governments, in 1959–60. Thus the main objective of the new organisation was to 'stabilise' prices. Its member states recognised that this would require limiting levels of production, and considered schemes for allocating production levels among the different producers. It was able to reach a tentative agreement on a set of criteria for deciding how much each member should produce (the area and population of each country, its historical levels of production, the percentage of oil income in government revenues and total expenditures on development). But there was no agreement on the precise levels to be established and the authority the organisation should have in imposing them. It did succeed, as we have seen (p. 151), in securing some marginal concessions from the companies. It encouraged producer governments to secure local participation in the operations of foreign companies or even full national ownership of domestic operations. It proposed their increasing involvement in down-stream operations – refining, petrochemicals and distribution – as well as diversification into non-oil activities. Finally, it aimed to increase the technical expertise of member governments, partly through the provision of joint research and other activities, so as to improve their bargaining strength in relation to the companies.

Membership of OPEC is restricted to countries having a substantial net export of crude oil and with similar interests to existing member countries (thus Britain and Norway, whose membership has sometimes been, only half jokingly, proposed, might well not qualify even if they wished to join). Some important producers, such as Mexico, have not joined. The organisation has a board of governors, in which every member is represented, with responsibility for overseeing the general running of the organisation, meeting at least twice a year; a secretariat, undertaking research and public relations activities, as well as normal executive functions; and, by far the most important, the Conference, which meets usually twice a year, once at the headquarters and once elsewhere. This is usually attended by oil ministers, occasionally by prime ministers and heads of state. It reaches the essential decisions on policy matters: above all on prices. Each member state has a vote and in theory decisions are unanimous. In practice the countries with the largest production, such as Saudi Arabia, have a dominant influence, since their decisions on their own production levels can determine the price which can be sustained in the market. Each government, however, continues to reach independent decisions concerning premia and discounts; and to this extent all are still able to determine the exact price level set for their own oil.

OPEC is not the only organisation of producer states. Another which has had considerable influence at certain times is the Organisation of Arab Petroleum Exporting Countries (OAPEC). This was established in January 1968 in the aftermath of the Six-Day War. During that war some of the Arab states attempted to impose an embargo on the United States, Britain and West Germany, which had been accused (without foundation) of providing military assistance to Israel during the war. The countries affected were in fact easily able to obtain oil from other sources; and, as Saudi Arabia quickly admitted, it was the producers themselves that finally suffered. Saudi Arabia, Kuwait and Libya therefore decided to establish a new organisation to co-ordinate their oil policies. This was at first confined to the more conservative Arab states. Iraq and Algeria, angered at their exclusion, signed an agreement with each other for co-operation between themselves. To overcome this division between the two groups, in 1970, the membership of OAPEC was broadened to include Algeria, Abu Dhabi, Bahrain, Dubai and Qatar. At the same time Algeria, Iraq and Libya signed an agreement for co-operation among the Arab producers in the Mediterranean area.

Decisions in OAPEC are in effect unanimous: though initial decisions can be reached by majority vote, they must be ratified by all members to have effect. The organisation has a court which can decide disputes on oil matters. And it has considered the establishment of a joint tanker company, a finance corporation, and other projects.

Under its charter the policies of OAPEC are not supposed to be in conflict with those of the wider organisation, OPEC. Even so, some members of OPEC, and especially Iran, resented the establishment of OAPEC, which, it was believed, would weaken the cohesion of the wider organisation. In some cases, however, decisions that were originally reached in OAPEC have proved of considerable value to members of

OPEC. For example, it was the decision of OAPEC in 1973, in response to the October war in that year, which led to the large increase in posted price and tax revenues which were finally enjoyed by the members of OPEC generally. As the power and effectiveness of OPEC have increased in recent years, however, the importance of OAPEC has diminished sharply.

There are one or two other regional organisations which are concerned with oil. In 1961 the Latin American states, following the establishment of OPEC, set up an organisation linking the state-owned oil companies of the sub-continent. Once again Venezuela took the lead. Her Minister of Mines and Hydrocarbons, who had taken the initiative in founding OPEC, was also responsible for proposing the Latin-American body. This was supposed to help with the economic and technical integration of Latin America and with the development of local oil organisations. Sooner or later most of the national oil companies of the region joined. But there was a sharp conflict of interests between the three or four countries that were significant producers and exporters of oil, and the majority, which were importers. The organisation has, therefore, in practice done little more than facilitate the exchange of information among member states.

The development of these various organisations representing producers stimulated a demand for corresponding bodies to promote co-operation among consumers. Even before 1973 the OECD had had a Consultative Oil Committee, which had responsibility for considering the problems faced by member states concerning the supply of oil. After 1973 it was felt that a more formal organisation among consumers was required if the bargaining power of the producers was to be matched. As a result, in November 1974 the International Energy Agency (IEA) was set up in Paris. This includes most industrialised countries other than France, which, for the sake of her relations with Arab countries, preferred to remain outside. It is concerned with co-ordinating the policies of the chief consumer countries, organising a system of oil-sharing for use in emergencies, promoting energy conservation, stimulating domestic production and the development of alternative fuels, and undertaking discussion and analysis of energy policies. Decisions are taken by weighted majority, with a different type of majority required for particular kinds of decision. The organisation spent much time at first discussing a proposal for a minimum price of oil, which it was believed would be required to provide the incentive to invest in alternatives. Since the price in fact (contrary to the expectations of some) soon shot far above the proposed minimum, this idea has never been pursued. But the Agency did agree on an emergency oil-sharing scheme and, in theory, on the establishment of stockpiles of oil (p. 166 below). It has also set successive targets for levels of oil consumption and oil imports for the industrialised countries. Some of these have been endorsed or modified at the economic 'summits' among the developed states.

One of the weaknesses of the organisation is that it is confined to industrialised countries. Its capacity to influence the policies of oil-producers would undoubtedly have been greater if, from the beginning, it had included the great majority of consumers which are developing countries. The latter therefore are only able to put their views either in bilateral contacts with the producers or in larger international gatherings (such as UNCTAD meetings) and have been generally reluctant to confront the producers publicly.

In addition to these wider bodies, there are regional bodies among countries that are mainly consumers which have an interest in this field. The EEC, for example, has for years in theory been developing an energy policy, though this has never got very far.

Over the years there have been intermittent discussions about the establishment of some wider international body for discussing energy questions. Energy matters receive occasional attention in UN bodies which have general responsibility in the economic area, such as Ecosoc, UNCTAD, and the regional economic commissions, each of which has undertaken studies of energy needs and capacities in their own area. Aid-giving agencies, especially the World Bank, have also devoted considerable attention to providing assistance in the energy field.

In recent years there have been proposals for a more direct UN responsibility in this area. Kurt Waldheim, UN Secretary-General, suggested in 1978 the creation of a UN energy 'institute', which would at least be in a position to *study* some of the problems, without necessarily having any power of decision or recommendation. Such proposals have, however, always failed in face of the stubborn refusal of the oil-producing countries to accept that there should be any degree of international responsibility in this field. This resistance has been based on the fear that any such body might acquire the power to influence decisions on pricing, which they are determined should remain firmly in the hands of OPEC. On these grounds those governments have consistently rejected successive proposals for the creation of a new UN agency with responsibility in this field. Surprisingly, the non-oil developing countries, which have a strong interest in the creation of an international body within which the views of consumers would carry substantial weight, have not proved energetic or persistent in pursuing this proposal. No progress has therefore been made.

As a result, although the decisions concerning oil, especially the price of oil, have a greater effect on the international economy than those in any other field, at present they are reached (in the case of crude) by an organisation representing a few producers and (in the case of products) by a few major companies, each acting to promote its own interests, unconstrained by consideration of the needs of the world economy generally or by the views of the consumer states. If a more rational way of managing the international economy is to be devised, there is a clear need for some institutional arrangements that would allow a broader view of the needs of the world economy to be reached.

6.4   AN INTERNATIONAL OIL STRATEGY

At the beginning of the eighties, therefore, there were many manifest deficiencies in the world trade in oil. A large proportion of world production was in the hands of a small group of countries which, by their joint decisions on taxation, largely determined the price at which oil was traded. In consequence, during a single decade the price of a barrel of oil had multiplied by almost 40 (from about $1 a barrel in 1970 to $39 in 1980). The increases that took place were not only very large, but also abrupt and unpredictable. They brought in their train both rapid inflation and severe recession, each affecting the whole world economy. They had particularly serious effects on poor countries, which were obliged to spend very large parts of their total foreign-exchange earnings on imports of oil. And there existed no international institution to seek to formulate the kind of international energy strategy which was increasingly required.

During the previous decade a total transformation of the world energy situation, and especially of the market in oil, had taken place. If oil had been underpriced, taking account of its long-term availability, before that decade began (its price fell 20 per cent in real terms between 1950 and 1970), it was clearly overpriced at its end, even by the same criterion. The current price meant that alternative fuels were, with technological developments, becoming increasingly more economical than oil. In the developed countries consumption of oil, previously rising fast, was now declining. The producers risked being left with large reserves on their hands which might well not all be sold when totally new forms of energy (such as that from fusion power) or totally new vehicles (such as efficient battery cars) became available 15 or 20 years later.

For one effect of the price revolution had been a reduction in demand for energy generally. Within developed Western countries, energy consumption was now rising considerably less fast than GNP. Energy consumption per unit of output had declined sharply.[6] Consumption of energy generally was now rising by only about 3 per cent a year against double that a decade or so earlier.

In 1980 oil still represented something like half of all energy consumption (about 20 per cent each was represented by coal and gas and 5 per cent by nuclear power, the rest by hydroelectric and other forms of energy). But the proportion of all energy taken by oil was now rapidly declining. While total demand for oil had risen by 7 per cent or so a year in the decade up to 1973, during the next five years demand rose by only 1 per cent a year on average.[7] In 1980–1 there was a significant net *decline* in the demand for oil – by about 7 per cent a year – and an even stronger decline in demand for oil imports. The decline resulted partly from world recession. But in part it stemmed from the higher relative cost of oil and the switch to alternative fuels. The switch to oil had been less marked in poor countries (even though the effect of the oil-price rise was even more serious) because the availability of alternative fuels was less (oil represented 55 per cent of energy use in poor countries against under 50 per cent for rich countries) and the costs of conversion and conservation were high. Thus demand for oil in such countries continued to rise by 6–7 per cent a year, though, since they counted for only about a fifth of non-communist consumption, the effect on the world market was considerably less. Moreover, these countries too were likely to switch increasingly to other fuels as the opportunity arose.

The result was that demand for oil, even if economic growth resumed, was likely to rise very little during the eighties. Total demand at that time was about 50 million barrels a day in the non-communist world, with a further 10–12 million in the Eastern bloc. Demand among poor countries, it was believed, might rise in the next decade by about 8–10 million barrels a day (half of this among the OPEC countries themselves); while there would probably be a decline in demand among rich countries. New sources of oil were rapidly being developed outside the OPEC countries. And it was thus likely that OPEC production, though by far the cheapest in cost of production and requiring little further investment, would decline significantly (partly because of the desire of consumers to avoid dependence on them and partly because of the efforts of their governments to maintain the price) and be replaced by far more expensive supplies from other sources.[8]

From an international point of view it was irrational that new supplies should be sought from the most expensive sources, while large untapped resources that were far cheaper were allowed to remain idle. There was an urgent need for a more sensible way of managing the world's scarce but valuable remaining sources of energy.

Any new system would have to take account of the radical changes in the way the oil market worked. Thirty years ago, most oil production all over the world was undertaken by a relatively small number of major companies which were therefore able to control both its supply and its price. In every respect this situation was now changed. Production, volume and price were now all largely controlled by the governments of the producing countries. Through 'participation' and nationalisation, OPEC governments now themselves undertook about four-fifths of oil production in their states. They were themselves responsible for selling about half the oil. A considerable proportion of this was not sold on the oil market at all, but sold direct to companies and governments under long-term contracts. Many consumer countries (including, for example, France, Italy, Spain, Portugal and Greece among the rich countries, and India and Brazil among the poor) preferred such deals to safeguard the security of their supplies to relying on commercial operations by the companies, which no longer had secure access to crude supplies.

Producer governments were also able to control directly the total *level* of production. Here too power had passed from the companies to the governments. While companies had maintained supplies at the levels necessary to meet an ever-growing market, the governments sought to maintain them at the levels necessary to ensure ever-rising prices. In the eighties the capacity of the OPEC countries to exercise this control would probably decline. The proportion of oil produced in their territories would go down. A rapid increase in the total number of producing countries had taken place already: to over 70 in 1980. Each price rise stimulated new programmes of exploration. Some of these programmes were supported by the World Bank, which planned to finance still more through a proposed energy affiliate. As a result, by 1980 OPEC countries were providing only about half of the non-communist world's supplies (the United States and the Soviet Union alone provided more than half the rest). During the eighties that proportion was likely to decline to 40 per cent or less. The producers could not maintain prices during a severe recession, as in 1981–2, because each was unwilling to reduce its own production proportionately. But, as world economic activity revived, so would the capacity of the main producers to control the market. And, even though new producers have a greater need for revenues for development, it was by no means sure that their demand for offtake would be sufficient to reduce real prices over the long term.

A more rational system for managing the world's energy supplies is clearly needed if the excessive power now exercised by a small number of major producers is to be diminished. Some means of providing a more objective assessment of the world's energy needs and capacities must be created. There is a need for some international body to be established, representing consumers and producers alike, to oversee the world energy situation. It is an anomaly that, while in almost every other economic and social sphere – including the monetary system, development, labour, health, education, and several kinds of communication – specialised agencies have been established within the UN system to organise international action, there still exists no such body with responsibility in the field of energy. The only organisations at present operating in this field are, as we have seen, partial bodies, representing only producers or consumers. There is clearly a need for some kind of international energy agency in which all governments that so wished could be represented. Such an agency would no doubt, like the other specialised agencies, have an assembly in which all countries would be represented, to meet every year or so to discuss general policy; a council with perhaps 25 or 30 members, to undertake day-to-day responsibility, keep under review the world energy situation, institute negotiations of particular issues in dispute, and undertake research and information work; and a secretariat to undertake the executive functions for the intergovernmental bodies.

What would be the responsibilities of such an agency? First, there is a clear need for collective action to maintain a reasonable balance of supply to demand, over both the short and the long term. Over the short term, what is needed for this are measures to reduce the pressure on supplies at times of crisis or feared shortage. At present, in any such situation both companies and governments, fearful of a threat to their supplies in the future, frantically compete for all available sources, so forcing the price rapidly upwards. Each of the major price increases of the 1970s followed such a sudden restriction in supply (the closure of Tapline in 1970, the embargo and production cut-backs in 1973, the Iranian revolution and the Gulf war in 1979–80): in each case this caused a sudden upsurge in demand by companies and a rapid rise in the spot price, inevitably stimulating a demand for higher prices by OPEC. Oil companies have no incentive to show restraint in this situation. Their immediate concern is to fulfil their supply obligations and maintain their markets, and they know that any consequent rise in price, far from damaging them, will normally bring them higher profits than ever. Governments too (as those of Japan and France have several times shown) are more concerned at such times to avoid the possibility of serious oil shortage than to avoid pressure on prices. So, under this competition, the initial pressure on supplies is magnified many times, producing a matching pressure on prices.

If large price rises are to be avoided, therefore, an essential condition is collective action to bring about greater stability in supply. One obvious measure, much discussed but still not adequately implemented, is to ensure a higher general level of stocks which could then be used to reduce the pressure at times of crisis. In theory an agreement to bring this about was reached among the main consumers in 1974. The United States determined to establish a strategic reserve of a billion barrels. Most other Western countries place the obligation to create stocks on the oil companies, which were to ensure 90 days' supply. But for a number of reasons (including, it is alleged, pressure from Saudi Arabia) the United States has so far failed to create a reserve of the size planned.[9] In other countries the companies have held adequate stocks only at times of oil glut, as in 1980–1. Normally the supplies have been maintained largely in tankers and pipelines, much of which constitutes part of the normal supply channel. Even the surplus is not in practice available to relieve pressure on prices at times of shortage: at such times companies are more than ever anxious to hold onto all the stocks they can, both to avoid a situation of shortage and to benefit from the expected rise in price.[10] Neither their governments nor the IEA have the authority to require them to release stocks in any situation short of an acute international emergency, such as the boycott of 1973:[11] an emergency which has never yet recurred. One possible way of meeting the situation would be the establishment of a full-scale commodity agreement, not unlike that operating for tin, under which oil would be released automatically onto the market once the price on the spot market had reached a certain level. There are, however, many difficulties about reaching such an agreement: above all, the likely opposition of the producers. It is therefore essential to ensure at least that there exist adequate emergency stocks in consumer countries and that these can be quickly and effectively released onto the market at any time of shortage.

Even more important, however, is to increase the availability of *long-term* supplies. This requires securing a greater diversity of sources than exists today. This is needed partly to reduce the degree of market power at present exercised by a small number of producer countries. But it is needed equally to reduce the huge balance of payments costs of oil supplies for very many consumer countries, especially the poorest of all. At present imports of oil take a substantial proportion of the export earnings of such countries: for Tanzania the proportion today (1981) is 50 per cent, for Brazil 60 per cent, for India 75 per cent (the average for poor countries is nearly 30 per cent).[12] It is not unlikely that substantial quantities of oil remain to be discovered in the territories of poor countries. They have so far been explored far less intensively than those of most developed countries; and according to the World Bank, even though at present only 2 per cent of proven reserves are in their territories, they may possess about 15 per cent of ultimately recoverable reserves.

A greater diversity in sources would make it less likely that a severe interruption of supplies, whether to particular countries or to the market generally, could be imposed, either for political or for other reasons. The world energy situation would be less under the direct control of a small number of countries, often, anyway, unable to spend their oil revenues, and therefore with little incentive to increase supply. The long-term supply situation a decade or two hence would be better safeguarded. And, because a large number of countries would be both producers and consumers, there would be a less rigid and clear-cut division than exists at present between the two groups, and therefore a greater possibility of creating stability in supply and price.

Any systematic effort to develop new sources will be extremely costly. Available supplies of crude in the United States and the Soviet Union that can be economically exploited are almost exhausted. Heavy investment in expensive supplies in other parts of the world might therefore be required (at present it costs about 25 times as much to produce a new barrel of oil from the North Sea as it does to produce one in Saudi Arabia). According to some estimates, the investment required to develop new supplies might cost about $800 billion in the eighties alone. Something like $15 billion a year in developing countries would be required. The World Bank is hoping that its proposed energy affiliate, if established, will spend about $25 billion over five years.[13] This would help at least to identify favourable deposits which could then be subject to commercial exploitation.

It is unlikely that the development of new sources would be undertaken on the scale and at the speed required without the participation of major companies, which at present control most of the available technology, staff and equipment. But many poor countries at present feel understandable hesitation about making themselves too dependent on such companies for the development of their precious natural resources. There is thus a case for the establishment of a new organisation that would supply funds to third-world countries to enable them to engage the necessary experts, or even hire the companies, under service contracts, to locate the oil and establish the necessary wells, storage and other infrastructure. Such an organisation might also help poor countries acquire the expertise to formulate energy programmes, to organise their own exploration programme and eventually to participate in production, refining and marketing. The interposition of an impersonal agency of this kind might help to depoliticise the relationship between the host countries and the companies, and to reduce the mutual suspicion which at present deters mutual involvement.[14]

A rational international strategy would be concerned not only with the development of conventional oil supplies. At current prices non-conventional sources of oil could begin to be economic: for example, the large deposits of shale oil available in the United States, which are expected to produce significant quantities of oil before the end of the decade; the tar sands of Canada; and the production of oil from coal, for which the techniques have been known for years and which could now become more economic. The use of ethyl alcohol (ethanol), produced from sugar and other products, as an additive to petrol or even as the sole source of power in motor-cars, already widely used in the United States and Brazil,[15] could be far more generally adopted to reduce import costs. And there will be increasing attention to alternative energy sources altogether. The development of a battery car which does not need to be too frequently recharged now appears a feasible objective. Above all, the so-called renewable sources of energy, those that do not involve the depletion of scarce natural resources, such as power from the sun, wind and waves, or nuclear fusion power, become, with every new increase in the price of oil, increasingly attractive alternatives on which much much more research expenditure should be undertaken. An international energy agency could help stimulate co-operative research projects in this field.

Equally important in any rational oil strategy is the encouragement of the most efficient use of the supplies that are available. At present there are huge variations in levels of oil consumption, even among countries at similar stages of economic development. Consumption a head is, for example, about one-third higher in the United States than in most other countries at the same level of development. This results partly from heavy use of energy for air conditioning and central heating, and partly from the failure of US governments for years after the increase in price of 1973–4 to expose US consumers to higher energy prices. Over the long term, higher prices will be the main factor in promoting greater conservation. But an important part can also be played by appropriate government policies on power generation, building regulations, insulation programmes, regulations on maximum petrol consumption of cars, and similar measures. Among the industrialised countries, the IEA has attempted to promote such policies and established successive targets for energy saving which have had some effect. But, as the energy consumption of developing countries increases as a proportion of the total, effective conservation policies may increasingly need to be established and implemented at a global level.

But an international oil policy would need to be concerned above all about questions of price. The oil-producing countries have continuously asserted that such matters cannot be the subject of international discussion. It is on these grounds that they have strenuously refused to consider the creation of any international body with responsibility in the energy sphere, however limited or carefully defined its powers. Oil companies too, which have benefited so much by the present pricing system, are probably almost equally reluctant to see such matters become the subject of international discussion. No new system of regulation will be able to operate against fundamental economic forces; nor is it necessarily desirable that it should do so. But prices are not now determined by normal commercial factors. They are determined mainly by the decisions of a small group of governments, each with a very strong vested interest, acting alone. There is clearly a need for the representatives of consumer governments to have the opportunity (as under commodity schemes) to influence such decisions. Regular discussions in the appropriate body could help reconcile conflicting interests on such matters. And it should make it possible at least to avoid too sudden lurches in the oil market, to safeguard security of supplies, and so to maintain greater stability in the world economy as a whole, frequently rocked in recent years by the movement of oil prices, to the benefit of producers and consumers alike.[16]

A new agency with special responsibility for energy matters should be able to keep a continuing watch on the trends in supply and demand, on the level of stocks and on arrangements to cope with emergency interruptions of supply. It could consider the volume of investment in new production and the long-term supply situation. In this way it should prevent a situation in which prices were established on the basis of a short-term imbalance in supply and demand, arising from crisis situations, as has happened over the last decade. Before each round of negotiations on price, it could seek to assess and to publicise the likely effects on the world economy, and especially on the economies of very poor countries, of a particular level of prices. It could estimate the balance of payments deficits and surpluses which would flow from proposed price increases, the effect on world rates of inflation and the ultimate consequence in restricting world growth. Finally, it could seek to estimate the future energy requirements of the world economy as a whole, the level of available energy reserves and the amount of investment in new sources which might therefore be required to sustain the international economy in the future.

For years, individual governments have exercised a general overview of the energy needs of their own economies, and sought to regulate or influence the availability of energy supplies in consequence. Today the world as a whole is as small as were many nations only a few decades ago. The international economy is now therefore sufficiently integrated to require, at the international level too, some effort to establish an energy policy for the world as a whole.

7 Food

7.1 THE PRESSURE OF POPULATION ON FOOD SUPPLIES

Until recently there was no world food problem. There were food problems for individual villages; more often for whole districts, suffering from flood or drought; occasionally for entire countries. But for most of the time most nations were able to meet their own essential food needs. Trade in food was mainly in luxuries: such as spices, sugar, tea and coffee. Even where trade in essential foodstuffs developed – as in the grain trade from the Baltic to Western Europe, or from south-west China to the east coast – it was relatively marginal in relation to the needs of the receiving areas. Because populations were only a fraction of their levels today, most countries, even with very low yields for each acre sown, were able to feed most of their population most of the time.

It was only during the nineteenth century that trade in food began to be more significant. The development of large-scale and efficient grain production in North America and meat production in Argentina, together with the advent of steamships and refrigeration, brought about a substantial trade in food from the Americas to Europe. In Asia the prosperous rice-bowl of South-East Asia began to be a substantial exporter of grain to other parts of the area. So, for the first time, a few countries became permanently dependent on imports for part of their food needs. Britain, in particular, adopted from the 1870s a deliberate cheap-food policy, relying on substantial imports, and allowed her own agriculture to decline in consequence.

The First World War revealed the strategic disadvantages of dependence on external food supplies. There was some attempt to revert to self-sufficiency. Some countries in Europe prohibited the export of food altogether. Even Britain took a few steps to revive her agricultural industry. With reduced demand, world trade in food declined significantly during the depression, and commodity producers, dependent on the export of foodstuffs, found world prices too low to yield them a living. In 1939 only Western Europe was to some extent dependent on imports from elsewhere, mainly from North America. Every other continent was either self-sufficient or a net exporter of food.

In the 35 years after the Second World War this situation was transformed. By 1980 most continents of the world were net food importers, often on a large scale. Europe, West and East alike, the Middle East, Africa, Asia and Latin America now all depended on imports for a significant proportion of their food needs. Only North America and Australasia were self-sufficient.

This change had come about with dramatic speed. In the early 1950s, imports of food to Asia, Africa, Latin America and the Middle East, where most of the world's population lies, was still insignificant. Most individual countries in each of those regions were able to feed their own populations. By 1960 imports to those four developing regions had already reached 20 million tons a year. By 1970 their average imports were just over 30 million tons a year. By 1980 they were about 80 million. On current trends, it was estimated, their total imports could be 150 million tons by 1990.

The surplus countries remained highly concentrated. By 1980 a great part of the food needs of the rest of the world were met from a single source, the grain belt of North America. 70 per cent of the grains entering into international trade came from the United States and Canada, and much of the rest from Australasia. This unbalanced situation could not continue. Even if production in those areas could go on increasing in line with the rapidly growing needs of other parts of the world (which was not unlikely), many of the deficit countries would not have been able to pay for the imports. If world needs were to be met, it was generally recognised, it must be mainly by increasing productivity and production in the importing countries. This meant mainly in poor countries where yields were low and where there was therefore greater room for improvement.

In fact the crisis in world food supplies had not come about because of an overall decline in food production in any part of the world. On the contrary, production had increased everywhere. Even in developing countries, though agricultural productivity often remained low, total production, partly because of extensions in the cultivated areas but mainly because of improvements in techniques, was increasing by nearly 3 per cent a year. The growth in production a head varied from 4–5 per cent in the most successful (Brazil, South Korea and the Philippines, for example) to 1 per cent or less per year in other cases (especially in Africa). In a few cases (as in Ghana, Togo, Morocco and Cuba) there was an absolute drop in production during the course of the seventies.

But during the same period population was increasing in those countries at about the same rates as elsewhere. Potential demand for food, because of an increase in the proportion of young people in the population and some improvements in levels of nutrition, was increasing still faster than population.

But the real problem concerned distribution, both between countries and within them. The averages, both for population growth and for growth in agricultural production, concealed huge variations. Some developing countries were self-sufficient in food and a few were net exporters. Others had raised production by 5 per cent or more a year. But in others, including the poorest countries of all (where the growth in population was often highest), the growth in production was only about 1 per cent a year. It was here that agricultural productivity was lowest. Yet it was these countries that could least afford to buy food from elsewhere. So the growth of production was slowest where the needs were greatest.

If the world was to avoid food shortages, therefore, either there had to be a decline in the rate of growth of population; or there had to be a rapid increase in the rate of food production, especially in the poorest countries, where the shortfall was greatest.

Let us look, first, at the essential facts about population growth. It is easy to forget how recent, and how phenomenally rapid, has been the increase in world population over the last century. Figure 7.1 makes dramatically real the size and speed of the increase. This is not merely the effect of compound growth from a relatively small base. It has come about above all because of better health facilities, leading to lower death rates. Over the last 25 years, death rates in developing countries have declined from 25 per thousand to 12 per thousand. Expectations of life at birth have risen in many of them from under 30 to 50 years (against 70 in rich countries). It is this development, more than any increase in birth rates, or changes in agricultural production, which has affected the growth of population and in the adequacy of food supplies.

As a result the rate of world population increase has risen sharply over the last two centuries: from about 0.4 per cent in the eighteenth century to 0.5 per cent in the nineteenth, 1 per cent from 1920 to 1950, 1.8 per cent in the fifties, and 2 per cent in the sixties. Since 1970 there appears to have been a slight decline and the rate of increase is now estimated to be about 1.8 per cent. Since death rates will not go up, and will probably come down still further, it is only a decline in rates of birth that can reduce the levels of population in the future.

There is little doubt that such a reduction in birth rates will occur. The

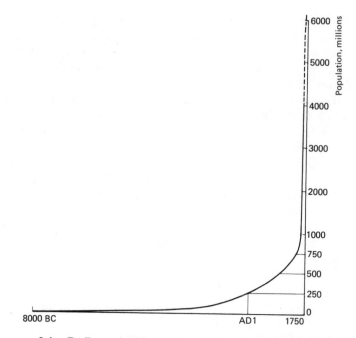

SOURCE John D. Durand, 'The Modern Expansion of World Population', *Proceedings of the American Philosophical Society*, vol. 3, no. 3 (1967) p. 139.

FIGURE 7.1   *Growth of world population, 8000 BC – AD 2000*

probable trend can to some extent be extrapolated from developments within advanced countries. In those countries, from a century or so ago, a large decline in death rates took place as medical standards improved. This occurred over a longer period, and to a lower level, than has yet occurred in most poor countries: so that today death rates are at a level of about 10 per thousand or a little less. This reduction in death rates was accompanied by an even more dramatic decline in birth rates, also over a longer period and to a lower level. These began to go down in most Western countries during the nineteenth century. After the turn of the century, as living standards improved, they fell further: from 35 per thousand in 1900 to under 30 by 1910 and below 20 between the wars. After the Second World War there was some increase everywhere, followed by a subsequent, though somewhat erratic, decline: to levels around or a little above 20. In most rich countries today, therefore, there is either no increase in population at all; or a situation in which population should stabilise once the current generation of children and young people, born at a time of higher birth rate, have ceased to be of child-bearing age.

There is good reason to hope that among poor countries too a similar reduction in birth rates will occur as standards of living rise. The crucial question concerns the speed at which this will happen. It is already certain that the world's population will rise from about 4 billion today to about 6 billion by the end of the century (see Fig. 7.2). This will occur even if the birth rate continues to drop significantly, since those who will become parents within the next twenty years are already born. But, if the world population were to grow thereafter at 2 per cent annually, it would still grow to 15 billion by 2050, nearly four times the present level. If it grew at 1 per cent the population would be only 10 billion in 2050. The precise level of birth rate in coming decades is therefore crucial in determining whether reasonable living standards are to be provided for future generations.

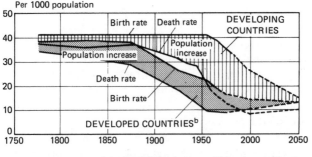

Rate of population increase = birth rate − death rate

[a] Crude birth and death rates. The projected increases in death rates after about 1980 reflect the rising proportion of older people in the population.
[b] Include industrialised countries, the USSR and Eastern Europe.

SOURCE   World Bank, *World Development Report, 1980*, p. 64.

FIGURE 7.2   *Trends in birth and death rates, 1775–2050 (births and deaths per 1000 population)* [a]

There are a number of factors which may encourage a decline in birth rate over the coming years. First, a reduction in rates has already taken place in a number of developing countries. Such a reduction normally results automatically from higher living standards: perhaps because of later ages of marriage, greater knowledge of the possibility and advantages of small family size, more knowledge and advice about contraception, higher educational standards especially among women, easier abortion and, possibly, lower fertility. This has already occurred in, for example, Sri Lanka, Colombia, Singapore, Taiwan and Hong Kong (though in a few cases birth rates have remained very high *despite* higher living standards – for example, in Mexico, Libya and Kenya). In other cases, considerable reductions have come about, usually through intensive population programmes, even where living standards remain low: for example, in Indonesia. Secondly, the religious objections which have traditionally deterred both populations and their governments from the use of modern birth-control methods have proved much less significant in recent years: even in some Catholic and Muslim countries governments have introduced extensive family-planning campaigns, which have sometimes had dramatic results (in Colombia and Costa Rica among Catholic countries, for example, and Indonesia among Muslim countries). Thirdly, there exists an increasing range of international assistance programmes, both multilateral and bilateral, to assist local governments in implementing population policies: including the UN Fund for Population Activities and the large US programme. Fourthly, there is now a real hope that new, simple and relatively cheap methods of contraception may shortly be widely available which will make such programmes increasingly attractive and practicable for many poor countries. It is the *desire* to limit family size which is essential in reducing population growth; but help in making it easier to do so, once desired, assists the process.

It still remains to be seen, however, whether these factors will bring birth rates down within the time available, or in the places where it is most needed. By early in the next century, many developing countries may be approaching the living standards already achieved in rich countries today. Levels of food consumption per person are certain to increase. Even where birth rates go down, therefore, pressures on food supplies will be great. But in the poorest countries where food needs are greatest the birth rates will remain highest. Thus it may not be sufficient that birth rates continue to decline at present rates. A more drastic international effort to promote family limitation may be required.

7.2   THE CURRENT WORLD FOOD SITUATION

Whatever success this may achieve, however, it will need to be accompanied by a new attempt to increase world food supplies. World population, as we have seen, will increase by a half in the next 20 years, regardless of any reduction in birth rates. And because of the large numbers who will come into the world in that time (at least a third of the world's population will be under twenty in the year 2000) the population will probably increase by 50 per cent again within the following 25 years or so. Yet today a population little more than half what will then exist is already not properly fed.

The number of people who literally die of starvation in any one year is normally relatively small. The consequence of inadequate food is that enormous numbers of people in the world – perhaps hundreds of millions – suffer from such severe malnutrition that they will die in consequence: because they are far more vulnerable to many diseases – including simple diarrhoea and dysentery – as a result. Every year millions of people become blind because of deficiencies of vitamin A. About 20 million children die each year before the age of five, partly at least because of inadequate diet. More food is needed, therefore, not only to feed very many more mouths than exist today, but also to ensure that many others secure for the first time a more adequate diet than they now have.

For this reason world agricultural production will need almost to double in the next twenty years. It is generally agreed that there are no technical reasons why this should not be attained. Yields in many parts of the world are so low that they could be increased several times (as was achieved, for example, by Japan in a relatively short period) if new techniques and greater inputs were applied. The current aim of the FAO is to increase food production by 4 per cent a year from 1980, which would roughly double the amount produced by 2000.

That aim, however, is far from being achieved at present. During the sixties the increase in food production in developing countries was about 2.9 per cent a year and the figure during the seventies was barely more (see Table 7.1). But these averages are very misleading. Some developing countries have secured increases in food production far above the average: for example, South Korea, Brazil and the Philippines. For many others the increase is much lower. The increase in food production in the low-income countries declined from 2.5 per cent in the sixties to 2 per cent in the seventies. This meant that food production a head declined by 0.4 per cent a year in those countries. In parts of sub-Saharan Africa the situation was even worse: there food production a head dropped by nearly 10 per cent during the seventies. Only imports on an increasing scale have prevented mass starvation. And they are imports that such countries are increasingly unable to afford.

TABLE 7.1   *Average annual percentage changes in food production (crops and livestock) and in food production a head between 1971 and 1980*

	Food production 1971–80	Per capita Food production a head 1971–80
Developing market economies	3.2	0.5
Africa	1.8	− 1.1
Far East and Southern Asia	3.2	0.7
Latin America	3.9	1.2
Near East	3.3	0.5
Developed market economies	2.3	(1.6)
World	2.5	(0.7)

SOURCE   OECD, *Development Cooperation, 1981*, p. 140; drawing on Council of the FAO, *The Present World Food Situation*, 79th Session, Rome, 22 June – 3 July 1981, CL 79/2 (except for the figures in parentheses, which are estimates).

Thus it is not sufficient to increase *world* food production. A further rise in agricultural production in rich countries – even if this could be achieved, which is by no means certain given the high rate of productivity already attained there[1] – would only intensify the imbalance in supplies which already exists. There would be large surpluses in advanced countries which do not need them, and large deficits where the need is greatest.

Most poor countries will remain without the foreign exchange to import food on any significant scale. The continued use of 'food aid', the giving of food by rich countries to poor, can overcome this problem. But it creates others almost equally serious. Its effect depends crucially on the way the food is distributed. Without adequate supervision it often never reaches those most in need. It can adversely affect food production by lowering food prices. And it leaves poor countries dependent on a form of charity. Food aid, though still necessary at present, can therefore never be more than a short-term solution.

The only long-term answer is a substantial increase in the production of food within developing countries, especially within the poorest countries of all, where the food deficit is greatest.

What would need to be done to accomplish that objective? Though there is little doubt that it is technically possible, there are many problems on the way. Some of the essential preconditions for increasing agricultural productivity are fairly well known, even if not easy to fulfil.

One essential need is the creation of a working market for food products within each country. Above all, an adequate price level for food is required. At present in many poor countries the main objective of governments is to keep prices down. This is partly to restrain inflation generally. But its aim is above all to reduce the cost of living for the populations of the towns. Since their goodwill is often essential to a government's survival, these urban populations are vitally important politically. To keep prices down, governments create monopoly purchasing agencies, impose strict price controls, or introduce consumer subsidies. But the effect of low prices is that farmers decide to hoard their produce; to smuggle it abroad; or make little effort to increase production which is so poorly rewarded. So the effect of the policy is to reduce the general availability of food.

Creating an effective market does not depend only on adequate price levels. It demands, secondly, good communications: adequate roads and vehicles to enable farmers to get their products easily to market (and to enable purchasers to travel there). It demands good storage facilities. It demands the availability of attractive consumer goods which farmers will wish to buy in exchange for their products: without these the farmer has no incentive to produce more and sell more. It demands a wider trading network, so that merchants and wholesalers come from further afield to buy produce for sale in the towns; the market can thus be broadened beyond the immediate production area (where most potential purchasers anyway produce the same crops). Finally it requires, in some cases at least, adequate outlets to international markets beyond the borders.

Thirdly, an effective market requires that sufficient purchasing power be available among those needing food. The *need* for food will not create a market without ability to *purchase*. The more unequal the distribution of income, the weaker is the market for food. Higher purchasing power in the hands of a small wealthy elite may increase demand for certain factors of production *used* in agriculture, including land, water and labour (and so raise their price); but, since the amount of food that any one family requires does not vary greatly, it will not increase the demand or price of food itself. The surest way to increase effective demand for food products (and so raise prices), therefore, is to bring about a more equal distribution of purchasing power among the population as a whole. It must therefore be a major aim, both of national governments and of international organisations seeking higher food production, to bring about more equal purchasing power.

Fourthly, inequality among producers too may deter higher production. Land and water, for example, the two essentials of production, are often unequally shared, so that the maximum use is not made of either. A more equal distribution by allowing a more intensive system of cultivation, will nearly always raise production. Though this is not always so, at least in the the short term, for plantation and other cash crops, it is production of food which is mainly required in most developing countries today. Thus an essential precondition for growing more food and especially of more food consumption, is often land reform, leading to a more equal distribution of land, water and other inputs, and so to a more intensive cultivation.

Fifthly, improvements in techniques are required. Even if effective *demand* for food is raised, production cannot always immediately be increased enough to meet it. Agricultural producers are often deeply conservative in their ways. They may be reluctant to abandon traditional techniques or systems of social organisation. They may be inclined to prefer the safety of familiar subsistence farming to the unstable prices and other uncertainties of production for markets. Social structures and systems of land tenure may discourage innovation and enterprise. Traditional methods of storage may lead to large crop losses, yet are expensive to replace. Credit facilities, which production for the market usually makes essential, may be lacking or expensive; and, even if available, they may more easily be obtained by the richer farmers who need them least than by the poorer who require them most. Only considerable education and training through extension services can overcome these problems.[2]

Sixthly, improved production requires that many governments give more attention to agriculture. Since industrial development has been seen as synonymous with modernisation, liberation from traditional activities, and reduced dependence on Western countries, governments in poor countries have been concerned above all to develop industry. Available investment funds, development aid, administrative and managerial talent, energy and skills, have therefore been channelled more to that task than to the slow, tedious and unexciting work of raising agricultural productivity in the villages. In some countries today, agriculture still takes under a fifth of development funds, even though most of the populations are engaged in it. Though most poor countries are now increasingly aware of the need to develop their agriculture, they are sometimes reluctant to take the necessary steps – such as the raising of agricultural prices – which may be the essential precondition for increasing production.

It is not only national governments, however, that need to give increased attention to the problem, but international institutions as well. Any significant increase in food production in poor countries depends on a very high level of investment. In most such countries, though substantial new areas have been brought under cultivation in the last 20 years, the uncultivated land that remains is mostly of marginal quality and cannot be expected to produce high yields. Increases in production today, therefore, depend mainly on increasing yields on land already cultivated. This can only be brought about through better water control and irrigation, increased use of fertilisers[3] and pesticides, better rural communications and electrification (see Table 7.2). All of these require large investment funds. On some estimates, to achieve a 4 per cent increase in food production a year (the FAO target) in developing countries, more than double the present investment – which is nearly $5 billion a year – would be needed. Moreover, the costs of such investment increase all the time: nearly all the inputs required – in fertilisers, pesticides, irrigation, storage and communications – are energy-intensive; and energy costs may still continue to increase rapidly in the years to come. Only international assistance on a scale far larger than is provided today could bring the improvement required.

There are other problems, of a social character. The most dramatic increase in food production over recent years has resulted from the use of new high-yield varieties of wheat and rice in conjunction with large quantities of fertiliser and improved irrigation: the so-called 'green revolution'. This has brought dramatic increases in food production. India, for example, has been transformed in a few years from being a major importer of food to being a marginal exporter today. But this has been achieved at heavy cost: it has increased substantially the numbers

TABLE 7.2 *Consumption of fertilisers per hectare of permanent cropland (kilograms)*

	1961–5	1975
Developing countries	5.7	19.6
Africa	1.7	5.6
Latin America	10.6	31.9
Near East	6.6	24.7
Far East	5.7	21.2
Developed countries	66.9	100.4

SOURCE FAO, *Annual Fertiliser Reviews.*

of landless and workless labourers in the countryside, and may have increased the numbers without food. Though this is not an inevitable effect of the 'green revolution' – in South Korea rapid increases in productivity have been obtained without much affecting the system of small peasant proprietorship – it is a result which frequently occurs in practice. Poor countries may therefore believe themselves faced with the unhappy choice between tolerating stagnant food production and facing mounting social inequalities in the countryside.

Only an international effort on a substantial scale, therefore, is likely to overcome the difficulties which these countries are experiencing and bring about a more balanced pattern of agricultural development throughout the world. The problem is how this international effort should be organised.

7.3 INTERNATIONAL AGRICULTURAL INSTITUTIONS

From the time of the Second World War it had been recognised that it was no longer enough for food questions to be considered only by individual national governments acting in isolation. A measure of international responsibility had to be taken. Some international body was required which could keep the world food situation under review and stimulate the necessary action to improve it. Gradually over the years thereafter there emerged a proliferation of international bodies and activities related to food and agriculture, a system more complex and profuse than exists in any other area.

The first body to be created was the Food and Agriculture Organisation (FAO). This was set up at the end of the war as one of the United Nations' specialised agencies: part of the UN family but autonomous and outside the control of the United Nations itself. It was supposed to be concerned with improving the production and distribution of food, as well as other agricultural products; with fisheries and forestry; with levels of nutrition; and with providing assistance to governments in all of these areas. It quickly became one of the largest of the UN specialised agencies. It was also (in the view of many) one of the most bureaucratic and ineffective. It has made some effort in recent years to decentralise its activities and relate its work more directly to the key task of raising agricultural production in poor countries. But it continues to be heavily engaged in the compilation of statistics, the organisation of conferences and meetings, and the co-ordination of many small programmes, which occupy much of its time and energies.

And four-fifths of its staff continue to be based at its headquarters in Rome.

Today the FAO has 140-odd members and is active in almost every country of the world. It now spends over $300 million a year. A third of this comes from its regular budget: while much of this goes to finance activities at headquarters, a quarter goes on assistance work. The rest is financed mainly from voluntary programmes, especially the UNDP, and these sums are almost entirely spent on aid to poor countries in the field.

The FAO has a wide range of activities which are designed to assist governments in the task of increasing agricultural production. Its Investment Centre assists poor countries in preparing development projects in the agricultural field: for example, in land reclamation, irrigation work, roads and bridges, water supply or plantations (such projects may later be executed by the FAO with funds provided by the UNDP or the World Bank). It runs an International Fertiliser Supply programme under which fertilisers given by donor governments are supplied to the governments of poor countries at reasonable prices. It helps with the vaccination of livestock against foot and mouth disease, pest control, soil management and conservation. It runs a global information and early-warning system to give advance warning of impending food disasters and take the necessary precautions. The Organisation also provides credit facilities and extension services (partly from the profits of sales of the donated fertilisers). To help prevent the large losses of food which result from bad storage facilities, leading to deterioration and destruction by rats, it runs an Action Programme for the Prevention of Food Losses, to provide advice and assistance on storage. It gives considerable help for forestry work, and with the construction of related projects such as sawmills. It organises and services the main fisheries commissions, which are responsible for the management and conservation of fish stocks in different parts of the world. It finances research into the development of new seeds and livestock. And it provides poor countries with advice and training on nutritional questions.

But these efforts had only a marginal impact on the agricultural situation within poor countries, and by the early sixties many had begun to import food on an increasing scale. Because of the heavy balance of payments costs of this, there was a desire to establish an international programme of donated food. A considerable amount of food aid was already being provided bilaterally, especially through the US PL 480 programme. In 1963 the United Nations' World Food Programme was established. Donor countries pledged themselves every two years to provide a certain amount in food or in services (such as shipping space). The food is used to help with emergency relief in areas of famine; for refugees; for especially vulnerable groups such as children, pregnant women and nursing mothers; and especially for food-for-work programmes (under which food is provided for workers engaged on construction programmes). In 1967 this programme was supplemented by the Food Aid Convention, since several times renewed. Under this, donor countries commit themselves to provide a certain amount of food aid, through either bilateral or multilateral programmes: the amount committed under the latest convention is 7.6 million tons, still substantially below the target figure of 10 million tons.

Such programmes dealt with the *consequences* of food shortages. They did nothing to prevent their occurring in the first place. The major food crisis of 1973–4 induced a widespread concern to improve international efforts to raise production. As a result the World Food Conference was called in Rome in 1974 to consider what new arrangements should be made to prevent such a disaster recurring. The first and most important objective, it was agreed, must be to provide more assistance to poor countries to help them to raise the level of their own food *production*, so that they became less dependent on supplies from outside. The second aim must be to improve food *security* by creating an international reserve that could be called on in an emergency and by increasing the volume of food aid.

To help achieve these two objectives, the Conference created new institutions. The first was the World Food Council, a body of 36 nations representing a cross-section of the world community. It had no executive functions and no funds to organise development work. But it was to meet regularly to keep the world food situation under review and to make recommendations to governments. It was to be independent of the FAO (it reports to the General Assembly through Ecosoc and its Executive Director is appointed by the UN Secretary-General). But it is based in Rome, like the FAO and other food organisations, and seeks to work with them. It monitors the food security situation, the level of food aid and the progress made in establishing an emergency grain reserve. It has set as its overall aim, like the FAO, an increase of food production in poor countries of 4 per cent a year. It identifies 'food priority' countries which most heed help in increasing food production. And it has been above all concerned to persuade individual developing countries to give greater priority to agriculture and to adopt 'food strategies', covering the production, storage, marketing and distribution of food.

At the same time it was decided to set up a new International Fund for Agricultural Development (IFAD) to undertake practical assistance work. This was to finance assistance to very poor countries to develop their agriculture and so help to ensure that a larger proportion of total development assistance went to agriculture (previously the proportion of aid going for that purpose was only 5 per cent). The Fund finally came into existence in 1977, with a budget of $1 billion for the first three years.[4] Three-fifths of this money was provided by developed Western countries (no communist nations have joined), a quarter by oil-producing countries and a small amount by other developing countries. Control of the Fund is shared, in equal parts, by these three groups. It provides assistance primarily to the least developed countries. Most of its loans are highly concessional: that is, they carry a rate of interest of only 1 per cent. Of the rest, most are 'intermediate' in that they carry an interest rate of 4 per cent. So far virtually no loans have been made at market rates of interest. Most of IFAD's projects are designed especially to help small farmers and the rural poor. It also provides funds for agricultural research within developing regions. Some of its projects are cofinanced with, for example, the World Bank, regional banks, the OPEC fund and the EEC. IFAD is now constituted as a specialised agency: that is, it has a status equal to and separate from that of FAO.

A third new initiative resulted from the Rome Conference. Concerned to prevent a recurrence of the acute shortages which had occurred in 1973, the Conference wanted to see the creation of an adequate world food reserve which could be called on to meet shortages in an emergency. It therefore decided to set up an International Emergency Food Reserve. Producer countries would contribute stocks which would be held, and rotated where necessary, to be available in emergency situations. In 1975 the UN General Assembly approved this proposal. The FAO therefore prepared an international undertaking on world food security and the Reserve was formally established in the following year. Donors agreed to contribute to the stock when able to do so. By 1980, however, contributions had only risen to about 350,000 tons out of the 500,000 tons originally called for. Even the latter figure is considered by many experts to be inadequate, and the FAO has calculated that emergency needs, due to crop failure, average over 2 million tons a year. The state of the food reserve is considered on a continuing basis by the FAO Committee on World Food Security.[5]

There are other bodies which have some responsibility in this area. The International Wheat Council supervises commodity arrangements for wheat, of which there have been a number during the post-war period. These are designed to preserve reasonable stability of prices for producers and consumers alike. For much of this time, however, neither the United States, the chief producer, nor Britain, one of the chief consumers, has participated in such schemes. At present there is no scheme governing wheat prices, though there are arrangements for regular consultation. Recently there have been attempts to negotiate a wider 'international grains arrangement'. This would include a wheat trade convention to stabilise wheat prices, with national stocks under international supervision, and would increase the availability of grains for the emergency reserve. The negotiations have, however, been stalled for several years on the question of who would pay for grain purchases and storage facilities in developing countries. The latter would probably need to hold 5–7 million tons out of a total reserve of 20–30 million tons. The total cost of this is estimated at nearly $2 billion. Rich countries have agreed that a study should be undertaken to examine the storage needs in each developing country and to make recommendations to donor governments and to international organisations. But poor countries have called for a clear commitment from the rich states that they will bear the full cost.

This is by no means a complete account of all the international bodies concerned with food questions at the present time. It does give some idea, however, of the extent and complexity of the existing institutional structure. This has grown *ad hoc* in response to immediate critical situations. There is inadequate co-ordination at present of the activities of the various bodies involved. If world hunger is to be reduced, there may be need for a better system for supervising and improving world food production and distribution than exists today.

7.4 THE MANAGEMENT OF WORLD FOOD SUPPLIES

During the seventies the world food situation grew worse. Though production increased, large numbers remained hungry. Mass starvation occurred with increasing frequency: for example, in the Sahel, in Cambodia, in East Africa. Elsewhere hundreds of millions were severely malnourished. At the end of the decade the world had a smaller margin of reserves than at any time since the famine of 1973. Only a much better management of world food supplies could bring this situation under control.

The main problem was one not of production but of distribution. Enough food was produced in the world easily to feed the whole of its population. But it was produced in the wrong places. Some countries produced far more food than they needed and others far less; and the latter could not afford to buy the surplus of the former. More fundamental was the maldistribution of purchasing power: within nations as much as between them. This had the effect that hundreds of millions of people were unable to purchase food even when it was available; and so, still more disastrously, could not create the demand that might make it more available at lower prices in the future.

There are thus two essential conditions for raising food production within poor countries. First, there is need for a more equal distribution of purchasing power. Here, above all, a distributionist strategy is required: on grounds of equity and efficiency alike. It will help many who at present go hungry to purchase food, and so prevent the situation which exists today (for example, in Southern Asia) where there is an overall surplus of food but very many have not enough to eat.[6] It will also make it easier, by increasing effective demand for food, to meet the second condition. This is that food prices are sustained at a level which encourages higher production.

Perhaps the most important way in which international bodies can promote production, therefore, is by seeking to ensure that these conditions are met. They can direct their own assistance to the poorer peasants, most lacking in techniques or access to resources. They can use their influence with governments to ensure that they direct their policy to making and, water and fertiliser more equally available and raising incomes among the landless labourers. In this way they may make it easier to ensure the other condition is met: the raising of agricultural prices. Aid donors already sometimes use their influence to persuade receiving governments to raise food prices. The influence of international organisations on such questions could be greater. The example of those countries which have secured higher production with higher prices – South Korea, Thailand, Ivory Coast – can be used to encourage imitation.

Inequalities in purchasing power occur not only between classes but also between one region and another. In many poor countries rural poverty occurs above all in particular areas: often those which are geographically disadvantaged in terms of quality of soil, communications, resources, water availability and geographical remoteness, or are neglected for political or other reasons. The provision of roads and other infrastructure in remote areas is often especially expensive. Even if they wish to provide them, it may be beyond the means of the local administrations. Here too, international bodies may be able to ensure that the assistance they provide is used to overcome the special disadvantages of such areas. Regional funds may be well equipped to bring about redistribution from the more favoured to the less favoured areas within the whole region.[7]

It is equally important for international bodies to ensure that the needs of agriculture receive adequate attention in each country's development policy. International institutions and bilateral donors now usually recognise the need to devote more resources to agriculture. Total agricultural aid has increased from about $2.5 billion in 1974 to over $5 billion at the end of the decade.[8] The governments of poor countries too have begun to increase the proportion of their development funds allocated to agriculture. But that shift in emphasis needs to go much further. The total sums available at present are still only a fraction of what is needed for improving food production. According to one calculation, the total investment funds, from all sources, would need to be more than doubled to enable poor countries to approach the target of a 4 per cent a year increase in production which has been set internationally.[9]

If new assistance on this scale can be found, much will no doubt be channelled through the World Bank and, to a smaller extent, the FAO. But it is to be hoped that a substantial proportion will be given to IFAD. That fund gives the kind of aid that is most needed: help to raise food production within the poorest countries of all and among the poorer sections of the agricultural population, where the need for improvements is most urgent. At present the scale of its operations is much too small to have any significant effect. It is thus important that its funds should be enlarged (the latest replenishment barely increased its resources in real terms).

Another aim of international management in this field must be to ensure that adequate *research* effort is focused on the special agricultural problems of developing countries. The total volume of research devoted to agricultural questions has increased many times over the last two or three decades. But the great majority of this is undertaken within rich countries: to resolve the problems that are met by agricultural producers within those countries. The production of new high-yield strains of wheat and rice over recent years has shown the spectacular effects which can result from even modest research efforts devoted to the problems of agriculture in poor countries. That effort needs, however, to be multiplied many times if a more significant impact is to be made on food production in the third world. Most of the increase over the coming years will have to be through improving yields on land which is already cultivated. This makes it the more necessary to increase research on better strains and better techniques. One way to do this would be providing more support for the Consultative International Group on Agricultural Research, which supports and co-ordinates research in a number of centres throughout the third world.

Since it will take time to increase production in poor countries significantly, it remains urgently necessary, meanwhile, to create an international emergency reserve. Adequate emergency supplies cannot only prevent starvation in the worst deficit areas. They also relieve pressure on prices at times of shortage, and so can eliminate the huge price increases which occurred in 1973–4 with disastrous results. To work effectively, however, a substantial part of the reserve needs to be situated close to the areas where the shortages arise. To depend on emergency relief being flown in from great distances after mass starvation has already begun (as has been necessary in recent years) is the worst of all options: it may lead to the loss of hundreds of thousands of lives and involves the highest possible cost in transporting the food. Storage capacity thus needs to be built in the areas of shortage and a part of the grain surplus grown elsewhere transferred there (perhaps through the World Food Programme or bilateral food-aid programmes). If this requires the rich countries to undertake most of the financial responsibility for purchasing the grain (or providing it in food aid) and building the storage capacity (or allowing the IMF to lend for that purpose) many would feel this was a cost worth undertaking if the result were to reduce significantly the risks of famine in the future. If the task cannot be undertaken on a fully international basis, there is still a good case for the creation of regional food banks, of the kind that the Economic and Social Commission for Asia and the Pacific (ESCAP) is now considering for Asia.

Even if major emergencies are met in this way, it seems likely that for some years to come additional programmes of food aid for deficit countries will be required. It is essential that far better supervision of such programmes is undertaken than in the past. This could reduce the known defects of such programmes: that they can lower prices and so reduce local production; that they may not always reach the poorest sections of the population most in need of help; and that they can be used corruptly or for political ends. The depression of prices can be avoided if food aid is sold only in the deficit areas where acute shortages exist, and only in amounts that will sustain the price in the market. Distribution to those most in need can be ensured if those who provide the aid insist on the necessary arrangements to that end. And corruption can be prevented if the donating agency, preferably an international institution, exercises effective control of the distribution of food aid right to the point of final purchase (at present the food is usually handed over to the receiving government to distribute).

If these aims are to be achieved there may be need for a reform of the various international agencies concerned with food. At present there is some overlap and confusion among them.[10] Possibly the simplest solution would be to accord much greater authority to the World Food Council, so that it was in a position to give direct instructions, or at least very strong recommendations, to the FAO, to IFAD and to the World Food Programme. While these latter organisations would retain operational control in their own fields, overall direction would be placed in the hands of the Council. This would prevent duplication and bring about a greater coherence in food programmes. There are great difficulties in bringing about major institutional changes of this kind in the UN system. But without such a reorganisation it is unlikely that international efforts to meet the world food crisis will be successful.

There are thus two fundamental tasks to be accomplished in this area: to improve the distribution of the basic agricultural inputs – land, water, fertiliser and credit – and above all of the capacity to buy food; and to improve agricultural productivity, and so production, especially in the poorest countries. How far these two aims are realised will depend crucially on a new and more purposeful approach by the international organisations responsible, and a more rational distribution of tasks between those organisations than exists today.

8 Unemployment

8.1 UNEMPLOYMENT IN RICH COUNTRIES

Traditionally unemployment has been regarded as a national rather than an international problem. If it aroused concern at all, it was seen as a matter to be coped with by individual governments. Even this is a fairly recent development, dating back little more than fifty years. Before that, unemployment was seen as an act of God, beyond the control of any human authority.

Governments have been concerned with relieving the *effects* of unemployment for far longer. In England the Elizabethan poor laws were introduced largely to ensure that assistance was provided for the workless; and at the end of the eighteenth century the so-called 'Speenhamland' system in the same country placed on the parishes the responsibility for paying a subsistence income to families without wage-earners – a system much criticised at the time but in fact anticipating (in the provision of a minimum standard of living for all) some features of modern social security.

During the course of the nineteenth century unemployment began to take a more obviously visible form: with a rapid growth in population, accompanied by a large-scale movement from the countryside to the towns. For the first time there came to exist in many industrialising countries a considerable section of the population who not only *lacked* work but actively searched for it. Even then, until the end of the century there existed in most countries no system for registering the unemployed and so measuring their numbers; still less for assisting them to find employment.

Whether or not work could be found depended mainly on the uncertainties of the business cycle. Because hiring and firing were relatively simple, and the needs of business very variable, there was a wide variation in the numbers employed in boom times and in depressions. US unemployment rates varied from about 2 per cent in boom years to 10 per cent or more during the downturns, and reached as high as 28 per cent in 1894. Among European countries, large-scale emigration abroad – over 40 million are estimated to have left Europe, mainly for North America, in little over a century – helped to absorb some who would otherwise have been workless, so that the rates were generally somewhat lower. But neither in North America nor in Europe, still less elsewhere in the world, was there yet any conception of action by governments deliberately designed to reduce levels of unemployment.

The growth of the number without work, and increasing concern about the hardships they suffered, did lead, however, to more systematic measures to mitigate their difficulties. An unemployment insurance scheme, covering workers in a few industries, entitling them to a modest benefit in time of worklessness in return for contributions when at work, was introduced in Britain in 1911. It was eventually widely copied elsewhere. Such schemes certainly reduced the privations experienced by those who took part in them (for long only a part of the working population). But they did not affect, and were not intended to affect, the root causes of joblessness. For these were still generally regarded as beyond the capacity of governments to influence.

Even so, some began to foresee that increasing intervention by governments might be required in the future. The development of the industrial system, and the increasing investment in machinery to which it led, it was suggested, would bring growing unemployment. At the turn of the century such writers as J. A. Hobson in England looked ahead to the type of economic and social policies which would be required to create increased purchasing power and so higher levels of employment when the trade with colonial territories, and the opportunities this provided for European industry, declined, or at least ceased to grow further.

Any crisis that might have emerged, however, as a result of the inadequacies of world demand was postponed by the coming of the First World War. It was not until the emergence of mass unemployment on a huge scale, with the depression of the 1930s, that governments began to think seriously of adopting policies deliberately designed to create jobs. The Swedish government then increased government spending and allowed a large budget deficit for the express purpose of reflating the economy. Nazi Germany and Fascist Italy introduced large-scale public works schemes which (together with rearmament) brought about dramatic reductions in unemployment. Roosevelt's New Deal in the United States (where at one time unemployment had reached 35 per cent of the workforce) for a time reduced the scale of unemployment in that country (though in 1940 the level was again, at 14 per cent, higher than in

1936). The economic rationale of such measures was laid down in Keynes's *General Theory of Unemployment, Interest and Money* in 1936. This suggested that, when an excessive level of savings reduced the level of demand below that required to sustain full employment, only deliberate action by governments, through monetary and fiscal measures to fill the gap, would succeed in lowering unemployment, by restoring equilibrium at a higher level.

For a time the Second World War once again found employment for all. At the end of that war the maintenance of 'full employment' became a major aim of governments. In 1944 the British Government issued a White Paper declaring its determination to pursue policies to that end in the post-war period. In 1946 the US government passed an Employment Act committing it to a similar policy. Everywhere the reduction of unemployment had become a widely declared aim of policy.

Whether or not because of these intentions and the new policies adopted to fulfil them, or because of other factors in the international economy at the time (p. 8 above), unemployment in developed countries was lower during the next 25 years than at any period in modern history. Though there was some fluctuation in rates of growth, levels of unemployment were kept far below those of earlier times. Average rates of unemployment in Western Europe were about 1–3 per cent, and were sometimes even below 1 per cent (for example, in West Germany). In Japan the average was 1 per cent. In North America the recorded figure was 4–5 per cent, but, if the European system of measurement had been used, that level would have been significantly lower. These rates had been maintained, moreover, despite the fact that there were far more people seeking work. There was a large increase in the number of people of working age, a very substantial movement of labour from the countryside to the towns, an increase in the number of women working and in many cases a significant immigration from other countries. During the 1960s the total number of new jobs *created* in the industrialised (OECD) countries as a whole was 29 million. This was an increase of 11 per cent over the decade (17 per cent in the United States, 13 per cent in Japan and 4 per cent in Western Europe).

With this success, preoccupation with the problem of unemployment everywhere declined. During the next decade, however, there was a dramatic change in this situation. New jobs were still being created: almost as fast as in the previous decade. In the 1970s there was an overall increase in employment within the OECD countries of 28 million (only 1 million less than in the 1960s). In the United States alone, 12 million new jobs were created. But the number of people needing jobs rose still faster:

because of the large number of young people reaching working age, a smaller number reaching retirement age and still more women looking for employment. So, while employment rose fast, unemployment rose still faster: to 23 million within OECD countries by 1980.

One obvious reason why those coming onto the job market could not now be so easily absorbed was the slower rate of economic growth among most such countries. The economies of these countries no longer had the dynamism which had earlier made it possible for them to find employment for rapidly growing workforces. But, if this had been the only reason for increasing unemployment, there would have been room to hope that, as growth resumed, unemployment rates would come down. There were, however, a number of other reasons for the substantial increase in unemployment in rich countries during this period.

One of these was that over the previous quarter-century there had been major structural changes in the economies of developed countries. Many traditional industries which had been very large employers of labour now declined: textiles, mining, shipbuilding and the railways. Agriculture, the largest employer of all, though not declining in output, was shedding labour even faster. Other important industries, such as iron and steel, motor manufacture, and the engineering industry generally, even if not losing jobs to similar industries in developing countries (and even in those industries this began to happen towards the end of the period), were producing as much as before with a smaller workforce. Even construction, which with the large growth in house-building and industrial development had expanded rapidly before, now began to decline as an employer, with cuts in government spending, in house-buying and in industrial expansion. Though the services sector was increasing, and fairly fast, the expansion was not nearly enough to create employment for those displaced elsewhere; and here too, with the growth of self-service in retailing and catering and the mechanisation of banking and accounting, labour-saving was now taking place.

A related development was the rapid growth of investment, much of it of a highly capital-intensive type. Rapid economic growth had stimulated high levels of investment in equipment and rapidly rising levels of productivity: even in the United States and Britain, though less high than elsewhere, they were still very high by historical standards. The fact that unemployment had been low during that period, and the labour market therefore tight, had inevitably promoted this style of industrial investment. The strong bargaining power of unions had the effect that wage costs were high; and to the level of wages themselves had to be added increasingly large social security payments, redundancy payments, holiday pay, sick pay, maternity pay and other obligations on the employer. Strong unions and strict labour legislation restricted the employers' right to hire and fire. Conversely, there were many inducements from governments to invest in equipment. Since productivity growth was seen by many as the key to economic success, large tax concessions, investment grants, depreciation allowances, regional grants and industrial subventions were offered to industry to promote investment. Companies, as much as governments, saw high productivity as the key to competitive success; and, with lower taxation on undistributed profits in many countries than in those distributed, they had no hesitation in spending them on capital improvements. Huge sums were spent on research and development. Machines appeared both more reliable and less strike-prone than men. Mechanical robots, each replacing at least three or four human workers (and costing about $40,000 each in 1980 or about $5 an hour, against $15 for a human worker) increasingly appeared a more attractive workforce. Computers, transistors and microprocessors replaced fallible human intelligence. And, where mere mortals could not be dispensed with, it was often cheaper and more profitable to place production facilities in developing countries where wage rates were far lower: so US firms placed their textile and footwear factories in South Korea and Brazil, US motor manufacturers their engine production plants in Mexico, West European firms their assembly plants in Iran, India and elsewhere.

One effect of these changes was a sharp decline in the demand for unskilled labour. The jobs which the unskilled had previously undertaken were now increasingly performed by machines. Conversely, the industries which grew in rich countries were those – electronics, computers, components, teaching and the social services – for which substantial skills were required. Even in the engineering industries it was always in the skilled trades that supply bottlenecks appeared. For the unskilled and semi-skilled jobs, the number offering themselves for work always exceeded the vacancies available.

There were other, less significant reasons for the increase in unemployment during this period. There was greater 'frictional' unemployment: a longer time spent between jobs. Job-seekers were much more particular about the employment they took; and, with higher unemployment pay, were better able to be choosy. There was greater immobility of labour: because many workers were tied by their pension rights, their tenancy of a council house, by mortgage obligations, by children's schools and by greater reluctance to abandon friends and locality, they were much less prepared than many had been in the thirties to roam the country in search of work. For many workers the 'poverty trap' – low wages in the only occupation they could expect to find, coupled with a sharp drop in social security benefits and increase in tax liability if employment was taken, leading to a very small resulting increase, and occasionally a drop, in take-home pay – meant that those without skills had little financial incentive to work. In other words, the problems resulting from lack of *demand* for labour were sometimes matched by problems relating to *supply* as well.

Whatever the real causes, high unemployment was often attributed to other factors, whose effect was often marginal. For example, it was widely believed to result from the rapid increase in imports from abroad, especially those, such as textiles and footwear, coming from low-cost countries. Since these often replaced the products of domestic industry which had been large employers of labour, it was tempting to suppose that, by cutting off the imports, domestic employment could be easily increased. In fact a series of detailed studies within industrial nations showed that most of the loss of jobs, for example in textiles, resulted from changes *within* the domestic industry, such as the use of more capital-intensive methods, rather than from bigger imports from abroad (which according to some calculations accounted for only a thirtieth of the decline in available jobs).[1] Indirectly, moreover, the increase in imports *increased* the availability of jobs: the earnings which the increased exports generated were spent (since there was insatiable demand among poor countries for the products of the rich) on other goods, creating new jobs in other industries, usually more advanced and more appropriate for developed countries than those they replaced, and with better prospects for growth in the future.

Whatever the causes, from 1970 unemployment relentlessly increased among developed countries. During the course of the decade the average level of unemployment doubled (see Table 8.1). From having been exceptionally low in the previous 25 years, it now became exceptionally high: probably higher than at any time except the 1930s. By 1980 the rate had reached 6–7 per cent in Western Europe as a whole, 9–10 per cent in Britain and France, and 7–8 per cent in North America. The total number without work within the OECD countries had grown from about 8–9 million in 1970 to 25 million in 1980. Moreover, in *particular* areas and among *particular* groups the rates were very much higher. While, for example, in the middle of the seventies the average ratio of unemployment to unfilled vacancies was 6.1 per cent in the United Kingdom as a whole, in Wales it was 12 per cent, in North-East England

TABLE 8.1   *Unemployment rates in Western countries, 1960–82[a]*

	United States	Canada	Japan	France	West Germany	Italy	Britain
1960	5.5	7.0	1.7	1.8	1.1	3.8	2.2
1965	4.5	3.9	1.2	1.6	0.3	3.5	2.2
1970	4.9	5.7	1.2	2.6	0.8	3.1	3.1
1975	8.5	6.9	1.9	4.2	3.7	3.2	4.7
1980	7.1	7.5	2.0	6.5	3.8	7.6	7.4
1981	7.0	7.2	2.3	7.2	5.6	8.4	10.7
1982	9.5	10.2	2.4	8.3	7.6	10.3	12.2

[a] Rates for 1960–75 adjusted to place them on a comparable basis. 1980–2 figures as reported.

SOURCE   1960–75 figures from R. T. Kaufner in International Economic Association, *Unemployment in Western Countries*, p. 6; 1980 figures from ILO, *Yearbook of Labour Statistics, 1980*, pp. 315–29; 1981–2 figures from the *Economist* economic indicators for the relevant periods.

it was 14 per cent and in Northern Ireland it was 20 per cent. Similarly, while at the same time average unemployment in the United States among adult males was 7.3 per cent, among adult females it was 8.6 per cent (even among those registered), among teenagers it was 22 per cent and among black teenagers it was 40 per cent.

Unemployment had become, once more, the prime economic and social problem of the age. And, because it stemmed partly from international causes, it was one that it was increasingly difficult for individual nations to cope with in isolation. An international approach to the problem was increasingly required.

8.2   UNEMPLOYMENT IN POOR COUNTRIES

But if the level of unemployment in rich countries had become serious it was still nothing to the level which existed, and had existed over a much longer period, within many poor countries.

To a small extent unemployment in poor countries was the inevitable result of that existing in rich. Since the economies of developing countries had always been highly dependent on those of rich countries, the level of employment in the former was affected by the slow rates of growth in the latter: especially, for example, among those working in the export sector, whether in industry, mining or agriculture. But these groups accounted for only a very small part of the population of poor countries, and for the most part the causes of unemployment in those countries were wholly independent of the rise of worklessness in developed states.

Until recent times there has been no system for measuring levels of unemployment in most poor countries. But it is reasonably certain that in most of them levels of open unemployment have traditionally been low. Most people lived a subsistence existence in the countryside. Though many were underemployed for long periods of the year, and may barely have secured a living, almost all had some work to do during the course of the year. At least they had a recognised place within the family or village which afforded them a share in the work and food available, however inadequate; and usually had little inclination to search for alternative occupation elsewhere. Few therefore, until recent times, have been *conscious* of being unemployed: in the sense that they actively expected and sought more employment from that which they had.

Over recent decades this situation has changed for a number of reasons. First, total populations have increased rapidly (p. 173 above). In some countries populations have doubled within only three decades; and in a few cases have multiplied by three or four within fifty or sixty years (the population of Mexico, for example, has quadrupled from 17 to 72 million in 36 years). Yet there has usually been no corresponding increase in the amount of land that could be cultivated, nor in the availability of alternative occupations elsewhere. Secondly, while the capability of the countryside to sustain its growing population has declined, the consciousness of possible alternative work in the towns has increased: so more today are *aware* of being unemployed and actively seek work than before. Thirdly, the effort to record the numbers of unemployed by governments has increased. Not only do the workless seek work: governments seek the workless, as they did not before. Together these factors mean that within almost all such countries very large numbers are now recognised as being unemployed.

In the countryside, recorded unemployment often remains low. This is partly because there is usually no system for measuring unemployment there: there are no employment exchanges in the villages, nor, often, in many small towns. It is partly because most women, and other dependants living within families, however little they work (and most do share the work that is available) will not appear, even to themselves, as unemployed, since they seek no other work (if only because they know it does not exist). But it is also because even those without regular work or support – for example, heads of families who are landless – will often, if they remain in the countryside, be able to find at least some occasional and sporadic employment, sufficient to provide some sort of livelihood: either in working for others or in working in the 'informal' economy as a pedlar, small trader or craftsman. For this reason the recorded levels of unemployment in the rural areas of poor countries are nearly always low: in India, for example, one of the most overcrowded countries of the world, census figures record only 1 per cent of the population of the rural areas to be unemployed (though that figure omits beggars, who are effectively unemployed, as well as dependants who live at home without work).

Such figures may be delusive. While there may be little overt unemployment in the Western sense (that is, people who actively seek work and take steps to register themselves as such), there are many who would work more or differently if other opportunities were available to them. There are, for example, very large numbers of men and women who live within a household who undertake only the little work available to them and who subsist at a very low standard of living, yet who have no means or inclination to travel or are deterred by strong social and family pressures from seeking work elsewhere, even if it were easily available. There are others who work only seasonally, mainly at harvest time. Some who seem to work continuously only a few hours a day or a few days in the week. Others who work in theory are rarely fully occupied, for example street pedlars. Some, craftsmen and workmen, work only when work is offered to them. Casual labourers are not regarded as unemployed, but may receive pay for only a few days in the month or a few weeks in the year. Some do not seek work, and therefore do not appear in the statistics, only because they know there is no work available in the vicinity.

The apparent full employment in the countryside is therefore misleading, since many – a third to a half – are at least underemployed. But it remains true that overt unemployment in poor countries is primarily an urban phenomenon. This does not mean that unemployment *results* from urbanisation. It is mainly because those who lack work in the countryside seek it in the towns. A large proportion of those who are unemployed in the towns grew up in the country; or at least are the sons and daughters of those who went there from the country to find work. In other words, the capacity of the towns to *attract* those desiring work is much greater than their capacity to *provide* work. Of those who migrate to the towns only a very small proportion will find work of the kind they seek: for example, in manufacturing industries, in a government department or, best of all, in a high-paying Western firm. Some will eventually be content to work instead within the traditional economy, at low rates of pay. But many will find no work at all.

As a result, the level of unemployment in the towns is usually very high, often 20–25 per cent of the workforce (and even in the towns not all unemployment is recorded).[2] A large proportion of those who are workless are young. This is not only because those joining the workforce are inevitably mainly young. It is also because many of those who are willing to move from the country in search of work are young. Against this, the number of older workers made unemployed through dismissal or structural change (as happens in rich countries) is relatively small. This leads to a situation in which many of those without jobs are better qualified than those who have them. Growing up more recently, they have had better educational opportunities than their elders. And it is the most well educated who leave the villages and the small towns to seek work in the big cities; or who grow up in cities but scorn employment in the traditional economy. The number with qualifications has increased much more than has the number of jobs for which those qualifications are suitable. There is therefore (as in rich countries) an increasing gap between expectations and available employment; between ambitions and opportunities.

Higher levels of demand in the economy would do little to relieve the problem. In many poor countries rates of growth are anyway high, and inflationary pressures strong. Even if still higher rates of growth were attainable, they would, if secured by traditional means, have little effect on employment levels. The total numbers engaged in manufacturing, where the effect would be greatest, is tiny.[3] In agriculture, increased production alone would have little effect. It could most easily be procured by additional inputs of water, fertiliser, pesticides and so on, without additional labour. Indeed, that process could easily, as in the past, bring about an increasing concentration of holdings and so even *increase* the number of landless labourers seeking work. Where this has not happened those who possess land have already often, with increasing sub-division, plots so small that they provide neither adequate work nor an adequate living. Where, on the other hand, large landholdings survive in the hands of rich landowners, usually as plantations or large estates, labour is still less intensively used and the standard of living of the majority is often lower.

It is not, therefore, to inadequate growth or insufficient demand that the high rates of unemployment in poor countries can be attributed. The levels of employment have been affected above all, as in developed states, by the strategy of development which has been adopted. Development policies have been heavily influenced by the demonstration effect of rich countries. Consumption patterns and production models have been borrowed from richer states. Technology, production facilities and assembly lines have been directly imitated (or directly transplanted by foreign companies). As a result, investment of a highly capital-intensive type has been undertaken: a type still less appropriate to the situation of poor countries than of rich. External aid, usually provided only for the imported (normally the capital) element of a project, encourages similar types of investment. Countries that are poor in capital resources but rich in labour thus create facilities – steel-mills, motor assembly plants, oil refineries and petrochemical plants – requiring large capital resources but little labour. Huge inducements – tax holidays, investment grants, advance factories, and other benefits – are given to attract still more investment of the same type. Low or negative interest rates resulting from high inflation, overvalued exchange rates and very heavy protection provide still further inducements. Yet such investment has not only provided employment for relatively few; it has done so at wage levels far beyond the capacity of local firms to imitate. And it has therefore only increased the magnetic attraction which the big cities exert on those living, on quite inadequate incomes, in the countryside.

In poor countries, as in rich, there are problems relating to the supply of labour as well as to the demand. Labour-intensive development is sometimes unattractive because much of the labour force is without the skills and aptitudes which would be required even for simpler types of production. A substantial part of the labour force is, because of malnutrition, internal parasites, severe ill-health, illiteracy and deficiency in skills, unproductive or even unemployable. Without the housing, health care and other essentials for a decent life, workers may lack the energy or the ambition for a sustained work effort. Certainly they are not always the most suitable work force for precisely the type of employment which the capital-intensive development mainly favoured primarily supplies.

For all these reasons unemployment in poor countries is already vast (see Table 8.2). According to some estimates about 300 million people are fully unemployed in such countries throughout the world. Probably about as many are severely underemployed. In the next decade or two these figures will increase substantially. In most developing countries today, 50 per cent of the population is under 20 (against 27 per cent in rich countries), and most of these have still to reach the labour force. A

TABLE 8.2   *Estimates of unemployment and underemployment in developing countries, 1975 (per cent)*

| | Unemployed | | Underemployed | | | |
	Total	Urban	Total	Urban	Total	Of which urban
Asia	3.9	6.9	36.4	23.2	40.3	30.1
Africa	7.1	10.8	37.9	25.1	45.0	38.9
Latin America	5.1	6.5	28.9	22.8	34.0	29.3

SOURCE   ILO, *Employment Growth and Basic Needs* (Geneva, 1975) p. 18.

much larger number of women will seek work outside the home for the first time. With changes in agricultural techniques and growing landlessness, an increasing number of adult men too will leave the land to find employment elsewhere. On these grounds the labour force in poor countries is expected to increase by another 450 million or so in the next decade. The task of finding work for all that number is a formidable one.

Certainly the chance of creating new employment for such a huge number by traditional means is small. Manufacturing industry, though it will undoubtedly grow, in some cases rapidly, will not employ more than a very small proportion of the total. There is, as we have seen, little new land to be brought into cultivation. And some already cultivated may provide work for fewer in the future.

If employment is to be found for the hundreds of millions of people who will come onto the labour market in the next two decades, therefore, a wholly new development strategy may need to be employed. And an international as well as a national effort may be required to implement it.

8.3   THE EMERGENCE OF INTERNATIONAL CONCERN ABOUT UNEMPLOYMENT

It is only slowly, and mainly within the last 50 years, that a sense has begun to emerge that the international community as a whole, as well as national governments, should be concerned about unemployment questions.

When the International Labour Organisation (ILO) was established in 1919, its main purpose was to raise standards of labour protection and conditions of employment throughout the world. It was to that task that it devoted most of its efforts. But it always had some interest in the question of unemployment. And, when, a dozen years later, unemployment in Europe and North America reached levels never previously known, the organisation devoted considerable time and effort to considering the ways in which this could be counteracted. At its annual conference in 1932, the workers' group put forward a resolution calling, first, for the convening of world conferences to consider the international monetary system and to examine the questions of production and trade; and, secondly, for a world-wide programme of public works, to be co-ordinated by the ILO, so as to provide employment for the workless all over the world. This resolution, slightly amended, was carried and the organisation proceeded to try to get it implemented. Instead of the two separate conferences originally called for, a single World Economic Conference took place in Geneva in 1933 to consider the world slump and the revival of trade. But this had little effect in restimulating the world economy, partly because of the non-co-operation of the United States with the Conference, and partly because of the general reluctance among most countries to lower tariff barriers as a means to expand trade. The proposal for a synchronised programme of public works, to be introduced simultaneously in a number of member states, got nowhere. It was considered in detail in a number of League committees, as well as at the World Economic Conference. But nothing came of it, because a number of countries, especially Britain, were unwilling to see the expansion of credit or the budget deficits which would have been required to implement it.

When employment eventually revived, in the second half of the thirties, therefore, it was as a result of the action of individual governments (including their decisions to rearm) rather than of any concerted international effort. But the belief that the ILO should be partly concerned with the need to sustain high employment levels became stronger than ever. When the organisation was revived at the end of the Second World War, it committed itself more emphatically than ever before to that goal, just as individual national governments were doing (p. 193). In the Declaration of Philadelphia of 1944, which effectively relaunched the ILO after the disruption of the Second World War, the requirement to create and maintain full employment levels was recognised as a 'solemn obligation'.[4]

This did not at first seem an onerous commitment. During the years that followed, unemployment, at least in developed countries, was lower than at any time in recent years. Even so, the organisation demonstrated its concern on the question when in 1964 it adopted a convention (together with corresponding 'recommendations', less binding in character) about employment policy. The Convention obliged ratifying countries to 'declare and pursue, as a major goal, an active policy designed to promote full production and freely chosen employment', to consult with representatives of workers and employers about the application of the policy, and to decide on the measures necessary, within the framework of a co-ordinated economic and social policy, to fulfil that aim. The Governing Body of the organisation was to report from time to time to the Conference on the working of the Convention and the need for revision. The recommendations set out the general principles that should govern employment policy, including the need to define its objectives, in the form of quantitative targets where possible, based on an analysis of the future size and distribution of the labour force, the need to provide adequate training and education, to improve qualifications for employment, to organise employment services to help people find jobs, to provide for unemployment pay, to promote an expanding economy and to even out seasonal fluctuations in employment, to counter structural unemployment and promote industrial adjustment, to introduce adequate regional policies and so on.

There were a number of corresponding regional initiatives. In 1966 the Conference of American States Members of the ILO adopted the Ottawa Plan on human resources development for the Americas. In the same year the Asian Advisory Committee of the ILO made recommendations for an Asian manpower plan, endorsed later by the Regional Conference for Asia. In 1967 the African Advisory Committee proposed an African jobs and skills programme. Arrangements were made for reporting on and evaluating the programmes for each region; while member states were called on to adopt 'comprehensive employment programmes', including specific targets for the numbers in employment, to be progressively achieved, and laying down the means by which they were to be accomplished.

In 1969, as a culmination of all this activity, the ILO launched its World Employment Programme. This recognised the organisation's special responsibility and committed it to a long-term programme of activity to help alleviate the problem of mass unemployment. It was mainly designed to influence the policies of governments within their territories: in the words of its Director-General, it would 'assist governments in devising measures not only to promote employment but also to adjust labour supply, qualitatively and quantitatively, to employment needs'.[5] The role of the organisation would be in analysing the nature of the problems faced, the type of development strategy which could best reduce them, and advising countries individually on the best ways of meeting their own difficulties in this field. It sent missions to a number of countries – Sri Lanka, Colombia, Kenya and others – which came up with proposals, more or less radical, for coping with the problem.

The reports of these missions, as well as the more general advice provided by the organisation at this time, reflected the new approach which it had adopted towards these questions. It saw the level of unemployment as being to a substantial extent the effect of a wholly unequal distribution of wealth and income within the society concerned. This led to a pattern of consumption which was often oriented towards imported Western products, to a concentration of landholdings that provided inadequate employment opportunities in the countryside, and to inadequate encouragement of the informal sectors of the economy which would have been likely to create more job opportunities than the modern sectors which traditional development strategies favoured. This approach, emphasising the 'basic needs' of the mass of the population, stressed the vital importance of securing a wider distribution of purchasing power if existing levels of unemployment were to be brought down. Conversely, the only way to relieve poverty, in conditions where there were few social services, was to create jobs. The organisation stressed the importance of policies in other fields – agriculture, trade and aid – which would have most effect in creating jobs. It called for more assistance for rural development programmes, small-scale industry, and rural handicrafts. It wanted more research on labour-intensive methods of production. Meanwhile it offered advice on training programmes, manpower policy, youth employment schemes and development strategy generally. And its Turin Centre for Advanced Technical and Vocational Training helped provide suitable training, established courses for instructors and administrators, distributed training materials and sent experts into the field.

In 1976 the ILO, as a culmination of this activity, called a World Employment Conference. This was intended to draw attention to the scale of the unemployment problem faced all over the world and to persuade governments and international organisations to adopt strategies which took account of the overriding need to create jobs. The Conference adopted a declaration of principles and programme of action calling for more intensive efforts in this direction. Though it may be doubted whether these (like most of the other high-sounding documents issued at the end of major international conferences) exerted any very profound impact on the action of governments, they at least served to focus attention on the need to keep employment needs very much in mind in formulating development strategies.

Over the last few years, other international organisations have begun to show some awareness of the importance of these considerations. The World Bank, for example, has increasingly recognised that the type of capital assistance it provides should be of a kind appropriate to countries which are rich in labour but poor in capital and technology: an increasing proportion of World Bank assistance today goes to agriculture, education and population programmes rather than large-scale industrial or infrastructure projects. Similarly, the UNDP and other organisations have been more willing to finance programmes in the field of agriculture and rural development and the traditional sector as a whole. And, as we saw in Chapter 7, new organisations such as IFAD have been set up specifically to provide assistance for the least privileged sections of the population within rural areas.

The periodic economic summits among the heads of government of the industrialised countries have also given some recognition to the seriousness of unemployment questions. But for the most part such meetings have demonstrated much greater concern about the problems of inflation than of unemployment, and have been notably chary of making recommendations that could be interpreted as favourable to reflationary policies. They have certainly showed little interest in the problems of poor countries. The EEC and the OECD have shown somewhat greater awareness of the unemployment problem; and the latter has undertaken a study specifically directed to the means of discouraging excessively capital-intensive types of investment. But in general it cannot be said that any of these international organisations has yet directed to the problems of world unemployment an attention that is in any way proportionate to the urgency and scale of the problem.

8.4   AN INTERNATIONAL EMPLOYMENT STRATEGY

Responsibility for action to reduce unemployment has thus until recently been held to lie with national governments. They have been expected both to relieve the hardship which unemployment causes, and to manage their economies in a way that will maintain high employment levels. It is only now beginning to be recognised that it is today beyond the capacity of *individual* governments, rich or poor, to maintain, through their own policies alone, high levels of employment within their territories. Unemployment has been the consequence of developments within the international economy as a whole. The attainment of full employment in the United States as in India, in Zaire as in Britain, depends as much on international as on national policies. If workless-ness is to be reduced, therefore, it is necessary for governments to devise together the *international* policies necessary to bring that about.

What should be the elements of such a strategy? Some of the policies required have been discussed in earlier chapters. If more jobs are to be created, there will be a need for more effective measures to manage international demand so as to secure reasonably sustained growth in the world economy in place of the stumbling stop–go – with much more stop than go – experienced in the last few years (Chapter 1 above). There will be a need to run the world's monetary system in a more flexible, and when needed in a more expansionary, way, so that countries with severe balance of payments or debt problems (that is, most poor countries and some rich ones) are able to secure credit without being forced in return to accept severe deflation, and for more adequate resources to be available for that purpose (Chapter 4 above). There will be a need to bring about an expansion of world trade, by reducing the barriers which at present inhibit it, so as to help promote employment at the world level as effectively as it was promoted, largely by the same process, among the developed countries for 25 years after the Second World War (Chapter 4). And there will be a need for policies on investment and development assistance that will facilitate the transfer of resources to those areas where there is the best opportunity, as well as the greatest need, of their productive use (Chapter 2).

All these measures together, however, even if they could in each case be successfully adopted (and it is scarcely probable that all will be) would not alone do more than marginally alleviate world unemploy-ment. For even a rate of world growth that was, as a result, consistently higher than before is unlikely to have a substantial effect on levels of employment, either in rich countries or in poor; still less would a cyclical upturn, of the kind that in the past might have been expected to secure a return to something like full employment in the developed world, today be sufficient. There are now long-term trends within the world economy, as well as structural developments within individual countries, that are likely, unless deliberate and specific policy steps are taken to counteract them, to leave hundreds of millions without work all over the world, even if boom conditions were restored and steady growth maintained; and, as we saw in Chapter 1, world growth is in fact more likely to be slower than before than faster. If unemployment is to be significantly reduced, therefore, in rich countries and poor alike, further measures are necessary. A strategy that is specifically directed to the creation of employment is required.

One of the reasons for high levels of unemployment all over the world is, as we saw earlier, the deliberate stimulation by governments, in rich countries and poor alike, of investment much of which is capital-intensive in character. That individual enterprises, whether private or public, are attracted to this type of development need not surprise us. Many factors today favour it: with the increasing size of many enterprises, large investment can be undertaken at low cost from non-distributed profits, which usually receive favoured tax treatment; large sums are available for the same purpose from the huge savings now undertaken through insurance and pension funds and through the banking system; high inflation reduces the real rate of interest on borrowing to low or negative levels; enterprises and governments alike devote large sums to research and development aimed at devising labour-saving improvements in technology; the cost of labour in manufacturing industry is increased by the monopoly power of unions as well as by government legislation on labour protection (for example, redundancy pay, sick pay and maternity leave) while recurrent industrial relations problems often make investment in machinery appear as a trouble-free alternative; trade unions themselves, which by definition only represent those who are in work, are more concerned, in practice if not always in precept, with raising the standard of living of those in work than of those without. The effect is that the 'iron law of wages', which was once held to condemn the workforce – because of competition between workers for available jobs – never to earn more than a subsistence wage, is now replaced by a contrary iron law which prevents real wage levels *declining* over the long term below any previous level, whatever the state of the market and the degree of unemployment.

In a sense, the predisposition to capital-intensive development, placing a greater value on the more efficient production of things than on the more satisfying employment of people, reflects the values of a society dominated by producers – whether capitalist firms, state enterprises or trade unions – in which the voice of the workless and even the voice of the consumer (both of whom must often pay the cost of capital-intensive investment) count for little. The 'public interest' is increasingly identified with the private interest of the producing classes. Only if government, national or international, were to adopt a wider view of the public interest, reflecting the social value of employment and the social costs of worklessness, are alternative types of development strategy likely to be adopted.

There are actions which individual governments could take if they wished to counter this trend. They could increase employment by reducing the cost of labour for employers: for example, by lowering the level of social security contributions required from employers, reducing their liability (but not necessarily the state's) to make redundancy payments or contribute to redundancy funds, reducing their responsibility for sickness pay, maternity leave and other benefits, relaxing some of the restrictions of employment policy, and increasing their freedom to hire and fire. They could reduce the cost of labour by other means: by shifting the burden of taxation from low-paid to high-paid (and reducing the proportion of indirect taxation to direct), so that the wage level required to maintain any given standard of living was lowered, by reducing the monopoly powers enjoyed by unions; or by appropriate incomes policies. They could ban moonlighting and reduce overtime. They could reduce the incentive to capital-intensive investment: by removing or reducing the many tax allowances, investment grants, depreciation allowances, grants for particular industries and regions which at present serve to promote it.[6] Conversely, incentives might be provided to encourage the type of investment which creates jobs: for example, by offering regional employment premiums, subsidies for retaining workers during recession, regional and industrial grants related to the numbers employed, more help for training and retraining, and similar methods. Employers could be encouraged to invest in people rather than machines, by granting them some sort of tax allowance for each worker trained comparable to that usually available for depreciation of equipment.[7] They could even be given a grant for each job provided equal to the amount now spent in unemployment pay.

Unfortunately, however, it is unlikely that individual governments, acting alone, will ever take such steps, beneficial though they could be. For each government tends to measure the economic success of its own country not in terms of the human satisfaction afforded to their populations but in terms of its national income, balance of payments position, productivity a head and similar measures, all of which are largely unrelated to aggregate human satisfaction; and these aspirations are believed to make necessary capital-intensive investment. Governments believe that this, by increasing productivity and technological development, must also increase long-term competitiveness and relative success. They therefore fear that measures to deter it, such as those just described, however valuable in increasing employment, could ultimately damage their nation in the contest about which they care most.

Such measures are not likely to be adopted, therefore, by any one government acting alone, but only in consequence of an international understanding that they were to be generally adopted. At the regional level there has been some tentative discussion of such measures: for example, in Western Europe. But, since an agreement within the EEC alone, for example, could still be held to risk a loss of market share to other regions, such as Japan and the United States, it would be insufficient in itself. Only international agreement on a far wider basis is likely to be effective in reducing the volume of investment which is capital-intensive in kind and in increasing that which is labour-intensive.

Such measures could be equally important for poor countries. A substantial part of the investment in modern industry in those countries, often coming from elsewhere, is capital-intensive in kind. Yet such investment is even more inappropriate to the situation of developing countries, where the surplus of labour is even greater. It is still more important, therefore, that they adopt strategies which favour labour-intensive development.[8] Before authorising investment projects, whether from domestic or overseas sources, they need to ensure that these are of a kind appropriate to their own economies: that is, will make use of their most abundant resource, labour. They could impose high duties or other restraints on imports of equipment which would reduce labour requirements. They could introduce credit controls or licensing systems which favour investment in labour-intensive projects. They could even, as the ILO has proposed, seek to establish lower interest rates for such projects.[9] They could specify maximum wage levels, both to safeguard their principal competitive advantage, low labour costs, and to reduce the distorting effect on their economies which very high wage levels in a small number of enterprises, usually foreign-owned, can bring about (for example, in attracting still more people to the towns in search of non-existent employment).

But here too international as well as national action is required. Agencies providing funds for poor countries, the World Bank and UNDP, as well as multilateral donors, need to ensure that the money they provide is used generally for labour-intensive rather than capital-intensive projects. They might grant more funds, on more favourable terms, for projects which create new employment.[10] They could support development plans which sought to assist the informal and traditional economies, assistance for agriculture, and large-scale construction work, as against Western-style manufacture.[11]

Such an international strategy should mean that the great bulk of investment and aid funds would go to the countryside. At least in the next few decades, it is only here that large-scale employment can be created while avoiding the high costs of urbanisation. This would go not only for labour-intensive agriculture but also for small industry, crafts and workshops based in the countryside. Assistance through local development banks and credit co-operatives, which lend for small-scale projects matched to local needs, may achieve this better than aid through national ministries and development agencies, concerned with prestige national projects and national production targets. More help could be given for the service sector, which is a large employer of labour and could be larger.[12] Labour-intensive energy development (for example, biomass) could be supported. Funds could be provided for programme lending: not tied to specific projects, but used for purposes that would sustain employment (for example, more assistance for the maintenance, spare parts and running costs of existing projects, help which will often do more to ensure that the available capital is used to maximum advantage, with maximum job creation, than the creation of yet more entirely new projects). Where industrial projects are thought essential, donors would seek to ensure that these operated on a multi-shift basis, providing the maximum employment for each unit of capital provided; and that those industries were favoured – garment manufacture, footwear, furniture and others – which were the largest employers of labour.

The same need for international agreement arises in respect of other measures to increase employment. One of the most obvious steps which could help is the wider sharing of the available work: through a reduction of the working week, the working year, or the working life. Here too only international agreement can bring progress. No nation acting alone can go very far (for example, in reducing the hours of the working week), because of the danger, of which employers warn only too vociferously, that its own industry's competitive position will be adversely affected. A nation which reduced its working week to 30 hours or the working year to 40 weeks, and did so alone, could not fail to be competitively disadvantaged.[13] Here too, therefore, there is urgent need of international understanding. Though there have been tentative discussions of such problems, for example within the EEC, there has been little momentum behind these, and few have regarded such agreements as practically possible. Yet there is no reason why there could not be agreement, for example, on a shorter working week; or the reduction of overtime except in exceptional circumstances (perhaps by a limit on the maximum number of hours per year). There could be agreement on a reduced retiring age. There could be official encouragement of voluntary early retirement: for example, by providing that this could be done with little or no loss of pension rights (since, however, most people prefer to go on working where possible, and certainly require occupation of some sort, it is important that for those who wish it, alternative, community-based employment of a non-commercial kind should be created). There could, more radically, be a move to encourage people of all ages to take voluntary periods of leisure or paid educational leave, for a year or more on unemployment pay, with the right to return to their former employment at the end of that period.[14] There could be agreement for much longer holidays, with further extensions at times of recession.

International action may also be required to organise and finance more research on labour-intensive types of development. The market economy in itself provides little incentive for such research. The social and human cost of unemployment is of no concern to individual enterprises, whether private or public, and it is such enterprises which undertake the greater part of industrial research and development today. Their research is undertaken on the assumption that capital is easily available for product development and often on the assumption of high domestic labour costs. Once the cost of development has been undertaken within a rich country, it is usually more economical, with the research and development costs already written off, to transfer the entire production system wholesale to a poor country, taking advantage of the investment incentives, tariff protection, import controls and other benefits which that country provides, than to devise a different technology altogether more suitable for the condition of the developing country. If research on alternative technologies which would take advantage of the factor mix available in poor countries is to be undertaken, it may need to be financed by alternative methods. International agencies could give loans to poor countries specifically for that purpose; or they could directly finance institutions, private, national or international, devoted to that objective.

Such research would be devoted, at least in part, to the technology appropriate to very small-scale production. The financing of many small-scale enterprises, including individual craftsmen, rather than a few large ones, may be the best means not only of securing more jobs in many poor countreis, but also of producing the kinds of products which will best meet the needs of consumers in such an economy.

But it is not only types of investment but also the supply of labour that needs to be adjusted to increase job opportunities. While unskilled labour is in oversupply, there is still a shortage of skilled labour in many countries. International assistance may therefore be needed to ensure the provision of adequate training and retraining to adapt workers to new requirements. School curricula may have to be adapted to make them more relevant to the likely adult life of many pupils. Adequate mobility of labour needs to be encouraged by reducing the costs of changing jobs: by securing transferability of pension rights and housing rights; and even by providing direct assistance for moving house and family (as undertaken for displaced miners by the National Coal Board in Britain). There is need for greater flexibility of pay so that those who are willing to accept lower income for a given job can more easily do so than current union attitudes will allow. Finally, there must be more effort to match abilities with available employment opportunities. At present, one of the major problems in both rich countries and poor is, as we have seen, that many people feel themselves overqualified for the type of jobs that are available. The best way to offset this is by a revision of wages and salaries: the attractive power of the most highly qualified jobs could be reduced through a lowering of pay, while higher incomes could be available to those who accept more humble jobs, which few at present wish to undertake. Here once more a distributionist strategy may provide the answer.

Equally important is structural adjustment within each economy. If adequate employment opportunities are to be established, both in rich countries and in poor, rich countries need to cease seeking to maintain industries more appropriate to poor. This may mean, as we saw in Chapter 4, international assistance to help them promote the necessary adaptation. Other types of structural change may be required. Technical assistance may be needed to help individual companies move into new labour-intensive technologies. Small firms may need to be encouraged to move to small towns and to the countryside to make use of surplus labour there. There is already international help for some such programmes: for example, through the EEC's Social Fund. But such help will increasingly need to be made available on a wider basis. And international guidelines may be needed to lay down the principles to govern such adjustment policies.

Finally, international action may be necessary to maintain a closer international watch on employment trends all over the world. As we have seen, the ILO's Convention on Employment Policy gave it responsibility for supervising the implementation of that convention, and so for noting the employment measures taken in ratifying states. But there is no reason why all governments, whether or not they are parties to the Convention, should not report regularly to the ILO on their employment situation; and to consult with other governments, at least in their own region and perhaps more widely, about the steps they are taking to improve the situation. High unemployment in one country, as was long ago recognised, is no longer the concern of that country alone. Because it depresses demand in the international economy as a whole, it contributes to creating unemployment elsewhere as well. This inter-relatedness is partially recognised when the countries of the EEC, for example, consider together the need for mutual reflation; or when at economic summits the chief industrialised countries together look at similar problems. But increasingly today such questions are problems for the world as a whole.

There is thus ample justification for the ILO or some other body (perhaps that with responsibility for world economic management suggested in Chapter 1) to keep under review the situation in every part of the world, and examine the performance of each government in creating conditions likely to promote employment, both in its own territory and among its neighbours. Such an international body should lay down guidelines concerning the kind of national policies necessary. It could seek to influence other international organisations, especially those concerned with aid, trade and monetary assistance, to adopt the policies that would help increase work opportunities. It could ask regional organisations to consider the steps needed (including regional development plans and regional infrastructure projects) to stimulate employment within their own areas. And it would remain, above all, the central institution where the problem of world unemployment would continue to be debated and new initiatives proposed.

For the interrelatedness of the modern world economy means that unemployment is no longer a problem for individual governments acting independently. Increasingly it becomes a matter of international concern. It is international bodies, therefore, that today need to be concerned with considering what policies are required to maintain adequate work opportunities for countless individuals all over the world, otherwise condemned to suffer the tragic despair of worklessness.

9 Efficiency in the World Economy

9.1 COULD THE MARKET DO IT BETTER?

Discussion of a managed world economy immediately invites the question: is management necessary or desirable? Would economic welfare everywhere not be better promoted by relying on market forces to maximise the welfare of all the world's inhabitants? The flow of trade and investment alone, if allowed to operate freely, should lead to the optimum allocation of world resources. This process would not only maximise rates of growth generally; it should also, if unimpeded, bring about an automatic transfer of wealth from those areas at present richest (and so most capable of buying and investing) to those capable of producing most economically and successfully. And, since production would usually be most competitive in areas where wage levels are lowest, it should thus bring about a rapid transfer of wealth and welfare from rich countries to poor.

The first answer to be made to this suggestion is that, even if the premise were accepted – that market forces can best maximise individual welfare over the long term – there is little evidence that such a market exists at present, or is likely to come about in the future, without some attempt at international management of the kind which we have been describing. Most of the evidence suggests the opposite. As we have often seen in this book, many of the problems of the contemporary world economy result from the interferences in free exchanges between states which are so widely and so deliberately undertaken by national governments. By raising barriers against imports, by subsidising exports, by assisting individual industries, by imposing exchange regulations, by manipulating exchange rates and by many other means, individual governments frustrate the operation of market forces: they seek to subvert the market in favour of their own interests. They are subject to strong pressure in favour of such actions from self-interested forces within their own territories. In the field of trade, interventions have for that reason increased rather than decreased over recent years. In the field of investment, governments have always been concerned to regulate capital flows, either outward or inward. Still less are they willing, with unemployment rising everywhere, to free the movement of labour into their territories, as a free market would demand.

Even if the alleged benefits of the free market system were accepted, therefore, it would not be an indication that there was no need for some system of international management. On the contrary, one reason why international management is required is precisely to prevent, or at least regulate, the constant interventions by governments which today distort the market.

But it is not only the power of governments that may distort the market. It is also the power of private corporations. Regulation may be necessary, therefore, at the international as at the national level, to rectify imbalances in market power. Within states it is widely accepted that government intervention may be necessary to restrain excess market power: for example, to control monopolies, restrictive practices and collusive agreements among companies; to protect consumers against fraudulent and misleading practices; to regulate the banking system and the stock exchange; to protect the rights of employees through labour legislation and in many other ways. Internationally, precisely similar needs arise. In the international economy as in the national, a small number of companies, operating transnationally, may acquire dominant power. And, because they are capable of slipping through the net of sovereignty and so escape national jurisdiction (for example, by setting artificial prices to minimise tax liability) they require some measure of control at the international level. This imbalance in market power may be reinforced by (and itself reinforce) the power of particular nations, so that the nationals of a few countries exert undue power in international discussions, effectively control the markets in particular products, or dominate the international banking system, capital flows, technology and its transfer, shipping and other communications. If other nations and their nationals are not to be disadvantaged, therefore, and a genuinely equal market is to be established, there may be need of international action to redress the balance.

Secondly, international measures may be necessary to reduce the instabilities to which a freely working economy may be subject. Just as national governments may need to intervene to check excessive instability in prices, interest rates, exchange rates, money supply and so on, so at the international level too some intervention may be necessary for the same purpose. Movements in commodity prices and the associated earnings may, for example, be so large and unpredictable as to cause serious hardship to countries, organisations and individuals unless action is taken to redress their effects. The movement of energy prices may be so sharp and extreme as to cause serious dislocation in the world economy as a whole. The flow of goods from low-cost to high-cost countries may, if no regulation occurs, be on a scale that will rapidly destroy entire industries and throw large numbers out of work. In such cases international measures may be needed to *slow down* economic processes that would otherwise occur so rapidly as to cause severe hardship and dislocation within the international economy generally.

Thirdly, international action is required, as is generally accepted, to regulate the world's monetary system. Such a system of regulation has existed now already for 40 years or so. There are few in any country who seriously believe that no international action in this field is necessary. Decisions concerning the management of capital flows, the use of gold in international transactions, the granting of credit to countries in balance of payment difficulties, and so on, are not ones that could today be left solely to the operation of the market. Controversy therefore exists only on *how* the system should be regulated, not on whether it should be so. With the large increase in the volume of mobile international capital in recent years, and the destabilising effects this can have, this regulation has today become more than ever necessary. The role of the IMF, or of some comparable body, in the world economy is likely therefore to grow rather than diminish.

A fourth reason why some measure of international regulation is likely to remain necessary over coming decades is the need to influence national actions affecting other countries. With the decline in distance and the consequent increase in transactions between states, the actions that are taken in one country have an increasingly important impact on economic developments elsewhere. The level of interest rates in the United States, for example, immediately affects the level in many other countries and therefore their rate of growth; and it equally affects the burden of debt repayments undertaken by many poor countries all over the world. Similarly, rates of inflation in Western countries are immediately fed into the economies of many poor countries to which they sell their goods; while the prices set for oil and other commodities have a crucial effect on developed states. The cycle of boom and recession flows from one country to another so that action to restrict or expand activity in one may have a rapid effect elsewhere. In all these cases economic decisions reached by one government have a vitally important impact on the economic welfare of other countries. On all such questions, therefore, the demand for joint discussions and joint decisions is likely to grow.

International regulation may also be increasingly required to influence the flow of resources, including development assistance, from one region to another. As there comes to be greater awareness of how unevenly these flows are distributed (p. 242 below), there will be stronger demands for some attempt to bring about a more rational and equitable distribution of resources and welfare about the world. The knowledge that they are at present so dominated by political factors – that, for example, one country may secure several hundred times as much development assistance per head as another – will cause increasingly insistent calls for a more objective assessment of needs and potentialities. Consciousness that private flows are predominantly attractive to those areas where capital, services and skills are already most abundant and markets most developed may bring increasing concern that public international funds should be used to redress the balance. Without such an effort the prospects of the least developed countries of all, with few resources and skills and inadequate markets, and the most underprivileged groups anywhere, would be almost beyond hope. Yet another reason for efforts to secure conscious and deliberate management of the world economy, therefore, is the need for a more even balance of development and living standards in different parts of the world than exists today.

Such management will be necessary, finally, because reliance on the market alone is unlikely to prove successful in coping with the most serious problems of all in the modern world economy: the huge levels of unemployment that everywhere prevail. Market forces left to themselves could even ensure that those problems get worse. They are likely to continue to promote a capital-intensive technology, which will increasingly replace human beings with machines. The large supply of funds available for investment in modern Western economies, through the savings of insurance companies, pension funds, and other institutions, the lending of banks and the investments of private individuals, over and above the vast internal savings of companies, together with the continuing technological advances produced by intensive research and development, have the effect that a free market will inevitably favour this type of development. Competition between nations inhibits the capacity of individual governments, acting alone, to counter that trend. For each fears that, by deterring capital-intensive investment, reducing investment in research and new technology, and other steps to encourage the use of labour, it may condemn its own country to fall behind in the race for 'progress'. And, since at present greater prestige is attached to high rates of growth and technical advance than to providing employment for the mass of the population in each country, there is no reason to expect that situation to change. Only international measures, affecting all countries alike, are likely to exercise any fundamental influence on the prevailing tendency.

These considerations do not of course mean that market forces should have no role to play in the way the international economy operates. They suggest only that market forces by themselves may not be enough: that they may need to be guided, controlled and in a few cases actively counteracted, by the deliberate action of regulatory agencies. On grounds of efficiency alone, therefore (over and above the grounds of welfare which we shall consider in the next chapter), some system of international regulation has become increasingly essential. The important thing is to ensure that it takes the most effective form.

9.2 A BETTER INTERNATIONAL DIVISION OF LABOUR

What then are the main tasks that a better system for regulating the world economy should seek to accomplish?

The first is to try to bring about a more efficient international division of labour than exists today. From the time of Adam Smith and Ricardo, economists have recognised that welfare will be maximised over the long term when the impediments to exchanges between states are minimised and when each seeks to meet its needs from those areas where the relative costs of production are lowest. Since trade is a voluntary transaction, it takes place only when both parties believe it to be in their own best interests. An increase in trade should therefore have the effect of making both parties richer than they would otherwise have been.

Though this is an oversimplified statement of the theory,[1] and the theory itself has rarely been accepted without qualifications, it is generally accepted that increased exchanges between states will normally bring about a better division of labour within the world as a whole and so promote the long-term economic welfare of all. As we have seen, such a division of labour is at present prevented by the deliberate actions of governments to restrict exchanges. Those restrictions are occasionally based on the justification first used a century and a half ago: that where industries are being first built up they may need to be temporarily safeguarded from competition from those already more developed elsewhere. Today, however, protection is more often provided for old industries rather than for new ones. It is usually these that are most threatened by competition from low-cost countries elsewhere which receive support. In this situation any industry may be regarded as deserving of protection if employment is threatened. And as we saw earlier, even where some of the old barriers (such as tariffs) are gradually removed, new ones, of entirely new kinds, are raised in their place (p. 75 above). Instead of a single integrated international economy, therefore, we have today a patchwork quilt, a series of separate national economies, linked together only as much or as little as each national government chooses to permit.

It can reasonably be argued that in many cases such interventions are contrary to the long-term interests of the countries which introduce them. Consumers in the home country are always adversely affected by such measures (since goods will only be imported if they are more desired by consumers than those produced at home). Inflation will be exacerbated; so that, if inflation is regarded as being the main threat to jobs and economic welfare, it can reasonably be held that measures of protection are self-defeating. Frequently, retaliation from other countries is provoked; so that the imagined benefits, for the balance of payments, for firms protected or jobs saved, may be immediately wiped out. Even if there is no direct retaliation, a more long-term process of world deliberalisation is encouraged, which will eventually inhibit trade and growth alike; and will also therefore bring a long-term loss of jobs.

The reason why governments continue, despite all the manifest disadvantages, to take action to exclude imports and to damage the international division of labour is that they are more conscious of short-term threats than of long-term advantage; and in particular more conscious of the interests of producers than those of consumers. Theoretical arguments showing the long-term benefits which more liberal policies should bring to the international economy will not always carry weight against the strong political pressures favouring less liberal action in practice. Only if consumers were to carry greater weight and influence in the deliberations of governments would these political pressures be reduced. Numerically, consumers are always the most important interest group in every country, since they comprise the entire population. Normally they are, however, less vocal and less well organised than the producer interests – both companies and trade unions; and the latter therefore usually exert far greater influence on governments. If better opportunities were provided within states for representatives of consumers at least to be consulted in cases where protective action was contemplated, the pressure on governments to interfere with normal trading flows would be reduced.

But, if the benefits of a wider division of labour are to be secured, it is institutional changes at the international level which are most required. Here what is mainly necessary is that governments should be made more subject to the influence and judgements of international bodies. Sometimes (if they are seeking to withstand pressures from vested interests at home) this can be of benefit to governments themselves. What is required is that all states should be, first, deeply committed to the general principle of maintaining a liberal trading system; and that in consequence they become committed, secondly, to accepting the necessary international rules and the necessary degree of international authority to achieve that. This would involve seeking international authority for any new measures to restrict free exchanges. International bodies would have to lay down as clearly and firmly as possible principles to govern trade policy (for example, on 'safeguard' action – p. 85 – or the provision of subsidies to industries in difficulty) and to secure explicit commitment to those principles by all member governments. We suggested earlier (pp. 89–92, 122–3) some of the institutional changes which may be necessary, both in the trade and monetary field, to make this possible. Whether or not the changes made take precisely these forms, it is essential to seek some improvements in the existing structure if a better international division of labour is to be secured.

Interferences in the natural division of labour between states may stem from completely different sources however. They may be brought about by companies combining together in their own interests: in arrangements to share markets, to maintain prices or to restrict supplies. There are a number of markets that today are dominated by a relatively small number of producers: oil distribution, aircraft, computers, chemicals, copper, aluminium, pharmaceuticals, to mention only a few. Frequently they are able to reach understandings, both formal and informal, enabling them to maximise their market power.[2] For some important commodities there are only a small number of purchasing organisations, which are therefore able to dominate the market.[3] The creation of a freer market must therefore involve international action to regulate restrictive practices of this kind. Although there has been some discussion of this question in the United Nations for about 30 years, it cannot be said that it has so far had much impact. Only if the international community can formulate and enforce regulations on such practices, comparable to those maintained by most national governments, will their effect in distorting free exchanges be significantly reduced. Similar measures may need to be taken to influence the actions of *individual* companies which restrict free competition: for example, the monopolistic control of technology, sometimes maintained by taking out patents in many countries where there is no intention of making use of the process concerned, or by special arrangements with subsidiaries to give them an unfair advantage over competitors (for example, by supplying them at below cost prices).

If progress is to be made in creating an integrated and liberal world economy, it is as important to regulate such arrangements among companies as it is to regulate tariffs and the other interventions of governments. The EEC has already recognised this in the institution of its competition policy, which is mainly designed to eliminate distortions of this kind. But, if a genuinely free-working world economy is to be created, such steps will need to be taken at the international level as well: it is a world 'competition policy' which is required.

A more efficient international division of labour is also inhibited by the restraints at present imposed on the movement of capital between states. Most of the theoretical advantages of an international market economy cannot be realised unless capital is able to take advantage of the most favourable investment opportunities all over the world, so encouraging the employment of underused and undervalued resources elsewhere (including abundant cheap labour). Even when the general ideal of 'liberalisation' was most highly cherished, in the years after the Second World War, it was not generally applied to the movement of capital abroad, which most countries reserved the right to control. And even those nations that attach the greatest possible importance to maintaining free market policies (such as West Germany, Japan and the United States) have in practice maintained strict capital controls for considerable parts of the post-war period. The right to restrict such movements is one of the most jealously guarded of the powers of sovereignty, a power many governments feel to be essential to their capacity to control their own economies. But eventually, if scarce resources are to be allocated more efficiently than today, and capital employed in its most productive uses, the ultimate aim at least must be to secure freer movement of capital (an objective that is likely to be all the more necessary if the flow of governmental aid from rich countries to poor continues to decline).

A final and still more long-term goal, if a more rational division of labour internationally is to be created, is to free the movement of workers from one country to another. Particularly if the flow of investment to low-cost areas is to remain inhibited, the ability of labour to move to high-investment areas should be facilitated. At present it is almost everywhere rigidly restricted. This does not mean that no movements take place. Such movements occur but under severely controlled conditions. There is, for example, a considerable movement of professional workers from one country to another, and of some other skilled workers, though nearly always controlled by governments. It is almost always the movement of the unskilled that is restricted. This is the worst possible combination for developing countries, since large numbers of their unskilled unemployed cannot secure work elsewhere, yet they may lose many of their most highly trained people.

Absolutely free immigration is not likely to be restored so long as living standards vary as much between countries as they do now. But there is scope for much more movement than takes place at present. At the regional level, considerable movement of unskilled workers does still take place. Within the EEC not only is there (in theory) free movement of labour throughout the Community; there was also for a time considerable inward movement of unskilled labour from the Mediterranean area (especially Turkey, Yugoslavia, Portugal and Algeria). In Africa, similarly, large numbers of workers move from one country to another, especially to more developed states in search of work. Between Mexico and the United States, even though such movements are in theory prohibited, it none the less occurs on a vast scale. But in all these cases the flow is limited, successfully or otherwise, and in time of recession foreign workers are usually the first to suffer, often losing their rights of residence as well as their work. The willingness of most states to open their doors to immigrants from elsewhere is likely to remain limited so long as unemployment is as high as at present. But, if and when the world economy begins to expand once more, there may be a greater willingness to accept that manpower as well as capital should move more freely than at present to those places where it can be used most productively.

Much remains to be done, therefore, before transactions within the international economy become anywhere near as free as those in most national economies today (within which goods, capital and labour travel almost without restriction from one place to another). Since it is difficult to see any natural forces operating to free the movement of goods, capital and labour between states, the process can only be brought about by the influence of external forces, concerned with the good of the whole rather than of individual parts: in other words, through the development of appropriate techniques of international management. And it is those who maintain the virtues of the market economy who should therefore most strenuously support, rather than as at present most strongly oppose, the development of a more effective system of international management.

9.3 STABILITY IN THE INTERNATIONAL ECONOMY

But the more efficient working of the world economy requires not only the removal of the various types of intervention, by governments or by private interests, which at present impede transactions within it. It also requires efforts to reduce the many kinds of *instability* which at present affect it.

By far the most important of these is that which results from the tide of boom and recession: what was once known as the trade cycle. Once upon a time that cycle, as its name implies, resulted from naturally occurring ebbs and flows in the level of economic activity. Though there have been many theories about the underlying causes of these, it is generally agreed that they did not result from the actions of governments. Over recent years there have been two major changes in the character of these ebbs and flows. One is that they are now to a considerable extent the result of deliberate actions by governments, reducing or increasing the volume of credit and activity within the economy, according to whether their aim is to counter inflation and external deficit or recession and unemployment. Secondly, the tide of boom and recession today, instead of being a *national* phenomenon, occurring largely independently in a number of different countries, has increasingly become a single *world* phenomenon, affecting almost all countries (though usually with some time-lags between them), rich and poor alike.

Because boom and recession now occur simultaneously all over the world, they are mutually reinforcing rather than mutually counteracting, so that each becomes more extreme. But, because the fear of inflation is generally much stronger than the fear of unemployment in the more powerful countries, periods of recession now predominate over periods of boom. There are thus three problems for those responsible for managing the international economy.

The first is to try to bring about the desynchronisation of the cycle among different countries, so that boom in one is counteracted by depression in another. The difficulty in achieving this has been at its greatest during the last decade, for it is the same phenomenon – high inflation, resulting partly from the increase in oil prices – which has caused all governments to react in the same way simultaneously. If the same problem is to be avoided in the future, it will be necessary to avoid the violent fluctuations in oil price which produced this effect. But in seeking desynchronisation it will not be sufficient to rely, as in recent years, on exhortations to the countries in surplus to expand their economies to ease the problems of the weakest. For the countries in surplus, whose position is strongest, have the least reason to comply. Only if they have been engaged from the start in a common effort to maintain surveillance of the world economy and so to time reflationary measures with that in view, are they likely to feel they share an interest in modifying their policies for the common good. Only, therefore, the creation of some new international body charged with that surveillance (as proposed in Chapter 1) is likely to be able to bring about the type of desynchronisation which is so badly needed.

Another major cause of instability in the international economy results from fluctuations in the prices of essential commodities. As we saw in Chapter 3, attempts over many years to stabilise prices through commodity agreements have not so far proved very successful. This is partly because, whether they operate by restricting the quantity of the commodity concerned reaching the world markets or by use of a buffer stock whose transactions counter market trends, they have mainly sought to influence the level of *prices* rather than the level of *production*. Where overproduction has continued to take place, or sudden shortages have arisen, it then becomes much harder to make the agreement stick: for example, to maintain agreements previously reached among producers about quotas, or between producers and consumers about price. It is difficult, if not impossible, to prevent prices from eventually reflecting variations in the supply of particular commodities in relation to demand; and it is arguable that prices *ought* to do so if they are to perform as signals, both to consumers and producers, as is their primary economic function. It is on these grounds that even producers usually accept that the price levels aimed at should reflect 'long-term market trends'. But these are often difficult to forecast.

Short-term fluctuations can be moderated. This can probably be done best by ensuring that there exist effective futures markets, whose function it is to constrain these fluctuations. But in this case it is important to prevent speculation and collusion among purchasers in such markets. International measures may be needed to supervise their operation: to ensure that they are not distorted by speculative transactions; to prevent cornering of the market by a few importers (as occurred recently in the case of silver); and even to establish new markets where they do not exist.

Commodity markets generally need to be reformed so that market power is made more equal: at present there are often only a very small number of purchasing organisations (as for bananas and cocoa, for example) against large numbers of disorganised sellers. Information needs to be more equally shared. Finally, sales need to be spread out more evenly over time (at present, lack of storage or of credit, or urgent need of foreign exchange, may compel producers to sell large quantities at the same time at very unfavourable prices).

But long-term fluctuations can only be prevented by a more effective international planning mechanism, to ensure that overall *production* matches the long-term trend in demand. It is this which has been so badly lacking in the past and has led so often to instability. Most of the problems surrounding commodities result from over-production: as with cocoa, tin, sugar and coffee today. Only better co-ordination of the original production decisions can overcome this. There may also be a need for better stockpiles and reserves to maintain supplies in cases where production falls. In the case of oil, the most important commodity in international trade, such measures are now being adopted. But even in that case the response among the international community is not co-ordinated. Efforts to diversify sources of supply by consumers are met with conflicting efforts by producers to hold down production. In this, as in other cases, an orderly market can only be achieved by some degree of consensus, between consumers and producers as well as between producers, about the long-term trend in demand and the required levels of production (which in turn will determine price). Such consensus is not easy to achieve, but at least the attempt must be made. Only some planning framework at the international level, comparable to those that now generally exist within national economies, to ensure that unilateral decisions are replaced by multilateral choices, is likely to create the stability in commodity prices so generally demanded.

But for many countries, especially developing countries, price instability results as much from inflation in Western economies as it does from that in commodity prices. The two are of course closely related. Inflation in developed countries is both a cause and an effect of inflation in commodity prices. But in part it results from internal factors within those economies. And some have argued that it is this factor which has brought about a long-term decline in the terms of trade for producer countries over the last 30 years. Though this argument is contested – the terms of trade for particular types of country depend largely on the dates chosen for comparison – it is certainly the case that non-oil developing countries have suffered doubly from external inflation over the past decade, having been hit simultaneously by higher oil prices and higher priced imports from the West. The fact is that inflation is a menace to rich countries and poor alike; and both have a common interest in containing it.

The policy of international bodies will reflect that concern. This does not mean that they must maintain a monetarist position, allowing all other aims to be subordinated to the control of inflation. It is doubtful if measures that hold down the production of goods and increase the number of unemployed receiving state benefits, while doubling the price of borrowing which recession makes more necessary, contribute much to holding down inflation over the long term. International bodies, in seeking to contain price instability, therefore, must be concerned also to maintain steady growth, while restraining inflation through other means – for example, by encouraging effective incomes policies and strict demand management (as were effectively practised during the fifties and sixties). Such a policy will probably do more in the long run to reduce price instability than the lurches of traditional stop–go.

Another type of instability which causes many problems for the world economy is that affecting currency values over recent years: especially since floating exchange rates became general in 1972–3. As we saw in Chapter 4, it is unlikely that there will be a general restoration of fixed parities in the immediate future. The extreme volatility of currencies which has become normal today, however, causes many problems: problems that affect traders, bankers and governments in developed countries and have serious repercussions for poor countries too. There is thus every reason to try to institute international measures which could lessen the fluctuations. At present, currency values are affected by very small changes in interest rates or monetary growth in individual countries, changes which may bear very little relation to long-term competitiveness. This leads to such irrational situations as the strength of sterling in 1978–80, when Britain's competitive position was declining sharply, and the weakness of the dollar in the same period, when US competitiveness was rising fast. The movements are intensified because of the large volume of mobile funds which jump from currency to currency according to short-term movements. Only a much greater degree of co-operation among governments about levels of demand and interest rates, as well as parities, and possibly a more important role for the IMF in influencing such decisions, are likely to reduce instabilities resulting from that cause.

Instabilities can also arise, however, from sudden changes in the balance of payments position of particular countries: as a result of the rising cost of imports, declining exports, or other factors. This has the effect that they are obliged to take emergency measures, because of the inadequacy of their reserves or alternative means of support: sudden restraints on imports, severe deflation, devaluation or repudiation of debts. Such emergency measures may have an adverse effect on other countries and can provoke a series of counter-measures. They will be prevented only if the IMF is able to provide more adequate balance of payments support to countries in deficit: whether through increased quotas, more SDRs, or larger 'facilities' to help states in difficulty. This could allow deficit countries to avoid restrictive policies, which are damaging to other countries and to the international economy as a whole. Credit will not, and should not, be provided unconditionally. What is important, however, is that the conditions imposed are not so rigorous that they reduce the level of international economic activity unnecessarily, so imposing deflation not only on the borrowing country but, indirectly, on many others as well.

Yet another type of instability can result from the huge volume of debts now incurred by many poor countries. When these reach a certain level they lead to a sharp reduction in their credit-worthiness and a reluctance among bankers and other institutions to lend further. This is a situation that has now been reached by a number of developing countries as a result of the large borrowing they have been obliged to make, at very high rates of interest, over the last few years. Unless given some assistance in undertaking these repayments, or in overcoming their shortage of foreign exchange, they could be obliged to default, with serious consequences for the international financial system. At the very least they will be obliged to cut back sharply on imports from elsewhere, with almost as dramatic consequences. There is a case for establishing a totally new financial institution which would be responsible for examining the financial position of very poor countries and recommending steps for dealing with their outstanding debts.[4] In many cases a rescheduling of debts will almost certainly be necessary, at least for governmental debts, and often some more substantial form of relief as well.[5] Ideally there should be agreement on a new set of principles governing such relief: on the circumstances when particular types of relief would be granted, on the types of country for which they would be reduced or written off, on the debt-servicing ratio regarded as tolerable, and so on. This would avoid the suspicion that the treatment accorded to debtors was influenced by political considerations. It could also reduce the sense among debtors that their economic fate was dependent on future, apparently arbitrary, decisions by the principal creditors, rather than on the application of accepted principles.

There are therefore a number of different types of instability affecting the operation of the modern world economy: fluctuations in general economic activity, in commodity prices, in export earnings, in currency parities, in payments, in trade balances and in debt obligations. Each of these can have serious effects not only for individual countries but also, in consequence, for other members of the international community. Only the development of appropriate international institutions and procedures is likely to succeed in reducing those effects.

9.4 EMPLOYMENT IN THE INTERNATIONAL ECONOMY

However, by far the most serious problem that will be confronted in any attempt to manage the world economy in the foreseeable future is that which we encountered in the last chapter: the very high levels of unemployment now experienced all over the world and the essential need in consequence to stimulate types of economic activity likely to create more jobs.

That problem will not be solved simply by maintaining the world economy at a higher level of activity. Even if the world were to enjoy a number of years of higher growth than in the last decade, which does not in any case seem probable, there would still be very large numbers of people, in rich countries and poor alike, who would be left untouched by that process and remain without employment. World economic policy in that situation would still have failed. For a widening gap between those people in the world fortunate enough to have jobs and those unfortunate enough to be without them would be no better than a widening gap between rich countries and poor. The creation of a relatively high, even of a rapidly growing, standard of living for a part of the population, while the rest were condemned to idleness and penury, would be as manifest a failure as a national health policy which provided admirable services for a part of the population and left the rest to squalor and disease, or an educational policy that provided schools for some and ignorance for the rest. Economic policy would have succeeded in its least important task – achieving a spurious overall growth, enjoyed by only a part of the population – while failing in the far more fundamental task of providing satisfying and useful employment for all who seek it.

If jobs are to be found for the large numbers at present deprived of them, it will thus not be enough to expand demand in a general way. As we saw in the Introduction, expansion of demand would need to be selective: to ensure that it had the greatest possible impact on the levels of employment. For that purpose it would also need to be redistributive. Demand would need to be expanded most among those where at present income was lowest; for these will spend the greatest part of the new income received, and so do most to expand demand elsewhere. Secondly, demand should be expanded most in those areas of activity which are least capital-intensive and most labour-intensive – for example, house-building, food production, road and rail construction and the traditional economy – rather than in modern industry, where demand for labour is low.

Though often it will be national economic policies which should reflect those priorities, international policies also should be influenced. For development assistance, for example, the policy implies a new approach altogether. Most aid in the past has been granted on the assumption that its purpose was to promote the fastest possible rate of economic *growth*. It was seen as particularly vital for that purpose to promote industrialisation and modernisation. It was here too that technical assistance and foreign equipment were believed to be most helpful. Projects were chosen on the basis of the capital–output ratio that could be anticipated, or the need to establish industrial 'growth points' to stimulate modernisation in the surrounding area. Those aims reflected the ambitions of receiving governments and donors alike. Yet the projects financed often provided benefits for comparatively few people, and contributed very little to employment.

If the object becomes the creation of employment, the emphasis will be quite different. First, aid would obviously go for labour-intensive rather than capital-intensive activities. An increasing proportion of aid would go for agriculture, since this is where the great majority of the population will continue to be employed. And it would go in particular to labour-intensive types of agriculture that will do most to create employment. It would be available for local procurement and not only for imported goods, including sub-contracting to the traditional economy. It would be supplied for many small projects, rather than a few big ones, because this too will do most to create jobs.

Secondly, aid would be designed to benefit the poorest sections of the population, since these will spend the greatest part of the new income received, and so do most to expand demand in other parts of the economy. Aid would thus become less directly focused on 'development' in the traditional sense. Some might be used for helping the most backward sections of the population improve their capacity to earn: by helping local co-operatives, local craftsmen and village infrastructure, so as to boost purchasing power where at present it is lowest and provide jobs of a kind many can perform.

The distribution of aid among countries too, would be affected. Traditionally many of the poorest countries have been low receivers of aid a head, on the grounds that their absorptive capacity is low. Most aid has gone to countries which already had substantial advantages, in terms of existing infrastructure and trained manpower, and were therefore able to attract funds from other sources. If the creation of employment is seen as the basic objective, a different set of criteria emerge. It is the poorest and least advanced countries which may require the greatest external assistance, both because they are least likely to attract private investment and because the pool of unemployment may be highest there (since population growth is usually highest). Their absorptive capacity is not lower but higher, because their need for population programmes, assistance in education and teacher-training, and for help in improving agricultural techniques, irrigation and soil fertility, is greater than that of more advanced countries. Because productivity is low in the poorest countries, especially in agriculture, external assistance may bring about the most dramatic increases in production (it is both easier and cheaper to raise agricultural yields in Nigeria and Bangladesh than in South Korea or Taiwan, because in the latter countries they are already high). The more aid is concentrated on the least developed countries, therefore, the more jobs it may create and the bigger the increase in production it may bring about.

Policy on private investment would be influenced in the same way. Over recent decades, most foreign investment has been undertaken by large transnational companies which have already developed a particular technology for the home economy and seek to extract additional returns by employing it elsewhere. Other investment is in undertakings that are by nature capital-intensive, such as the development of minerals and energy. Though such investment, by increasing foreign-exchange earnings, will bring benefits to the receiving countries (as well as to the international economy as a whole), it contributes little to reducing unemployment. If this situation is to be changed, a different strategy might need to be adopted, both by those international organisations concerned with investment (such as the International Finance Corporation) and by receiving governments. More jobs would be created if efforts were made to ensure that, instead of importing components and labour which could be acquired locally, the companies were committed to sub-contracting to local firms for many of their needs. Tax holidays and other investment incentives would be granted only for those types of undertaking which made the best use of local resources, especially of local resources of labour.

International trade policy would also be adjusted. Measures of liberalisation would be concentrated on trade in labour-intensive products. For example, since most agriculture in developing countries is fairly labour-intensive, more effort would be made to reduce trade restrictions in that field. Levies, duties and excise taxes on food imports would therefore be lowered or removed. Trade in handicrafts and other products of traditional industries would be promoted for the same reason. Finally, trade in simple manufactures, such as textiles, especially those produced by traditional labour-intensive means, would be liberalised faster than at present. If this strategy were accepted, the next round of negotiations in GATT would be deliberately focused on measures that would free trade first in the products which used the greatest quantities of labour in their production.

The monetary system too would be affected by the new policy objectives. In considering applications for credit, the IMF would be concerned with wider economic considerations than has often been the case in the past: not only the immediate response to a balance of payments crisis, but also long-term development needs. Already today it has begun to be concerned with structural adjustments as well as short-term measures. But it needs a still wider horizon. It would therefore be less disposed to demand measures – such as cuts in public spending, restrictions on credit – which may have the effect of reducing jobs in order to reduce inflation. The containment of inflation would remain a major objective of the Fund, but it may in future become less willing to buy this with the jobs of ordinary people who are unable to influence their own situation, and more through devising and demanding effective incomes policies and job-creation schemes to improve supply, often more appropriate to the situation of poor countries.

Whatever the particular policy adopted in each of these fields, an essential step would be the recognition, which scarcely exists today, that policies in all areas are closely interrelated. At present international decisions on trade, money and development questions are reached in wholly different organisations, with different representations, and quite inadequate attempts to integrate policy between them.[6] Yet decisions reached on international trade policy, including the negotiations undertaken in GATT, have an immediate impact on developmental and monetary policies in each country. Development policies, national and international, are deeply influenced by what happens in the trade and monetary fields. Monetary policy cannot be effectively conducted without regard to developmental and trade objectives. Thus, whether or not the objectives here described – the removal of intervention by governments in free exchanges, the reduction of instabilities affecting the world economy, and the promotion of employment all over the world – are accepted as the most important objectives, it is essential that some more integrated approach to world economic problems is established. This is unlikely to come about without the creation of new institutions exercising a more general responsibility for managing the international economy than is borne by the many specialised bodies which exist today.

10 Justice in the World Economy

National governments, in directing their economies, are concerned not only with improving overall efficiency, and so securing a high level of national growth. Even if this can be achieved, they know it will not necessarily maximise the welfare of all their people. However high the rate of growth, some, perhaps without jobs or without bread-winners, may still be left in a state of destitution. In other words, they are concerned with a broader range of goals than efficiency alone. They are concerned with the fate of *individuals* as well as of the economy as a whole; with equity as well as with efficiency; and with relative standards of welfare as well as with absolute standards. For that reason they all seek, in varying degrees, through social services and the tax system, to bring about a reduction of inequalities among society's members to a level that is generally acceptable.

In the international economy, likewise, there will be concern with other objectives than efficiency alone. At the international level too, the creation of a more efficiently working world economy, even if it can be achieved, may do little to promote the economic welfare of millions of people who live only at the fringes of that economy. The liberalisation of trade between states and the creation of a more efficient monetary system will benefit some people in poor countries, and perhaps help those countries generally. But it may have little impact on the welfare and way of life of countless individuals and families within those countries. The achievement of a higher rate of growth in the international economy, while it will clearly benefit some, may have little influence on the standard of living of many individuals and groups, of whole regions, and even of entire nations.

Those responsible for managing the international economy, therefore, will be concerned with the creation not only of a more efficient, but also of a fairer, world – one in which existing inequalities in welfare and ways of life may be progressively reduced. The two objectives are quite distinct. An economy may be extremely efficient yet at the same time very unjust. The slave economies of ancient Greece or Peru, and the semi-slave economies of the industrial revolution, may have secured high and growing standards of living for some, but at a cost in human misery that would today be regarded as insupportable. Similarly, in some societies today – where prosperity is based on subjugation or immiserisation for many – efficiency may be secured only at the cost of huge injustices. In such cases a choice has to be made between the two. If slavery (or 12-hour working days) were the sole means of securing economic growth, then a decision to abandon slavery (or 12-hour days) must be a decision to accept lower living standards for the sake of justice; and *vice versa*. In such circumstances a country can have maximum growth or justice but not both.

Usually the choice is not so clear-cut. The price of greater efficiency, it may be believed, is the adoption not of a totally unjust system, but of a marginally greater degree of inequality. This may be necessary, it is sometimes held, to provide greater incentives and rewards for enterprise; to secure greater saving and therefore greater investment; to provide lower wages and therefore reduced costs for industry; to economise in welfare payments and so in government spending. Much argument has been devoted to these questions and it is doubtful if definitive answers will ever be found. But evidence for a close correlation between inequality and growth is not strong. There are many countries where there are very large differences in standards of living that have secured little or no development; and some where differences are relatively small which have impressive growth records.

The answer would therefore seem to be that there is rarely a direct choice to be made between efficiency and equity. Both objectives are important, but they are not very closely related. Both nationally and internationally, the two are affected by quite different factors. Within nations rapid economic growth may be secured at a time when inequalities increase (as in the early nineteenth century); or at a time when they are reduced (as in Scandinavia in the fifties and sixties). Conversely, inequalities within a society may be sharply reduced or suddenly increased (for example, with a change in government) without any direct impact on its rate of economic growth. It is thus not sufficient, if there is any concern for equity, for economic policy to concentrate on securing economic growth alone, in the pious hope that, if 'development' can be achieved, the problems of distribution will look after themselves; or that prosperity can be relied on to 'trickle down' from the upper echelons of society to the lower. Efforts to promote equity have to be consciously undertaken, quite separately from efforts to promote efficiency. For the two are quite independent.

Internationally, there is still less connection between the two objectives. No reasonable person can maintain that wide differences in the standard of living of different states are necessary as an *incentive* to induce greater effort in the less developed countries: that India's poverty is the cost of securing higher economic growth in the United States, or that India will not seek economic advance without knowledge of the prosperity of the United States. Nor can inequality between states be held necessary to encourage *savings* and so investment. On the contrary, the attraction of greater prosperity elsewhere creates a constant drain of savings, legally or illegally, from the poorest countries, where they are most needed, to the richest, where they are already greatest. Similarly, inequalities between states, far from encouraging a more rational allocation of manpower, bring about a drain of talent and skill from the poorest countries, where they are most scarce and can bring about the largest increase in welfare, to the richest, where they add only marginally to existing resources of that kind.

The fact is that inequalities between states are more comparable to those between regions than to those between individuals within states; and none of the arguments traditionally used to justify inequalities between individuals can be equally applied to the inequalities that exist between regions. Inequalities between states, like those between regions, derive usually from historical accidents: different starting dates, varying resource endowments, differing social structures and attitudes. For the most part they are neither the *effect* of varying efficiency, nor the *cause* of efforts to attain efficiency. And here too, as within states, measures that promote efficiency are indifferent in their effects on equity. Though some measures to reduce inefficiency – the liberalisation of trade, for example – may also reduce differences in standards of living between states, others will have no such impact: for example, the creation of a more efficient international monetary system. In other words, internationally as nationally, the creation of a fairer economic system between states has to be pursued at the same time as, but quite independently from, the creation of a more efficient world economic system.

It is inevitably much harder to win political consensus for the measures required to promote equity among states than for those needed to promote efficiency. The reduction of inequalities between states, like the same process within them, involves costs for some to match the benefits of others. It is not always the case that the steps required can be justified as being in the 'mutual' interests of all states. Measures of which the primary effect is to increase efficiency (such as those we examined in the last chapter) may promote mutual interests. Rich countries and poor alike may be expected to benefit (though not necessarily in the same way or in equal proportions) as a result of measures to liberalise trade and payments, for example: low-cost countries will benefit through access to increased scales abroad, high-cost countries through the increased availability to them of low-cost goods and through increased purchasing power abroad. Even here there will be differences in interest among different groups in each country. In the low-cost countries those in exporting industries will gain directly, some others indirectly, while many will benefit hardly at all, and a few may be adversely affected (for example, if their land is taken to provide export crops); in the importing country all consumers will gain, exporting industries may gain less directly, while a few who work in the industries whose goods are displaced by imports will suffer severely. Between countries as a whole, however, the long-term benefits may be fairly evenly distributed.

In many other cases, however, no such mutual interests exist. It cannot reasonably be argued that many changes which directly benefit the poorer countries bring no cost to the richer ones. If larger aid programmes are provided to poor countries than before, if debts are re-scheduled or written off, if interest rates are reduced by subsidies, there is a direct transfer of resources from one group of countries to another. There may be some *indirect* benefits to rich countries (because poor countries are enabled to buy more of their goods) but these will not necessarily outweigh the cost of the resources transferred. It is for this reason that a decision to increase such transfers may depend ultimately on the political goodwill or moral responsibility of rich countries, rather than on their economic rationality alone. At best it might be said that rich countries have an enlightened self-interest in being generous on such matters: if they are not, various problems will be caused – economic and political – which could be held contrary to their long-term interests. In the same way, a rich man might be said to have some long-term advantage in giving his money away: because his conscience will feel clearer or because he will gain in reputation. But that interest is not strictly an economic one. On a pure calculation of material advantage, the interests of different states (as of different groups within them) often conflict.

It is perhaps more accurate to speak of a mutuality of *concern* between rich countries and poor. Given the complex and interrelated character of the modern world economy, every country is to some extent involved in the prosperity of others. When, as today, rich countries do 30–40 per cent of their trade with poor countries, the economic fortunes of the latter must be of considerable importance to the former.[1] Where poor countries owe $500 billion in debts to rich countries, their economic future must matter to some extent to the latter. Where the raw materials and energy sources on which rich countries rely come in substantial quantities from poor countries, the former must have some interest in the economic affairs of the latter. On these grounds – that is, because of the close interrelatedness of the modern world economy – no country can afford, even apart from its moral responsibility, to be altogether indifferent to the economic conditions prevailing in other parts of the world.

It is not only rich countries which do not always recognise this interdependence. Some in poor countries, because of the difficulty of competing on equal terms in a world economy dominated by countries far more advanced than they, because of the fear that by opening their countries to outside forces they may expose themselves to increased dependence on the strong, see the way to salvation in isolating themselves from external economic forces: in policies, that is, of 'self-reliance' or 'de-linking' (p. 52 above). Under that strategy foreign investment is spurned, foreign borrowing renounced, aid forgone and trade reduced to a minimum. Industrial policy is devoted to import-saving rather than export development. Agriculture is given over to feeding the local population rather than growing crops which can be exported. Traditional rather than modern techniques are favoured. Even if overall growth is slower under such a strategy, this is felt to be a sacrifice worth paying for the sake of securing fewer disruptions of local traditions, less domestic inequality, and above all less dependence on foreigners.

There are obvious attractions in such an approach. The difficulty is that in purely economic terms the gains produced by contacts with the outside world – through trade, through inward investment, through the import of technology and skills – are substantial. Though these may benefit some sections of the population more than others, all the population will gain at least marginally. The sacrifice in living standards which is therefore involved in 'self-reliance' may be greater than the local population is prepared to accept. Since communication with the outside world cannot be eliminated, knowledge of the material progress attained in other countries by alternative means cannot be prevented and may erode faith in the strategy chosen. In other words, self-sufficiency is often an expensive luxury. A self-reliant country can depend on firewood and peat and other domestic sources of energy, rather than developing the exports needed to pay for oil; but for so doing it will have to pay a fairly heavy price. And, paradoxically, in the long run the loss of growth may mean that countries which follow the path of self-reliance become *more* dependent on imports, including imports of food (or food aid), energy and manufactured goods, than those that have followed the export-led pattern of development. Over the long term, poor countries as well as rich are affected by the simple law of comparative costs: all will usually benefit if they are able to import from the cheapest sources. Perhaps for this reason such policies, though passionately demanded by individuals, have almost never been pursued by governments of third world countries; or if attempted have been in time abandoned.

But the fact that all countries, rich and poor alike, become, with an increasingly complex world division of labour, increasingly inter-dependent, does not mean that they have an automatic motive to create a fairer world economy. The slave and the slave-master are inter-dependent; but they do not have a 'mutual interest' in changing their relationship. The slave-master has an interest in the slave's survival and physical health, but no interest in his ceasing to be a slave. Sometimes, it is true, rich countries benefit from increased prosperity among poor ones. This can produce larger markets abroad, or reflate the world economy with less inflationary consequences for themselves; can prevent debt repudiation and other major disruptions; can lower the rate of population growth; and (possibly) reduce political conflict throughout the world. But this does not mean that rich countries gain *more* from growth in poor countries than they gain from growth at home. And it does not therefore indicate that, on a calculation of economic interest alone, rich countries will benefit more by allocating resources to poor countries than by investing them within their own economies.

If a more equitable, as well as a more efficient, international economy is to be created, therefore, consciousness of 'mutual interests' will not be enough. A different type of motivation may be required: a conscious recognition of the injustice (as well as the inefficiency) of the existing world economic system and a concern to remedy that injustice. There is thus a need for a conscious desire, such as has long existed within states, that deliberate steps should be taken to reduce the inequalities that now exist; and that the international economy should be managed in such a way as will not only eliminate irrational barriers, instabilities and wasted human resources, but secure a more equitable distribution of the benefits of world growth as well.

These two aims are not necessarily in conflict. But they are different aims, to be pursued by different means. And we need to look now at some of the ways in which the management of the international economy may be undertaken to bring about the second aim: to create a more equitable world economy than exists today.

10.2 REDISTRIBUTION TO THE POOREST COUNTRIES

If the world economy needs to be managed in the interests of equity as well as efficiency, policies will be needed that will provide special assistance for the poorest *countries* within the world economy.

If the ultimate objective is to reduce poverty in the world, this is obviously a crude instrument to use. Not all the poorest people in the world live in the poorest countries. Not all the people in the poorest countries are very poor. Measures to help the poorest countries, therefore, may help a few people who are relatively well off. And some people who are very poor may not be affected by such measures at all (either because they do not live in very poor countries or because international measures that benefit such countries do not affect every group within them).

These are admitted shortcomings in any international efforts which pass through the governments of particular countries. But they should not be exaggerated. A large proportion of the poorest people in the world do live in the poorest countries (provided India, though not a 'least developed' state, is included among them). Most international aid given to those countries assists (or can be made to assist) the poorest people within them. If such measures are carefully selected, and if their application by governments is carefully supervised, it should be possible in practice to ensure that they go a long way to assist many of the people of the world who are most in need. And, since at present, whether we like it or not, power rests in the hands of governments, most international economic assistance has to pass through the hands of governments. Assistance to the governments of the poorest countries is at least more likely to help the poorest people than assistance to the governments of other countries. And, provided that it is selective and supervised in the right way, most of it can be directed to ensure that it assists those in the greatest need of all.

If special measures are to be taken to assist the poorest countries, the first question that arises is: which are the particular countries that deserve such special treatment? There is never likely to be universal agreement on the criteria to be used. The United Nations, in distinguishing the 30-odd 'least developed' countries, has chosen criteria that emphasise the degree of modernisation achieved. This has the effect that countries which are very poor in terms of income a head, such as India, are not included and do not qualify for certain concessions because they possess a small advanced sector within their economy. Most people will agree that, if human welfare is the ultimate consideration, income a head should be the decisive factor in the allocation of aid: the poorer the country the more help it requires. This does not mean it is necessary to use the same criterion for all purposes. For certain kinds of assistance income a head will be the most relevant factor; for others, the degree of industrialisation, the level of education, the volume of exports, or other considerations. Different international organisations may therefore need to reach their own definitions, according to their relevance to the kind of special treatment which they have in mind.

Even if there is general agreement about the relevant criteria, there may be disagreement about the way they are applied and where a dividing-line should be drawn: for example, whether the poorest 30 or the poorest 50 or the poorest 100 countries should be given special treatment. Such problems can be minimised (like the poverty trap within states) if sharp dividing-lines are avoided. There is room for a gradual spectrum ranging between the most favoured treatment of all and no special assistance at all: so, as countries progress, they should gradually lose certain rights and privileges. This principle of 'graduation', of adjusting concessions to the level of development reached, which is beginning to be adopted in the trade field, now needs to be much more widely applied elsewhere.

Nowhere is the need for clear criteria more obvious than in the field of aid. Though aid is the most specific, and usually the most concessionary, of all the measures that can be taken to help poor countries, at present the volume provided to each country bears frighteningly little relationship to its development needs. Table 10.1 gives some comparison of the amount of aid per head received by particular countries and particular categories of countries. As this suggests, the amount of aid which each country receives is based largely on the subjective preference of donors, traditional ties, and above all on the strategic importance attributed to each recipient country, rather than on economic needs, such as income a head. A small territory with close connections with a major indus-

TABLE 10.1   *Aid receipts per head:*
selected countries and territories, 1979

	GNP a head ($)	ODA ($m.)	ODA a head ($)
Réunion	3060	702.2	1404.4
Israel	3500	826.6	217.52
Tanzania	230	731.9	43.0
Egypt	390	1890.0	41.62
Kenya	330	559.5	36.3
Mali	120	186.6	28.73
Thailand	490	513.2	11.10
Bangladesh	90	758.4	8.7
Laos	90	18.7	5.05
Cambodia	n.a.	26.7	3.0
India	180	1267.7	1.91
Bhutan	100	0.7	0.53

trialised country, such as Réunion, may receive 3000 times as much aid a head as a very poor country with no wealthy partners, such as Bhutan. A strategically important country with a powerful friend, such as Israel, will get well over 100 times as much aid a head as a large country with few allies such as India. A strategically important nation, such as Egypt, will receive 20 times as much as a neighbouring country that is less favoured, such as Ethiopia, even though its existing income a head is three times as large. The result is that, far from the poorest countries of the world receiving additional assistance to help them cope with their special difficulties, they receive at present substantially less per head than the middle-income countries, whose problems are far less acute.

An international policy that was concerned about matching assistance to needs would, first, seek at least to ensure that attention within international bodies was adequately focused on this question. At present, extraordinarily enough, there is little effort to discuss and debate the *total* amounts received by each country (both from multilateral and bilateral sources) on a comparative basis. Bilateral donors each reach their own decisions on the issue, usually at least partly on political grounds, independently of each other. Multilateral institutions also make their own judgements, according to their own criteria (which are usually supposed to be non-political), but again independently of each other. If one country appears unimportant to all of them – say Bhutan, Burundi or Bolivia – it may receive very little; while another that all find deserving, perhaps for quite different reasons (Israel, Egypt or Tanzania, say), may be disproportionately favoured. Only if the question of distribution between countries (in terms of receipts a head) is given far more serious attention than it is today and on a much wider basis among donors will existing disparities be reduced.

Such a discussion would require an exchange of view between the major multilateral bodies (the World Bank, the UNDP, the European Development Fund and the Arab Development Fund, for example) as well as bilateral donors. An annual meeting of donors could be devoted to establishing what each country receives at present and to agreeing on criteria which should determine distribution in the future. Since political motivations play a larger part in determining the distribution of bilateral programmes, these would be more difficult to influence; but at least discussion in a wider context, and a greater understanding of the existing disparities, should do something to reduce the biases which at present operate, even here. There is now a greater disposition to recognise the special needs of the 'least developed'[2] (though that category urgently needs to be extended to cover all the poorest countries). Such a discussion should do something to reduce existing inequities of distribution. And it should ensure that the poorest countries of all, instead of receiving less a head than others, in future receive more. For the capacity of such countries to absorb external assistance of the right kind – communications, education, agriculture, population programmes, for example – is certainly no less and may be greater than that of more advanced developing countries.

But it is not only the amount but also the *type* of aid that is supplied which needs more international consideration. Far more than middle-income countries, the poorest countries need assistance on concessionary terms. Indeed, given their limited capacity to repay, most must be in the form of outright grants. The aid needs to be untied (spendable in any country), which in many cases is not so today.[3] It should be usable for maintenance or programme purposes, not always for major new projects. It should be available for local as well as for foreign purchases; for agriculture more than for industry: for small-scale rather than large-scale enterprises. Here again there needs to be far more discussion in an international context of the types of aid appropriate for particular kinds of country than is usually the case today.

The poorest countries of all also need special concessions in the field of trade. The best solution would be to grant totally free access to all their products. At the very least, future measures of liberalisation should be concentrated on the type of trade in which their interest lies. This would not be a very expensive concession for developed states, because the total manufacturing capacity of most of these countries is limited. For that reason such countries mainly get only a limited benefit from the generalised system of preferences, and from the quotas given under the Multi-Fibre Arrangement (most of the available quotas being taken by more advanced developing countries). To grant duty-free entry for the poorest countries of all would be to apply deliberate discrimination in their favour, giving them a preference over other poor countries, just as all poor countries are, under the GSP, granted a preference over competing rich countries. In other words, it would implement the principle of graduation which many rich countries themselves favour.

Special provision for the very poorest countries could also be given within the world's monetary system. At present many of the poorest countries receive only limited help from the IMF because, although their needs are great, their quotas are very small: the total quotas of the 30 poorest countries in the world amount to only about 1 per cent of all the quotas in the Fund. The simplest way of helping would thus be simply to increase their quotas (perhaps by establishing a larger minimum quota for all countries). There is also a case for creating a new 'facility' for assisting such countries *beyond* their normal quota limits. Finally, there could be special treatment of such countries in any measures of debt relief which are granted. At present their debt burden is usually not particularly large (because they have not been able to borrow heavily in the past, because most of their aid is now in the form of grants, and because some have already benefited from measures of debt relief). But, as their debts and so their borrowing increase, they may increasingly need official assistance, including subsidised interest rates, to help them maintain their repayments.

The precise type of measure that is adopted to help the poorest countries will vary from time to time in accordance with their special needs and with the changing structure of the world economy. The most important thing is that there should be a greater willingness to discriminate *among* developing countries. It is no longer sufficient to classify countries as 'rich' or 'poor', 'developed' or 'developing'. The 130 poor countries of the world comprise many different types of country, with greatly varying characteristics: those with energy supplies and those without; those with valuable minerals to export and those without; those with substantial numbers of technically qualified people and those without; those with a substantial manufacturing base and those without. Even the dual division here suggested, therefore, between developing and least developed, is too crude for many purposes; and eventually efforts will have to be made to adjust international and economic measures more precisely to the economic or other characteristics of each individual country.

This type of fine-tuning may be still a long way off. But, if considerations of equity as well as efficiency are to play a part in the running of the international economy, the amount and type of assistance given needs to be adjusted far more carefully to the needs of different types of country than is the case today.

10.3 REDISTRIBUTION TO THE POOREST PEOPLE

But more assistance to the poorest countries will not always ensure that more help is given to all the people in greatest need all over the world. Some of the poorest people in the world do not live in the poorest countries. Help given to the poorest countries may not always penetrate to the poorest people within those countries. Ideally, therefore, there is a need for international measures to provide *direct* assistance for poor people everywhere, rather than helping them only indirectly, that is, by courtesy of their own governments.

At present within many poor countries there remain huge inequalities. Squalor and misery for a large part of the population may exist side by side with opulence for a few. The political structure is often as inegalitarian as the economy. This means that in some cases the dominant elite within the country concerned will seek to use its power to ensure that aid from outside will mainly benefit, directly or indirectly, those classes which already wield power, or at least will not seriously damage their power (by, for example, reducing their control over land, water, taxation or industry). In such a situation an increase in governmental aid may, unless adequate care is taken, only increase the power and wealth of a few and bring limited if any benefits to the most deprived sections of the population, which are most in need of help.

There are a number of ways in which international organisations and other donors could seek to overcome this problem. The most obvious is simply by the choice of programme or project to be assisted. All donors can insist, if they are so minded, on providing finance only for projects that will bring benefit to the most disadvantaged of the population, whether in the towns or the countryside. Different projects provide help for different groups or different regions; and, each time a project is chosen for assistance, a decision is made to assist a particular group. The World Health Organisation (WHO), in launching an international programme to provide water supplies to urban shanty towns, is making a deliberate decision that the inhabitants of these towns are those they wish to help. The ILO, in instituting a programme to provide vocational training for the unemployed in the countryside, is deciding to give assistance to another deprived section of the population. The FAO and IFAD, in providing more extension services, improved seed varieties, or better water supplies to the poorer peasantry in the countryside, can ensure that help goes to another group in special need. In each case the governing bodies of those organisations make a decision to assist particular groups in need in the receiving countries (though they may subsequently need to exercise careful supervision to see that aid reaches the groups intended).

Bilateral donors, in deciding which programmes they are ready to help, make a similar decision. If they refuse to finance projects that will mainly benefit the better-off, and insist they will only provide help of a kind which reaches the very poorest, the governments of the receiving countries can only prevent those ends from being achieved by depriving their country of assistance altogether: a decision they will usually be reluctant to reach. More likely, they will seek to offer alternative programmes which benefit different groups – irrigation which helps the richer farmers, roads that provide fat contracts for particular firms, factories that benefit particular regions or towns (or particular industrialists) or prestige projects that bring glory mainly to the government. So long as the donors are insistent, they need not allow their purposes to be deflected in this way. So long as their commitment to assisting particular groups (rather than the 'country' generally) is sufficient, they should be able to ensure that their aid benefits those in the greatest need.

Donors may also be able to ensure that their help goes where it is most needed by working through local community organisations, rather than national agencies, if this is permitted. Sometimes it may be easier to do this if the money is channelled through a voluntary agency (such as Oxfam) which may have long-established contacts with local communities and which may be able to supervise the project on a continuing basis. Supervision of this kind may be far more welcome, both to the local community and even to the authorities of the receiving countries, than supervision by distant aid administrators, which can appear as a more overt interference in local decision-making, or by local officials, who may not always be fully trusted.

The relative benefits secured by different sections of the population in receiving countries will also be affected, of course, by decisions concerning the *volume* of expenditure to be undertaken by different development agencies. If the expenditure of the WHO rises more than that of the UN Industrial Development Organisation, of IFAD more than that of FAO, the balance of welfare within the world is marginally altered. At present there is little conscious attempt to balance the relative expenditure of different organisations, and certainly little public discussion of such matters; still less is there public debate about the relative amounts spent on different programmes by the same organisations (though this is of course discussed within the governing bodies of each organisation). Yet these are questions that can have an important influence on the benefits received by different groups and individuals in each receiving country. And, as the total volume of development assistance grows, and a welfare world begins to be superimposed over individual welfare states, it is important that the balance between the various programmes, as well as the policies pursued by different organisations (and by each government within such organisations) should be far more widely and actively discussed than is the case at present.

Another way of trying to ensure that a larger proportion of international assistance goes to the needier sections of the world's population is to vary the amounts going to different *countries* according to the policies they pursue. A general principle could be established that, where the policies of a developing country have the effect that aid funds benefit only a small elite in the ruling class, aid will be reduced. Where steps are taken to bring about a more equal distribution of income, it can be increased. In this way, without any overt arm-twisting or attempts to dictate domestic decisions, aid may be directed towards those who most need it (and, indirectly, the policies of receiving countries may be influenced in the direction desired). There are great difficulties in applying such a policy: for example, in reaching objective assessments of the policies pushed in each receiving country. However, there are already one or two bilateral donors that apply such a principle (Sweden, for example). If more were to do so, the policy might begin to have more influence worldwide. It will probably be last applied by multilateral organisations. These at present share out available funds on an almost indiscriminate basis, and their members would probably be unwilling to authorise such highly selective assistance. Only if a majority of governments represented in those organisations could be persuaded to adopt the new principle could they too become an influence in favour of more redistributive policies within developing countries.

At present the influence which international organisations can exercise on matters of this kind is relatively marginal. The distribution of welfare within each country still depends primarily on the decisions of each local government. Additional aid for the poorest sections of the population in the countryside – for example, through such organisations as IFAD – may have little impact unless there is a more fundamental shift of power: so that the underprivileged acquire a greater share of land, water, credit, fertiliser, and the other benefits that derive from power. The greatest benefit international organisations could bring, therefore, would be by changing the attitudes and policies within receiving countries and so adjusting the balance of power there.

Their capacity to do this by direct means is at present limited. The scale of the assistance they provide is for most countries so marginal that governments would normally prefer to forgo help altogether than submit to conditions they regard as unacceptable. It is unlikely, for example, that international organisations could, as has sometimes been suggested, ensure that measures of land reform were implemented in poor countries by threatening to withhold aid if no such action were taken. Such demands would be seen by many governments as a gross interference in their internal affairs and an unacceptable encroachment of sovereignty. And on those grounds a majority within such organisations would at present probably refuse to demand any such conditions.

Domestic policies are thus more likely to be influenced by more subtle methods. Help can be offered; but exclusively to independent peasant proprietors or co-operatives, or only in areas where land reform has already been undertaken. Help in establishing local health clinics can be granted; but only if control of them is left in the hands of representative community groups. New pumps and irrigation work can be offered; but only if the benefits of the water go to all cultivators, the poorest as well as the most prosperous. In all these ways the aid relationship can be used, even now, to influence the course of social development within the receiving country without resort to the more blatant forms of external pressure.

None of these various methods, however, is likely to achieve much unless the total *volume* of assistance provided by international organisations becomes far larger than it is today. At present the total amount of aid provided, from multilateral and bilateral sources combined, is so small that, even if it gets through to the neediest sections of the population, it provides only a marginal benefit for the assisted groups. For the same reason the threat of its withdrawal cannot represent a powerful inducement to governments to change their policies. If, therefore, international programmes are to become a significant factor in bettering the conditions of the poorest people of the world, it is not enough that their direction and character should be changed, important though that is: the total size of the international assistance programme needs to be radically increased.

In any case, those aims are unlikely to be achieved unless there is a far more thorough-going discussion about the content of existing aid programmes than occurs today. Attention at present focuses almost entirely on the total size of those programmes, rather than on their type. In so far as their distribution is discussed, it is in terms of distribution to different *countries*; rather than to different sections of the population or sectors of the economy. It is not the income a head of different countries that should primarily concern us: it is the income a head of different *groups*, regardless of country. Only when we begin to conceive of development efforts in a totally different way, not as aid from one country to another, still less from one government to another, but as assistance from groups of people in one part of the world to individual groups of people in other areas, is development assistance likely to go, more consistently than today, to those whose need of it is greatest.

10.4 ECONOMIC POWER IN THE INTERNATIONAL COMMUNITY

Ultimately, however, justice in the international community can be achieved neither by redistribution in favour of poorer states, nor by redistribution in favour of poorer individuals within states, unless that is accompanied by other changes of a more fundamental kind. For any redistribution of that kind could be quickly and easily reversed. Nor would the underprivileged, even if their material situation had been much improved, for long be content with a system that left them dependent on the choices and decisions of others in more privileged states and groups. Justice is always ultimately a subjective factor; a *sense* of justice. And that sense of justice will only be secured if there is at the same time a redistribution of the economic *power* that determines the distribution of wealth and welfare in the world.

The international community is in many ways at a stage reached within national societies a century or so ago. Until that time the reduction of inequalities and the distribution of welfare generally within states depended on the actions and decisions of individuals, determining to use their own wealth to provide charitable relief for the poor: in the form of schools, hospitals, sheltered accommodation, trusts and funds devoted to that end. Power remained with the wealthy; and justice was secured only in so far as the wealthy chose. It is only within this century that economic and political power has been more widely distributed; and in consequence the machinery has been developed to bring about, through social services, through progressive taxation and other means, a redistribution of society's assets in favour of the less privileged: a redistribution that occurs automatically through state agencies, and independently of the will of individual citizens.

Today the greatest disparities exist not within states but between them. But here the measures that can be taken to reduce those disparities – such as those described in this book – still depend mainly on goodwill and charity: on the express consent of individual governments – including many having a national interest entirely opposed to such steps. Economic power remains with states and so predominantly with the wealthier states. If a more just society is to be created, it can only be by establishing a machinery for redistribution within the world community that is as independent of the will of national governments as the redistributive system within states is of the will of individuals.

Even if their economies continue to grow, and even if they grow faster than those of the richer states, poor countries will not be able, acting as individual states, to bring about such a change. Even working together they may well be unable to achieve it. Diplomatically, their voices count for little. Economically, they have few levers in their hands. That is why long years of 'north–south dialogue' have so far brought few significant changes in the way the world economy works. Only through influencing the action of international institutions, able to influence economic developments in all states alike, are poorer countries likely to be able to bring about any significant change in that situation: a fundamental alteration in the balance of economic power in the world.

A shift in economic power depends on a shift in political power. Just as a fundamental change in the distribution of economic benefits within states had to await the extension of the franchise to the adult population as a whole, the establishment of political parties devoted to representing the interests of ordinary working people, and the creation of new institutions – planning mechanisms, welfare services, tax structures and so on – that would bring benefits to the previously dispossessed classes; so in the international economy any fundamental change in economic benefits will depend on a new sharing of power in the world community, and the creation of the institutions, for managing the international economy, through which that sharing of power can take place.

What changes would be necessary in the international economy if power were to be shared more equally?

First, existing economic institutions would need to be strengthened. This is a process that may in many cases be resisted by the richer countries of the world. For, just as the poorer states will see these institutions as a means of bringing about a redistribution of power in their favour, so too will the richer countries; and for that reason seek to prevent their acquiring significant authority. Since none of the organisations will be able, like the institutions of the national state, to call on coercive power to enforce their authority in the final resort, their influence can only be built up by gradual means. It will occur most easily in those cases where all countries can perceive, often for different reasons, some advantage in the development of stronger institutions. So, for instance, at the present time rich countries and poor alike might like, for varying reasons, to see a more powerful institution for managing the world's monetary system or a more effective body concerned with energy matters. And we have seen a number of other cases in this book where the conflicts and instabilities of the present world economy mean that most states would see some benefit in a greater measure of international decision-making and international authority.

But the strengthening of international institutions will only bring a significant shift of economic power if those institutions themselves are reformed. In many cases power within them is at present concentrated. The rich countries of the world were able to ensure when these institutions were established (before most of today's developing countries became independent) a system of voting rights which accorded the greatest power to the wealthier states. Within the IMF and the World Bank, as we saw earlier, the voting systems which operate today have the effect that 20 or so Western industrialised countries between them continue to hold a majority of votes, even though they represent only about a sixth of the membership. In many of the other specialised agencies there are comparable arrangements: giving, for example, a greater share of representation on the governing body to the 'chief industrialised countries', the chief ship-owning and ship-using countries, the countries of greatest importance in aviation, and so on. In the case of the financial institutions in particular, this weakens the authority which they would otherwise enjoy. They come to be suspected by the majority of countries from the third world as the instruments through which rich states exert their will, and their influence on the development and financial policies of developing countries is so reduced. If those bodies are to acquire the influence on poor states which the rich countries themselves would like to see them enjoy, it can only be through acquiring the legitimacy and authority of more representative institutions. The purpose would not be a total transfer of power, so that the dominance of the rich and powerful was merely replaced by the dominance of the poor and weak. It would be to create a system under which every decision demanded a considerable element of consensus: not unanimity, allowing a single vote to prevent any decision being reached, but a balance of voting power, so that two-thirds or even three-quarters majorities were required, so ensuring that a substantial majority, including both rich countries and poor, were reasonably satisfied with each decision taken.

The simplest way in which international institutions can alter the existing balance of economic power is by bringing about some redistribution of welfare from rich areas to poor. To some extent all international expenditure brings about such a redistribution (as does public expenditure within states); because it is financed mainly by richer states and benefits mainly poorer ones. At present, however, the volume of funds distributed in this way is minimal. A more substantial redistribution could come about only if there were far higher expenditure by international bodies than is the case today. And the simplest way of bringing about a more ample redistribution within the world would be to seek far higher levels of spending by such bodies – by specialised agencies generally as well as development institutions.

Since, however, some members, especially the richer ones, are likely to resist such an expansion, there is a need to seek alternative sources of revenue for international spending. At present virtually all the funds spent by international organisations derive from the contributions made by governments. This has the effect that the organisations are limited in what they can spend by the willingness of member states to vote the funds.[4] Over recent years the rich members in particular have sought to restrain the growth of the budgets of most international bodies. At the same time, any government can withdraw from the obligation to provide funds, as well as other obligations of membership, simply by withdrawing from the organisation. International organisations may therefore only be able to expand their spending in the future, whether for development assistance or for other activities, if they are able to draw on additional sources of funds.

One alternative type of revenue, independent of the will of governments, now seems quite likely to be established. This is a tax on the development of the resources of the seabed; a proposal that has been almost universally accepted in the negotiations for a new law of the sea over the last few years. But these revenues are unlikely to be large and will be used partly for financing the administration of the seabed area. A number of other types of international tax have been suggested.[5] These include taxes on international trade (comparable to purchase tax or value-added tax within states); taxes on air travel or all international travel; taxes on the use of space for communications; taxes on the use of radio frequencies; and so on. Perhaps the most discussed idea is for a tax on the arms trade, since many people would feel it just that the burden of taxation should fall on those countries which are anxious to sell or buy armaments. The revenues, however, are unlikely to be very great, and the idea has not proved popular with governments. The system which would undoubtedly provide the most adequate resources would be a system under which a proportion of the taxes levied domestically were made over for international purposes: for example, a percentage of VAT proceeds. This would be comparable to the system used to finance the EEC. Applied at the world level it could produce a more substantial volume of funds for international purposes than are available today.

An increase in the resources and power of international institutions will not, however, fundamentally influence the balance of economic power within the world unless those institutions are able to affect the power that is wielded by private institutions as well as that wielded by national governments. The largest private companies today, the big transnational corporations, wield a power that is greater than that of many governments. That power is based on their control over the flow of investments, technology, technically qualified staff, trained management, prices and other factors. Because they operate in many countries simultaneously, such companies are able to insulate themselves to a considerable extent from the control of individual governments. They can adjust internal prices to ensure that profits are made in a way that will minimise taxation. Only if governments act together can they effectively counter the power such organisations wield. For many years there have been discussions within the United Nations of guidelines to govern the activities of these companies.[6] But, even if these are finally agreed, it remains to be seen how much influence, if any, they will have on the operation of the companies.

If the existing balance of economic power in the world is to be genuinely affected, international organisations will need to acquire better means than they have today of ensuring that such enterprises operate in the international public interest and avoid policies that discriminate between countries – in pricing, procurement or employment policies – or otherwise abuse their economic power. It is the success of international bodies in that task that may, as much perhaps as anything else, determine the future balance of economic power in the world.

For the essential power we are concerned with here is the power of individuals. It is necessary to find means of managing the world economy at the highest level only because of the need to protect the economic interests of ordinary men and women, in the villages and in the cities, who are unable to protect those interests for themselves, and whose governments cannot or will not do so for them. A wider power is therefore necessary which can adequately master the powerful but unstable forces at work in the world economy. All will benefit to some extent from the taming of those forces and the substitution of a more rational order. But those who will gain most are those who at present suffer most from the irrationality and cruelty of the existing international economy: the underprivileged millions, scattered in many countries throughout the world, who cannot by their own efforts, however great, rescue themselves from penury; whose governments cannot or will not do it for them; and who depend therefore on a redistribution of wealth and power at the world level which only international action can accomplish. It is for that purpose above all that more effective international institutions for managing the world's economic affairs are today so urgently required.

Notes

NOTE TO THE INTRODUCTION

1. This is the main reason why conservative governments in Britain, Chile and other countries have found it so difficult, despite severely deflationary policies, to reduce the money supply in the way they intended.

NOTES TO CHAPTER 1:   GROWTH

1. See, for example, S. Kuznets, *Economic Growth of Nations* (Cambridge, 1961) pp. 11–14 and 24; A. Maddison, *Economic Growth in the West* (London, 1964) p. 28; W. A. Lewis, *Growth and Fluctuations, 1870–1914* (London, 1979) Appendices 1 and 2.
2. A. Maddison, 'Economic Policy and Performance in Europe, 1913–1970', in C. M. Cipolla (ed.), *The Fontana Economic History of Europe: The Twentieth Century*, pt II (London, 1976) p. 451.
3. For varying explanations of the high rate of growth at this period see A. Shonfield, *Modern Capitalism* (London, 1965); Maddison, *Economic Growth in the West*; International Economic Association, *Economic Growth and Resources*, Vol. 1 (London, 1979) pp. 23–51.
4. Though there are obvious difficulties of assessment, rates of growth in the Eastern bloc are estimated at about 9.5 per cent in the fifties, 6.5 per cent in the sixties, under 5 per cent in the seventies, and 3–4 per cent today.
5. The *World Bank Atlas* for various years; *World Bank Annual Report* for 1979. On average the growth in income a head of poor countries was believed to be more rapid than that of the rich countries at a similar stage of development: even that of Japan probably had grown only by about 2.5 per cent a year.
6. A number of categories are used to distinguish the poorer developing countries. The 'least developed' is a group of about 31 countries, mainly rather small, determined on the basis of income a head, literacy and degree of industrialisation: this does not include some of the largest poor countries, including India, Pakistan, China, Indonesia and Vietnam. The 'low-income countries' are a larger group of 58 countries including those just mentioned and over two-thirds of the population of developing countries, determined on the basis of income a head alone (under $370 in 1981). The 'most seriously affected' were a particular group of poor countries most badly hit by the oil-price rise of 1973–4.

7. For example, in the Redcliffe Report on the monetary system.
8. In 1980 it was over 30 per cent.
9. A scepticism that was not justified by the facts. In both the United States and Britain, inflation was at its lowest at the time when 'wage and price controls' or 'incomes policies' were in operation. It was at its worst at the time when they were removed. Logically this argued not that the policies were ineffective, but that they should be maintained on a permanent basis.
10. Club of Rome, *The Limits to Growth* (London, 1972).
11. For a more detailed discussion of the problems of co-ordination within the UN family, see E. Luard, *International Agencies: The Emerging Framework of Interdependence* (London, 1976) ch. 17.
12. World Bank, *World Development Report, 1978*, p. 16.
13. For a detailed analysis, see W. Rostow, *The World Economy: History and Prospect* (London, 1978) pp. 338–57.
14. In 1981–2 very high interest rates in the United States compelled European governments to maintain high rates too, at a time when all wished to lower them.

NOTES TO CHAPTER 2:   INVESTMENT

1. C. H. Jenks, *The Migration of British Capital to 1875* (New York, 1927) p. 413. At this time the distribution of British foreign investment is estimated to have been: government securities in Europe £45–55 million; French and Belgian railways £30–35 million; United States (various) £50–60 million; Latin America £35–40 million; Spain and Portugal £35–40 million.
2. A. H. Imlah, *Economic Elements in the Pax Britannica* (Cambridge, 1958) p. 180.
3. H. Feis, *Europe, the World's Banker, 1870–1914* (New Haven, Conn., 1930) pp. 18, 36, 40, 45n.
4. The distribution was about 20 per cent in the United States, 20 per cent in Latin America (about half in Argentina) 14 per cent in Canada, 11 per cent in New Zealand, 10 per cent in India and only 6 per cent in Europe – Royal Institute of International Affairs (RIIA), *The Problem of International Investment* (London, 1937) p. 117.
5. Feis, *Europe, the World's Banker*, pp. 133–42.
6. Ibid., p. 51.
7. RIIA, *The Problem of International Investment*, p. 142.
8. W. Ashworth, *A Short History of the International Economy since 1850* (London, 1975) p. 238.
9. RIIA, *The Problem of International Investment*, p. 215.
10. Ibid., p. 149.
11. P. Ady (ed.), *Private Foreign Investment and the Developing World* (New York, 1971) p. 17.
12. If portfolio investment and export credits are included, the figures become $3 billion and $6 billion respectively; but neither of these represent investment in the proper sense, the creation of new production facilities (see Ady, *Private Foreign Investment*, p. 8).

13. Brandt Report, *North–South* (London, 1980) p. 187. The total at that time was worth about $68 billion.
14. Ady, *Private Foreign Investment*, pp. 6, 13.
15. Something like two-thirds went to six NICs: Mexico, Brazil, South Korea, Taiwan, Singapore and the Philippines.
16. Published figures for debt–service ratios vary widely according to whether they cover private debt, short-term credits, income from remittances and exports of services as well as goods. The ratios are, anyway, not a sound guide to balance of payments strength, since they do not take account of capital inflows or the volume of imports. Countries such as Brazil and Mexico have high ratios because they have borrowed large amounts at high (often floating) rates of interest. Other countries which have financed their development out of export earnings have very low ratios: for example, Taiwan and Malaysia. Low-income countries as a whole, securing their external resources mainly from aid and export credits (sometimes subsidised) have fairly low ratios: the ratios for those countries declined in 1971–81, mainly because of substantial declines for India, Pakistan and Egypt.
17. World Bank, *World Development Report, 1980*, p. 27.
18. See OECD, *Development Corporation Report, 1980*: 'Bond borrowing is highly concentrated in the higher income and OPEC countries.' The largest bond borrowers during the last three years were Mexico, Brazil, Algeria and Venezuela.
19. Until the mid-sixties the US government persistently stimulated foreign investment by US companies through various fiscal devices, above all by placing a low rate of corporation tax on capital exports and by exempting unpatriated profits from tax altogether, so intensifying the balance of payments problems from which the country increasingly suffered. After that time it was increasingly controlled.
20. OPEC aid was given through about half a dozen separate funds. The money went almost entirely to Muslim and mainly to Arab countries.
21. In real terms the amount of aid received by low-income countries has declined since 1975.
22. The Brandt Report proposed using the proceeds of IMF gold sales to subsidise interest rates, but this was resisted by many poor countries which wish additional resources to be found for the purpose.
23. One form this co-operation might take is the general use of the 'universal' system of taxation, favoured by the state of California.
24. There are proposals that GATT should take responsibility for drawing up rules for private investment of this kind.

NOTES TO CHAPTER 3: TRADE

1. P. L. Yates, *Forty Years of Foreign Trade* (London, 1959) p. 166.
2. W. A. Lewis, *Economic Survey 1919–1939* (London, 1949) pp. 79, 94, 100.
3. Ibid., pp. 94, 100.
4. A third of all exports of manufactures from developing countries in 1973 came from three countries alone: South Korea, Singapore and Taiwan.

5. At this time the International Cocoa Agreement was ineffective because the main consumer (the United States) refused to join, on the grounds that the price level to be supported was too high, while the main producer (the Ivory Coast) equally rejected the pact because the price set was too low; the International Coffee Agreement had proved unable to support prices effectively because the quotas laid down (even when fully observed) were too large, so that prices remained generally below the floor price established; the International Sugar Agreement was ineffective because the EEC, a main producer, had not joined and had flooded the market with subsidised sugar, while the quotas of other producers were too large to sustain the price; the International Rubber Agreement had failed because the intervention price was set too low to provide remunerative prices when demand declined; and a new International Tin Agreement could not be brought into effective operation because the United States, the main consumer, refused to join on the terms proposed.

6. India, Brazil and Tanzania, for example, had to spend 50–70 per cent of all their export earnings on imports of oil in 1980–1.

7. Some limited liberalisation of agricultural trade was achieved during the Tokyo round; for example for trade in beef and in dairy products. The use of subsidies for agricultural exports was also deterred by authorising the imposition of countervailing duties against them. In addition, the EEC slightly reduced its tariffs on some agricultural imports (fresh fruit and vegetables, tobacco and some kinds of fish).

8. There has been lengthy controversy about whether such a long-term decline in terms of trade has occurred. Attempts to prove this depend crucially on the year chosen for comparison. There have certainly been substantial declines – for example, between 1875 and 1895, between 1928 and 1935, and from the early fifties to the early seventies. But there were substantial increases in such prices in the early years of the century, between 1939 and 1953, and during the seventies. There have also been big variations between commodities: for some, such as oil, gas, gold, silver and copper, there have been *rises* over a substantial period, while others – bananas and tea – have shown big falls.

9. More than half the developing countries earn more than half their export revenues from two commodities or less.

10. Manufactured exports from developing countries at present take under 3 per cent of the total market in developed countries.

11. The respectable goals of 'trade management' or 'planned trade' have been discredited in recent years by the use of these terms as euphemisms for trade restriction. It is important that advocates of trade management make clear that its objective is trade growth and not trade reduction.

12. For example, only 5 per cent of textile imports to the United Kingdom over recent years have come from the 50 poorest countries of the world.

13. There was agreement on safeguards for developing countries to allow them to withdraw tariff concessions on general development grounds.

14. An attempt at definition on these lines was contained in the US Trade Bill of 1970.

15. But this is partly because the *quid* to be gained for the *quo* is in this case less obvious: it will take the form not of tariff concessions offered in return, but

of better export opportunities resulting from the increase in poor countries' capacity to purchase in the markets of the North.

16. The Brandt Report pointed out that freight rates for processed rubber shipped from Malaysia to the United States are three times as high as for raw rubber; for processed leather they are twice as high.

17. A voluntary code covering restrictive business practices was negotiated at Geneva in 1980.

18. The opposition was partly on protectionist grounds and partly because colonial preferences were not abolished.

19. One of the oddities of the present situation is that liberalisation is normally conceived in terms of a percentage change from present unequal positions rather than as an advance towards a clearly perceived common end. There exists no objective measure of the degree of liberalisation actually achieved by each country, nor of the position towards which it should be moving. Neither the goal of 'linear' reductions, nor the alternative aim of 'harmonisation' of tariffs favoured by the French (the elimination of very high tariffs) sets any standard for the general level of liberalisation required. In future negotiations it would be preferable to set as a goal for industrialised countries not a percentage reduction from existing unequal levels but a specific average level of tariffs regarded as reasonable. If the total elimination of tariffs (which some demanded from the Tokyo round) is impossible, this might be, say, 3 per cent (most of the EFTA countries today already have outer tariffs averaging 2 per cent or less). This would at least set a recognisable standard to be aimed at. Comparable levels would then need to be set for other groups of countries, under the principle of graduation, according to the level of development they had achieved.

NOTES TO CHAPTER 4: MONEY

1. This can now be subscribed in SDRs or foreign exchange.

2. Less than a quarter of the members of the IMF have adopted floating rates: the rest are pegged to a floating currency or to the SDR.

3. One consequence was that for a few years poor countries had less need to seek help from the IMF itself. In 1977–8 the Fund was not a net lender at all, repayments exceeding new credits.

4. Poland has now applied to join.

5. By 1981 the US dollar represented 70 per cent of currency reserves, the mark 15 per cent, the Swiss franc 4 per cent, the yen 3 per cent and the pound 2 per cent.

6. Total debt servicing of the poor countries reached about $50 billion a year, at an average rate of interest (despite concessional aid from governments) of nearly 6 per cent.

7. A number of Western countries made drawings from the Fund in the fifties and sixties, but these were almost entirely within the first credit tranche.

8. Excluding drawings under low-conditionality facilities.

9. One proposal is that central banks should seek to maintain internationally determined 'reference rates' which would be revised at regular intevals: see

W. Ethier and A. L. Bloomfield, *Managing the Managed Float* (Princeton, NJ, 1975) p. 8.

10. They can be acquired by the World Bank, the IDA and the regional development banks at present.

11. For a discussion of these problems, see B. J. Cohen, *Organising the World's Money* (New York, 1977) pp. 121–2, 129–30.

12. Members of the IMF may no longer, for IMF purposes, define their currency's exchange value in terms of gold. Members are no longer required to pay gold to the Fund for any transaction – the obligation to pay gold can be discharged with SDRs or currencies. And the Fund will accept gold only with an 85 per cent decision to do so.

13. 55 per cent in 1981.

14. For example, the overseas deposits of US banks are not subject to US reserve requirements (except where these dollars are borrowed by their home offices). The same is true of a number of other countries.

15. Under new guidelines adopted in 1979 the Fund is supposed to 'pay due regard to the domestic and social priorities and circumstances of members, including the causes of their balance of payments problems'. This seems to have had little influence, however, on the performance criteria demanded since that time. In the eyes of receiving countries, these are often over-concerned about short-term monetary corrections and not enough about long-term economic adjustment.

16. Despite the theory, quotas have never been very closely related to economic strength: in 1981 Britain still had a much bigger quota than Japan, West Germany or France, for example, though the latter all had bigger shares of world production and trade.

17. Poor countries would also gain influence if those groups in which they are in a majority were represented by a poor country in the Executive Board, not, as at present, by the country, often rich, which wields most votes (see Table 4.1).

18. Since June 1979 the Managing Director of the IMF has been able to initiate confidential discussions with member governments if he believes their exchange-rate policies are inappropriate, and report to the Executive Board on the outcome; but there is little evidence that this has had much impact on government policies.

NOTES TO CHAPTER 5:   RESOURCES

1. The best known of these were J. W. Forrester, *Urban Dynamics* (Cambridge, Mass., 1969); A. and P. R. Ehrlich, *Population Resources, Environment – Issues in Human Ecology* (San Francisco, 1970); and D. Meadows *et al.*, *The Limits to Growth* (New York, 1972).

2. As in *The Limits to Growth.*

3. C. Freeman and M. Jahoda (eds), *World Futures* (London, 1978) p. 187.

4. Modern terminology reflects this distinction. 'Mineral resources' are concentrations of solids, liquids or gases, discovered or only surmised, that are or might become economic sources of raw materials. 'Mineral reserves'

are that portion of resources that have actually been identified and can be economically extracted. It is the size of the latter which matters.

5. W. Leontief *et al., The Future of the World Economy* (New York, 1977) p. 6.
6. United Nations, *Projections of Natural Resource Reserves Supply and Future Demand,* E/C7/40 (New York, 1971).
7. Quoted in W. W. Rostow, *Getting from Here to There* (London, 1978) p. 101.
8. The resources of which there is the greatest likelihood of shortage in the next 20 years are mercury, lead, tin, zinc and gold. In all cases there have been substantial increases in price leading to economies in use and the development of alternatives.
9. Such minerals include vanadium titanium, lithium, barium and tungsten.
10. In the first 30 years or so of its existence the Bank had lent $700 million for mineral development against more than 12 times that amount for energy projects, mainly electric power.
11. *Report of the UN Secretary-General on the Economic, Social and Environmental Impact of Mining Projects,* E/C7/97 (16 Mar 1979). Even among developing countries, a large proportion of exploration takes place in a small number where mining industries are firmly established, such as Chile, Brazil, Argentina, Zambia, Zaire and Malaysia.
12. The UN Secretariat proposed the establishment of an international minerals investment trust which would help to channel funds for investment to the exploration and development of mineral resources in developing countries.
13. In the study which he undertook on behalf of the Club of Rome, Jan Tinbergen proposed a world agency for natural resources which would have responsibility *inter alia* for managing commodity agreements and for advising and arbitrating on relations between producer nations and producer companies – *Reshaping the International Order* (London, 1977).

NOTES TO CHAPTER 6: OIL

1. Since the companies could not offset such royalty payments against their US tax liability, as they could tax payments, this was by no means welcome to them. The majors, however, accepted it relatively willingly on the ground that it would, as was generally believed, hit the independents much harder than them (and because they were allowed at the same time to base their tax liability on the prices actually realised, rather than on the artificial 'posted price').
2. In May 1981 it recommended, at a time of glut, a general production cut, but it remained for each government to decide what action to take.
3. In its Declaration of Petroleum Policy in 1968, OPEC had declared that member governments would 'endeavour, as far as feasible, to explore for and develop their hydro-carbon resources directly'.
4. The degree to which actual control, as against ownership of operations, was transferred depended on the technical capacity available within the producer states. It went furthest and fastest in Venezuela, Algeria and Iraq; at the other extreme, in a number of Gulf states companies continued to

undertake operations, though now as contractors to the government concerned.

5. Rather than build excess capacity, far from the markets, it would have been more rational for the producer governments to seek to buy refineries in the consumer countries.

6. Among OECD countries energy use per unit of output fell by 15 per cent and that of oil by 25 per cent.

7. Even in the United States, where for seven years consumers were largely protected from the rise in oil prices, the increase in demand slowed: demand for oil products rose by only 2 per cent a year in 1974–9 compared with 0.8 per cent a year in Europe.

8. Already by the end of 1981, demand for OPEC oil had declined to about 20 million barrels a day.

9. In 1980, the United States had an emergency stock of only 13 days' supply against 90 days agreed in the IEA.

10. One possible solution that has been suggested for this problem is a tax incentive encouraging the companies to hold high stocks in normal times, and a tax burden to deter purchases in times of shortage. More simple still is a heavy tax on windfall gains from stock appreciation.

11. 'Neither the IEA nor individual governments possess the power to require the sort of allocation of stocks necessary to smooth out the anomalies and shortfalls in any situation short of an extreme emergency. The lack of power exists at both national and international level and effectively contains the stockpile against any effective deployment other than for commercial purposes intended by the industry' – F. E. Niering, in *Petroleum Economist*, Dec 1980, p. 544.

12. According to World Bank estimates, the total energy import bill for developing countries could rise to $100 billion by 1990 unless new domestic energy supplies are developed much faster than at present.

13. Only about $3 billion of the $25 billion proposed is to be spent on oil development.

14. A proposal of this kind has been set out in detail in P. R. Odell and K. D. Rosing, *The Future of Oil* (London, 1980).

15. Brazil expects production of ethanol to be equal to about half its total expected demand for petrol by 1985.

16. Until now Saudi Arabia has been the only oil-producing country which has recognised the interests of producers in restraint in pricing policy, leading to a more prosperous world economy. One of the benefits of an international energy agency is that it might spread that wisdom more widely.

NOTES TO CHAPTER 7:   FOOD

1. See *Global 2000, Report to the President* (Washington, DC, 1980) vol. I, p. 18: 'Farmers' costs of raising – and even maintaining – yields have increased rapidly in recent years. The costs of energy-intensive yield-enhancing inputs – fertilizers, pesticides and fuels – have risen very rapidly throughout the world, and where these inputs are heavily used [mainly in developed countries], increased applications are bringing diminishing

returns. In the United States, the real cost of producing food increased roughly 10 % in both 1978 and 1979. Other industrialized countries have experienced comparable production cost increases. Cost increases in the less developed countries appear to be lower, but are still 2–3 times the annual increases of the 1960s and early 1970s. While there have been significant improvements recently in the yields of selected crops, the diminishing returns and rapidly rising costs of yield-enhancing inputs suggest that yields overall will increase more slowly than projected.' (The increase in food production in the period 1970–2000 projected in the report was 91 per cent overall, 43.7 per cent in Western industrialised countries, 74 per cent in centrally planned countries, and 148 per cent in less developed countries.)

2. Evidence from a number of places – Japan, South Korea, the Punjab in India – shows that resistance to change in agricultural methods can usually be overcome if the right incentives are provided.

3. The use of fertilisers in poor countries has increased by 15 per cent a year over the last decade or so, against 5 per cent in rich countries, but started from such a low level that the amount of fertiliser used in most poor countries remains only a fraction of that used in rich countries, above all where agricultural productivity is lowest, as in sub-Saharan Africa (see Table 7.2). Intensive use of fertilisers and pesticides use more energy per hectare but less per unit of food produced.

4. In 1980 a new and larger budget was approved for the next three years.

5. The US Government has now established a national food reserve of 4 million tons which could be used in an emergency for international purposes.

6. A more equal distribution of income between rich countries and poor would also have a significant effect in increasing food production: at present the higher purchasing power which exists in the developed countries has the effect that grain from poor countries is used for the relatively inefficient purpose of feeding animals for consumption, while within the poor countries there is inadequate grain to feed humans.

7. The EEC's regional programmes provide for just such a redistribution between regions. Similar programmes could perform the same function in other continents.

8. About $3 billion of this is given by multilateral agencies, of which about a half is concessional; about $2 billion comes from bilateral programmes and this is mainly concessionary.

9. The Brandt Report quoted estimates (by the International Food Policy Research Institution) that an additional $13 billion a year would be required if food deficits were to be eliminated by 1990.

10. One of the few conclusions of the North–South summit meeting at Cancún was the need for rationalisation of these bodies.

NOTES TO CHAPTER 8: UNEMPLOYMENT

1. See, for example, D. T. Healey, *The Export of Manufactures and Aid in Relation to Employment in Developing Countries*, Background Paper to World Conference on Employment, ILO, 1976.

2. A. Sen, *Employment Technology and Development* (Oxford, 1975) p. 20.
3. Healey, *Export of Manufactures and Aid*, p. 6.
4. Even the United Nations undertook in its Charter to 'promote . . . higher standards of living, *full employment*, and conditions of economic progress and development' (emphasis added).
5. ILO, *The World Employment Programme, Report of the Director-General to the International Labour Conference* (Geneva, 1969) p. 85.
6. A reduction in capital-intensive investment need not mean a reduction in investment generally; nor of investment in high technology. The development of microchips, for example, providing real benefits in better storing and retrieval of information, more accurate machinery of improved quality and reliability, may create as many jobs as it destroys; but relatively unskilled jobs, in factories, offices and banks, will be replaced by more skilled jobs – for example, as computer technicians and programmers.
7. At present, investment in *equipment* is held to increase the assets of the company (and so its borrowing power) while improvement of the *human* capital, training, is seen as a cost and so often deferred.
8. This might be a rational policy even if the overall growth rate were to suffer as a result. But there is no clear evidence that this need be the effect: see J. Mouly and E. Costa, *Employment Policies in Developing Countries* (London, 1974) pp. 21ff.
9. For a detailed survey of the kind of tax measures developing countries might introduce for this purpose, see ILO, *Fiscal Measures for Employment Promotion in Developing Countries* (Geneva, 1972).
10. ILO, *World Employment Programme*, p. 99.
11. For suggestions how aid programmes could be made more 'employment-intensive', see Hans Singer, '*International Policy and the Effect on Employment*', in R. Jolly, E. De Kadt, H. Singer and F. Wilson, *Third World Employment* (London, 1973) pp. 416ff.
12. For a discussion of the creation of more employment in the service industries, see Mouly and Costa, *Employment Policies*, pp. 76–89.
13. Unilateral reduction of the retirement age need not, however, have this effect, though it is expensive in budgetary cost if pensions or other allowances are awarded.
14. For suggestions about how such a scheme might be operated, see L. Emmerij, in International Economic Association, *Employment Problems in the Industrialised Countries* (London, 1980) pp. 58–69.

NOTES TO CHAPTER 9:　EFFICIENCY IN THE WORLD ECONOMY

1. For example, Ricardo recognised that it might be more efficient to purchase some things from abroad which were produced less efficiently than the same things produced at home if the difference was less than for other products traded.
2. Cf. G. K. Helleiner, *International Economic Disorder: Essays in North–South Relations* (London, 1980) p. 46: 'Among the restrictive practices which are most frequently found internationally, and for which there is

available evidence, are inter-firm agreements for the allocation of territorial markets; pooling and allocation of patents, trademarks and copyrights; fixing of prices or price relationships (including discriminatory pricing); allocation of total amounts of export business; and establishment of reciprocal exclusive or preferential dealing.'

3. Ibid., pp. 40–1.
4. This would be comparable to the role undertaken by the League of Nations in helping East European countries to overcome their debt problems in the period between the wars. The Paris Club undertakes the role at present, but, representing creditors only, is not a fully international body.
5. Debt relief can include the postponement of interest payments, the reduction of interest payments, the rescheduling of payments of principal, the reduction of the amount of principal to be repaid, and a total writing off of loans: the choice between them will depend on the economic situation of the debtor country.
6. The World Bank/IMF Development Committee is supposed to seek to reconcile policies on development and monetary questions; but because it meets so briefly and infrequently it is not at present well equipped to do this.

NOTES TO CHAPTER 10:   JUSTICE IN THE WORLD ECONOMY

1. Though here once again it is important to distinguish between *types* of poor country. Rich countries trade primarily with the more prosperous developing countries. Probably, the 50 poorest countries of the world could sink beneath the seas tomorrow, almost unnoticed (in a strictly economic sense) by the peoples of the north.
2. Both the IDA and the UNDP have adopted targets for the proportion of their funds which should go to the least developed (22 and 26 per cent respectively). At the Paris Conference devoted to the problems of these countries in August 1981, many bilateral donors, though not designating any percentages of total aid, agreed in principle to give 0.15 per cent of their national income to this category of countries.
3. The proportion of aid tied rose from 30 per cent in 1970 to 50 per cent in 1980.
4. The significant exception to this is the money which the World Bank devotes to lending at commercial rates: this it can borrow from the money markets of the world. For its concessionary lending, however, it is dependent on the funds contributed by governments in the successive replenishments.
5. For example, in the Brandt Report.
6. Guidelines have been produced by the OECD, the International Chamber of Commerce and the ILO and are still being discussed by the UN Commission on Transnational Corporations. These are mainly in such general terms that they have probably had little impact on the policies of the companies.

Index

DATE DUE
